Global Tarantella

FOLKLORE STUDIES
IN A MULTICULTURAL
WORLD

The Folklore Studies in a Multicultural World series is a collaborative venture
of the University of Illinois Press, the University Press of Mississippi, the
University of Wisconsin Press, and the American Folklore Society, made
possible by a generous grant from the Andrew W. Mellon Foundation. The
series emphasizes the interdisciplinary and international nature of current
folklore scholarship, documenting connections between communities and
their cultural production. Series volumes highlight aspects of folklore studies
such as world folk cultures, folk art and music, foodways, dance, African
American and ethnic studies, gender and queer studies, and popular culture.

Global Tarantella

Reinventing Southern Italian Folk Music and Dances

INCORONATA INSERRA

UNIVERSITY OF ILLINOIS PRESS
Urbana, Chicago, and Springfield

© 2017 by the Board of Trustees
of the University of Illinois
All rights reserved
1 2 3 4 5 C P 5 4 3 2 1
∞ This book is printed on acid-free paper.
Publication of this book was supported by grants from the
Andrew W. Mellon Foundation, and from the L. J. and Mary C.
Skaggs Folklore Fund.

Library of Congress Cataloging-in-Publication Data
Names: Inserra, Incoronata, author.
Title: Global tarantella : reinventing southern Italian folk music
    and dances / Incoronata Inserra.
Description: Urbana : University of Illinois Press, [2017] |
    Series: Folklore studies in a multicultural world | Includes
    bibliographical references and index. |
Identifiers: LCCN 2017017414 (print) | LCCN 2017019444 (ebook)
    | ISBN 9780252099892 (e-book) | ISBN 9780252041297
    (hardcover : alk. paper) | ISBN 9780252082832 (pbk. : alk.
    paper)
Subjects: LCSH: Tarantellas—History and criticism. | Folk
    music—Italy, Southern—History and criticism. | Tarantella.
Classification: LCC ML3660 (ebook) | LCC ML3660 .I57 2017
    (print) | DDC 781.62/51009457—dc23
LC record available at https://lccn.loc.gov/2017017414

To Heath

Contents

Acknowledgments

This project contains an ethnographic component, which was possible thanks to the generosity and patience of my interviewees as well as the practitioners and festivalgoers who took the time to talk to me and show me their work with tarantella and interest in the local festivals: in Campania—Raffaele Inserra, Giuseppe Dionisio, Ugo Maiorano, Antonio Matrone ('O Lione), Marcello Colasurdo, Pia Vicinanza, Le Ninfe della Tammorra, Raffaella Coppola, Salvatore Raiola, Luigi Coppola, Tiziana Torelli, Andrea Iozzino; the practitioners and festival promoters I met with in Milan—Filippo Renna and Ashti Abdo, Armando Illario and Francesca di Ieso, Rosa Maurelli, Valeria Lista, Armando Soldano, and Antonio Ricci; and on the other side of the Atlantic—Alessandra Belloni, Natalie Marrone, Michela Musolino, Mary Ciuffitelli, and Anabella Lenzu.

I also thank Luigi Coppola, Lenny Kaholo, and Lorenzo Rinelli for granting me permission to use their beautiful photos in this book and Giuseppe Laino for his help with Neapolitan-language orthography.

Besides these names, whom I explicitly acknowledge in the book, there are several others, since conducting an autoethnographic project also meant the direct involvement of my family and friends, both in my hometown of Gragnano and in the northern Italian city of Milan, including Enzo Inserra, Chiara Inserra, Mary Bernabei, Mario Giordano, Giovanna Sicignano, Giovanna Somma, Ida Brancaccio, Mariangela Aloe, and Raffaella Malafronte; my mother, who participated in the local festivals in my absence and reported back to me with anecdotes and contacts; and of course, *nonna* Ninuccia and her old-time stories about tammurriata, which accompanied me throughout this experience.

As for the book's scholarly component and critical framework, I am very grateful to folklorists Luisa Del Giudice and Dorothy Noyes for taking the time to read the book manuscript and for providing precious support and advice. Del Giudice's seminal work with southern Italian folk music in the United States has helped tremendously in the development of this project.

I'm also grateful to folklorist Joseph Sciorra for his help with my research and interviews in New York City and elsewhere in the United States; both Joseph Sciorra and Mary Ciuffitelli were valuable sources of information on southern Italian folklore in New York City and beyond. Moreover, scholars Sciorra's and Laura Ruberto's feedback was essential in the development of the final chapter on tarantella within the Italian American context.

I am solely responsible for any inaccurate or missing information.

Finally, I have deep gratitude for my adviser and friend folklorist Cristina Bacchilega, who has believed in this project since the beginning and kept pushing until it was completed. I couldn't have wished for a better mentor. Many thanks also to American studies scholar Donatella Izzo and her precious mentoring, which ultimately made possible these transnational encounters.

Global Tarantella

Introduction

Honolulu, April 26, 2006—it is a late-spring afternoon, and the hot air in the non-air-conditioned dance classroom reserved for our tarantella workshop is an evident reminder that the long Hawaiian summer is behind the door. There are about fifty workshop attendees in the room, many of whom are young college students taking my and my colleagues' Italian classes at the University of Hawai'i's Mānoa (UHM) campus; a couple of Italian American friends from the local community are there, eager to participate in one of the rare local cultural events related to Italian culture. The air is filled with humidity and growing impatience mixed with anticipation. To buy a little more time, I ask the crowd what they know about tarantella, their puzzled looks an unmistakable cue for the remoteness of Italian culture on this Pacific shore. Finally, our special guest, New York City–based Italian artist Alessandra Belloni, enters the room, her long pitch-black hair down, her long and flowing white skirt on a white top, her heavy gypsy-style makeup and ethnic jewelry—at first sight, the outfit looks like a mix of gypsy, hippie, and New Age.

Framing her dark features and Hawai'i-tan complexion, a Hawaiian hibiscus hair clip reminds the audience of the pervasive globalization of Native Hawaiian culture. As Belloni starts playing her southern Italian tambourine and singing southern Italian folk songs, the exotic yet realistic quality of her performance immediately comes to life. Her voice, her laughter, her whole persona is there to create the image of an extremely energetic, passionate, and seductive Mediterranean woman—undoubtedly a more familiar image than that of tarantella, especially given the similarities between the Native Hawaiian and the Mediterranean tourist paradise.

To make up for our late start, Belloni decides to continue the workshop beyond the allotted time; some rush out the door because they have other plans, but many decide to stay. We end up dancing and sweating for what seems like hours and hours, and the increasingly hot room resonates with many shrills of joy and shared laughter. I feel ecstatic to share singing, playing, and dancing from my hometown with friends and colleagues from other parts of Italy, the United States, and internationally.

Later that night, my Italian colleagues and I, most of whom belong to the Italian "brain drain" (*fuga dei cervelli*), stay longer to eat and chat with Alessandra.[1] As we share our life stories and the reasons that brought us all to the United States and to Hawai'i, I realize that Alessandra has not only been to all the music and dance festivals in my hometown and nearby areas but has also met local drummer Raffaele Inserra, one of the major performers in my region and from whom I bought my own frame drum in 2009.[2] Alessandra has visited him very often over the years, learned drum techniques from him, bought several handmade drums from his lab, and even asked his seamstress wife to make several costumes for her U.S. and international shows.

This was my first experience with "global tarantella," a music and dance phenomenon that, also thanks to our gathering that night, has traveled worldwide from a very localized tradition in southern Italy to far-off Pacific islands, passing by New York City and the West Coast, where Belloni has widely performed over the years for both Italian and non-Italian audiences. Having hosted Belloni's workshops for seven consecutive years, from 2006 to 2013, I have cherished our encounters not only because they offered me the possibility of singing and dancing tarantella far away from home, but especially for their cultural significance, as they played a role in introducing Italian culture to a U.S. and foreign audience. Ultimately, my experience as both organizer and participant in Belloni's workshops has made a strong impact on this project, since it raised a number of questions regarding the representation of (southern) Italian culture in the United States and within a globalized performance framework—how it is conveyed, how it affects global audiences' view of Italian culture, and to what extent it perpetuates or challenges certain stereotypes about Italian culture in the United States. It also raised questions regarding my own roles as a "local" removed from the southern Italian context and at the same time a representative of

ALESSANDRA BELLONI PRESENTS:

"RHYTHM IS THE CURE"

SOUTHERN ITALIAN DRUM AND DANCE WORKSHOP

SPONSORED BY THE FRENCH AND ITALIAN DIVISION

FEBRUARY 11, 2008 [5:00 - 7:00 PM]
UHM - KUYKENDALL HALL 410

CONTACT:
NADIA INSERRA INSERRA@HAWAII.EDU
9568548
VALERIA WENDEROTH VALERIA@HAWAII.EDU
9564166
FOR MORE INFO: WWW.ALESSANDRABELLONI.COM

BRING WATER AND WEAR CONFORTABLE CLOTHES TO ALLOW FREEDOM OF MOVEMENT

<<<DONATION ACCEPTED>>>

Figure 1. Flyer for Belloni's 2008 workshop at the UHM campus; flyer by Lorenzo Rinelli.

Figure 2. Local drummer Raffaele Inserra at the Madonna di Montevergine festival in the Campania region in September 2013. Photo courtesy of Luigi Coppola.

that culture within a foreign (and academic) context, especially one so removed and different as Hawai'i's. As Belloni often put it during the workshops, I was the only one in the room who knew southern Italian folk music and dances as they are performed at the southern Italian festivals and who had familiarity with their cultural context. Belloni's introduction would thus assign me a privileged position but also suggest the need for further reflection on my own as well as the performer's role (and responsibility) in presenting and translating southern Italian culture for both other Italians and foreign audiences.[3] This book is first and foremost an attempt at answering these questions.

Tarantella and Its Competing Images

The variety of southern Italian folk music and dance traditions that I examine in this book is more or less directly linked to the term *tarantella;* here I employ *tarantella* as an umbrella term to describe these various traditions, while keeping in mind major geographical and historical distinctions within the southern Italian context. The term *tarantella* therefore describes a complex folk system with a long history, which over time has given rise to several

Figure 3. Alessandra Belloni (*right*) demonstrates some of the basic steps of tammurriata dancing from the Campania region during her April 2007 workshop at the UHM campus, accompanied by the author (*left*). Photo courtesy of Lorenzo Rinelli.

and competing definitions of *tarantella;* this intricate history takes on new relevance given the increasingly global circulation of this term and of its kin term *taranta,* via world music marketing. Indeed, within the current context of global marketing, it becomes particularly important to understand why this term gets to circulate more widely than others associated with southern Italian folk music and dances and also why certain connotations of this term circulate more than others.

NEAPOLITAN TARANTELLA

Readers outside of Italy will probably associate the word *tarantella* with the music scene during Connie's wedding sequence in *The Godfather* (1972). The band plays an example of folk song from the Sicilian region of southern Italy called "C'è la luna mezz'o mare" (There is the moon amid the sea), usually performed on a brisk 6/8 tarantella and sung in southern Italian dialect; the song was often included in recordings of Italian songs released in the United States in the early twentieth century. Even though the song's comic theme and language belong to the southern folk tradition, the lyrics echo those of a well-known piece by Italian classic composer Gioacchino Rossini (1792–1868), titled "La danza, tarantella napolitana"[4] (The dance, Neapolitan tarantella), thus reflecting the mix of low- and highbrow cultural elements that are embedded in the Neapolitan tarantella tradition.

Generally speaking, Neapolitan tarantella (*tarantella napoletana*) refers to a specific music and dance form that is famous for its classic rendering by nineteenth-century musicians, from Mendelssohn to Chopin, and to Rossini, as well as for its literary references, such as the well-known play *A Doll's House* (1879) by Norwegian playwright Henrik Ibsen. Earliest traces of Neapolitan tarantella date back to sixteenth-century Naples; the seventeenth-century song "Michelemmà," with its allegro tempo in 6/8, represents the first well-known precursor of Neapolitan tarantella.[5] By the eighteenth century, Neapolitan tarantella seems to have become a popular form, as confirmed by the Neapolitan songs "Lo guarracino" and "Cicerenella," still well known today in the Neapolitan music scene (Paliotti 1992, 25–27, 37–41). Nineteenth-century illustrations clearly reflect the popularity of this music and dance form at the time (38) but also its folk elements, including the use of folk instruments like tambourines and castanets; this form would gradually give way to a more classic image of Neapolitan tarantella, via opera and ballet.

Neapolitan tarantella is also among the southern Italian folk music and dance forms that most people outside of Italy are familiar with through nineteenth- and twentieth-century Italian migration, a complex process that also included the migration of several Neapolitan musicians; this migration process thus helped give rise to a transnational (southern) Italian musical movement (Frasca 2014), whose echoes could still be heard in Dean Martin's 1953 hit song "That's Amore" and its reference to a "gay tarantella." Within Italian American communities, for example, this dance is still performed today at weddings and other social gatherings (La Barbera 2009; Rauche 1990). In addition, American popular culture features various examples of Neapolitan tarantella, ranging from *The Godfather* to Captain Hook's tarantella scene in the 1960 NBC version of the *Peter Pan* musical.

SPIDER DANCE

The presentation video for Alessandra Belloni's show *Tarantella Spider Dance* illustrates one of the most important scenes in Belloni's tarantella performances and workshops—the reenactment of ancient tarantella rituals, in which a sick person, often a woman, is lying on the floor, while musicians and other dancers form a circle around her ("Alessandra Belloni" n.d.). In the video, Belloni herself acts as the sick woman in the center and plays the drum, accompanied by another drummer, to the tune of a very fast *pizzica tarantata*, a music and dance form from the Apulia region of southern Italy and usually associated with the spider-bite syndrome. The woman twists and squirms, imitating a spider, and then slowly those movements transform into dancing steps that increase in speed in a frenetic crescendo—by the end of the song, the woman has risen from the floor, liberated from the spider's web and healed. Even a quick glance at this performance will immediately clarify the many differences (musical, conceptual, performative) between the more popular Neapolitan tarantella and this particular subgenre of southern Italian folk music, as well as Belloni's willingness to move beyond popular representations of tarantella.

The history of the term *tarantella* is indeed much longer than the one evoked by Neapolitan tarantella. Tarantella has been associated with ancient orgiastic rites in honor of Dionysus and in particular with a type of dress used during these rituals, called "vello di Taranto" or "Taranto's wool" (Romanazzi 2006, 142); others have considered the term *tarantella* to be directly related to the southern Italian city of Taranto, where this music and dance form probably originated (Sigerist 2003, 27). In any case, the close affinity with the terms *taranta* and *tarantula* has led most scholars to link tarantella to tarantism or spider-bite syndrome and its music and dance ritual system. This complex ritual is connected to rural healing practices most prevalent in the Apulia region of southern Italy, especially the cities of Taranto and more recently Lecce, but also present in other parts of southern Italy, in Sardinia, and on the Mediterranean coasts at least until the eighteenth century (Sigerist 2003; De Giorgi 1999; De Martino 2005). The ritual made use mostly of the tarantella rhythms and also of an archaic form of tarantella, the *pizzica-pizzica* or *pizzica tarantata* (De Giorgi 1999, 88), although tarantella's frenetic rhythm was not the only one associated with the tarantism cases observed by De Martino; in one case, the victims would dance to a waltz, for example (Romanazzi 2006, 142).

Early studies on tarantism, such as early seventeenth-century *Centum historiae* by Epifanio Ferdinando or *De tarantula* by Giorgio Baglivi, suggested that people bitten by tarantulas would engage in a frenetic dance in order to expel the insect's poison (Sigerist 2003); this dance would ultimately help them enter a state of trance, which accelerated the healing process. In his 1948 study, American medical historian Henry Sigerist argued instead that tarantism was not a medical condition derived by the spider's bite, but rather a type of mental neurosis (41). In any case, until the 1950s, most studies have explained the development of tarantella in relation to healing practices. Following his 1959 fieldwork research trip to the Apulia region of southern Italy, Italian anthropologist Ernesto De Martino was able to demonstrate how psychological factors, such as unrequited love, feelings of depression connected to puberty, or the economic and social status of *tarantati* (victims), must have contributed to this phenomenon. In his well-known book *La terra del rimorso* (1961; *The Land of Remorse*), De Martino defines tarantism as a "'minor,' predominantly peasant religious formation . . . characterized by the symbolism of the taranta which bites and poisons, as well as the symbolism of music, dance and colors which deliver its victim from the poisoned bite" (2005, xxi). The focus on "symbolism" particularly helps shed light on cultural aspects of tarantism and move away from previous studies, which had focused mostly on its medical aspects.[6] More important, De Martino claimed that tarantism was to be understood within the larger socioeconomic, cultural, and religious structure of the Italian South.

Within its southern Italian articulation, tarantella reflects both pre-Christian cultural roots common to the larger Mediterranean area and the strong influence of the Catholic Church, as well as a close relation with the southern peasant culture, particularly its "continuous contact with nature and its cycles" (De Giorgi 1999, 87).[7] According to Di Mitri, Sigerist has the merit of relating the phenomenon of tarantism and its music tradition to pre-Christian fertility rites, in particular to the festive rites in honor of the Greek god Dionysus (2003, 10). Considering the historically strong Greek presence in the southern Italian regions of Apulia, Calabria, Sicily, and Campania—an influence derived from Greek colonization—it is in fact possible to draw similarities between the tarantism music ritual and those related to the pre-Christian cults of Cybele and Dionysus: the same frenetic rhythms, flamboyant dressing, highly sexualized behavior, and extensive wine drinking (Sigerist 2003, 41–42). Nevertheless, organized religion seems to have played an important role in the later development and preservation of this cultural form, in that it helped contextualize a pre-Christian ritual system within Christian and Catholic frameworks; for example, the music and dance ritual, lasting several days, came to be practiced in the *tarantati*'s homes but also occurred in the chapel of Saint Paul in Galatina (De Giorgi 1999). According to De Martino, the local Catholic institutions encouraged *tarantati* to trust Saint Paul's power to liberate themselves from the tarantula-bite syndrome; in doing so, the church was able to combine the tarantula myth with the Christian cult of Saint Paul. Over time this synthesis deeply affected *tarantati*'s healing practices, since their yearly pilgrimages to Saint Paul's chapel in the city of Galatina became more and more frequent, while their use of healing rites through music and dance became less common. In some cases, the money that was originally destined to the musicians now came to be offered to the church.

Yet another important factor in the decline of this ritual is the emergence of the Enlightenment, whose theories largely contributed to view tarantism as an object of medicine; as a result, tarantism's mythical and ritual qualities were dismissed as an irrational mania that reflected the tarantula-bite syndrome (De

Martino 2005, 235).[8] Later in the 1950s, De Martino was able to trace what he considered the last remnants of a music and dance ritual that was dying out due to the increasing economic and social participation of the local church. Another important reason for this change was the 1950s–1960s call for industrialization and modernization in the South, which sought to purge those aspects of southern culture that were deemed unfit for a modernized Italy. Indeed, 1950s and 1960s tourist advertisement for the Apulia region "sought to ignore the last 'relics' of tarantism" (Apolito 2000, 141); this attitude was part of a larger political project that sought to "accelerate the modernization of the South" not only by "extending the lower classes' participation in the cultural life of the country," but also by eliminating those cultural "relics" that "slowed down" this process of modernization (139). By the early 1960s, then, tarantella music and dances had become mostly a symbol of the social and economic degradation and backwardness of those regions (De Martino 2005; Apolito 2000).

TAMMURRIATA

While Neapolitan tarantella remains very popular in the United States and internationally, the recent revival of southern Italian folk music is reaching an increasingly wide market, thus largely contributing to expanding the audience's view of southern Italian folk music and dances beyond Neapolitan tarantella. In the American TV show *The Sopranos,* Tony Soprano's cousin Fulvio moves from Naples, Italy, to New Jersey to work with his Italian American relatives in the family business. Fulvio's exotic character makes him the center of attention, especially among the women in the family, and it arouses the interest of Carmela, Tony's wife. An important scene in the show concerns Fulvio and Carmela's passionate dancing to the tune of a Neapolitan folk song. The song, titled "Vesuvio" and performed by the Neapolitan group Spaccanapoli,[9] features the slow frame-drum rhythm typical of the tammurriata music tradition from the Campania region of southern Italy; Fulvio and Carmela's dancing steps are very different from tammurriata's and resemble more flamenco; nevertheless, the use of the tammurriata rhythm in this scene testifies to the increasing variety of southern Italian folk music on the international music scene.

GYPSY-PUNK TARANTELLA

The international visibility of tarantella since the 1990s is also evident in the work of world-renowned gypsy-punk artist Gogol Bordello, particularly his 2007 album, *Super Taranta.* The song "Super Taranta," in particular, combines a frenetic tarantella rhythm with the use of violin, accordion, and drums, which are common to both the tarantella genre and to Balkan music, while also retaining elements of punk rock. Midway through the song, the tune changes

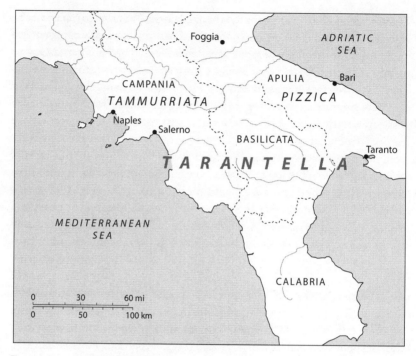

Figure 4. Southern Italy and its regions.

into a well-known pizzica song from the Apulia region; the tune is performed using only the violin and the tambourine, a small frame drum typical of pizzica. Bordello's international popularity has certainly contributed to the global circulation of the term *taranta* outside of folk music circles.

Figure 4 shows the southern section of the continental Italian peninsula, with the regions of Campania, Basilicata, Apulia, and Calabria; the map also illustrates the various music and dance traditions associated with the tarantella genre and the regions in which they have originated or developed. The Apulia region and in particular the Salento area (near the towns of Lecce, Brindisi, and Taranto) are home to the pizzica tradition; my fieldwork research concentrated on the Campania region, home to the tammurriata tradition.

Contemporary Definitions of Tarantella

Within the post-1990s tarantella revival, tarantella has been studied as a folk music and dance "family" (Gala 1999b; Romanazzi 2006) that is "neither morphologically homogeneous nor equally distributed over the Southern Italian territory; it is rather an ample and diversified family of traditional dances with some common elements" (Gala 1999b, 22). Over time the tarantella genre has come to include a variety of music and dance forms that are not strictly connected to the tarantism phenomenon. The pizzica tradition, for example, is common in the Salento area of the Apulia region and is also the form bearing the most direct link to tarantism even in its name (from the Italian *pizzicare,* "to bite"); this link is evident in the *pizzica tarantata* music and dance form, whose particularly frenetic rhythm and steps remind of the trance-inducing tarantism ritual. Elements common to the whole genre are the use of the drum to beat time—even as different types of drum are used—an extensive motion of the arms, and the couple-dance format. However, the complex choreographic pattern of tarantella is such that while most repertories feature couple dances (not necessarily man-woman), four-dancer, circle, and processional choreographies are also possible, depending on geographical context. Adding to such complexity, in the case of couple dancing, the dancers' movements can symbolize rites of fertility, initiation, and courtship, especially if the dancers are of opposite sexes. For Italian scholar Tullia Magrini, "The same kind of dance can take on different meanings in different contexts"; in fact, "when the partners are a man and a woman, the tarantella takes the meaning of a dance courtship rich in sensuality, although according to the traditional way of dancing, no bodily contact between the two dancers is allowed" (2003, 6). In the case of men-men and women-women dancing, the dancers' gestures can instead bear a variety of meanings, including strictly religious ones (Gala 1999b). As for the drum-based rhythm, different types of tarantella feature rather different rhythmic patterns, such as 2/4, 6/8, 4/4, and 12/8, and instruments, such as drum, bagpipe, accordion, violin, mandolin, and flute.

Neapolitan folk musician Eugenio Bennato identifies four elements that are characteristic of tarantella music, at least in its most traditional forms, and that go beyond its geographical, historical, and artistic variations. These elements are the performing style, the lack of a finale, the cyclic nature of its rhythm, and a disconnect between the rhythm of the music and that of the chant that accompanies it. The particular performing style of tarantella consists of the attitude of the musician, who appears disconnected from the audience, as if he were in fact in a state of trance. This attitude prevents any form of direct contact between the musician and the audience. This element arguably reflects the ritual energy of tarantella; in addition, traditional tarantella, Bennato continues, is a "music that never ends and the finale is at any rate non-musical, since it depends on two elements: the healing process or the death of the tarantati, or the end of the musicians' performance due to over-exertion" (2001, 89). This particular song structure creates extremely long performances, which will often take place from sunset to sunrise in the traditional village context and at least for several hours in a contemporary concert scenario. The lack of a finale is perhaps what mostly separates more traditional forms of tarantella from its contemporary remakings, as well as from its more well-known world music versions. As for the cyclic rhythm of tarantella, Bennato explains how the basic pattern of most tarantella forms repeats the same standard melody over and over, which not only provides tarantella with a trancelike obsessive quality, but also allows for a high degree of improvisation on the part of musicians and chanters. As one can imagine, this quality is more developed in traditional forms of tarantella than in more contemporary ones, partly because, Bennato suggests, today's composers tend to deviate from this simple pattern and, therefore, to reduce tarantella's possibilities of variation. Finally, the particular rhythmic pattern of most tarantella forms creates a disconnect between the music, which follows essentially a ternary pattern, and the chant, which follows a binary pattern. This element creates a sort of surprising effect in the audience.[10] The important lesson behind this dynamic is tarantella's tendency to disrupt and surprise, which allows it to transgress. Historically, this quality has served the healing role of tarantella; today it can favor new ways of disrupting the norms of society. In both cases, this disruptive potential seems to explain the large popularity of this musical form today. While Bennato's music performance is focused mostly on Apulian tarantella, and especially its pizzica variation, I believe that the rules described here can be applied to the tammurriata tradition, as suggested by local festival dynamics.

The Tammurriata Tradition

The term *tammurriata* refers to a folk music and dance tradition from the Campania region of southern Italy, with which I am familiar through festival participation since the late 1990s. Given its peculiar ritual, choreographic, and musical aspects, tammurriata differs in many ways from the forms most often associated with the tarantella genre. One of the major differences consists of tammurriata's slower binary rhythm, while most types of tarantella, such as pizzica or tarantella del Gargano, feature small tambourines and a much faster beat based on a ternary rhythmic pattern. Another major difference is that tammurriata bears no direct link to the spider-bite syndrome; while tarantism as a minor phenomenon has been noted to occur in the Campania region up to the 1950s and 1960s (Rossi 1994), these cases are associated not with the tammurriata rhythm but with other forms of tarantella.

Even so, the increasing popularity of tammurriata since the 1990s has followed a trajectory that is very similar to that of pizzica—that is, from localized to national- and international-scale festivals and performances; for this reason, Italian scholars have often included the revitalization of tammurriata within the larger post-1990s "neotarantism" (*neotarantismo*) phenomenon (Nacci 2001, 11). While my treatment of tammurriata as a subgenre of tarantella in this volume draws mainly on Italian scholar Giuseppe Gala's work, I am aware that this definition may not be accepted by all scholars of tammurriata. Therefore, I will use it as a provisional definition that allows me to trace the trajectory of tammurriata since the 1990s similarly to what other scholars have already done in relation to the more popular pizzica revival.

Tammurriata derives its name from the term *tammorra,* which indicates a frame drum still played today in several areas of the Campania region.[11] To accompany the drum(s) are the *castagnole* or *castagnette* (castanets)—a type of percussion

Figure 5. The tammorra drum that the author bought from local performer Raffaele Inserra in June 2009; the drum was made according to tradition, with goat skin, but instead of industrially made "cicere" (the little metal discs that appear on the wooden frame), it features cicere made out of tomato cans. This photo is particularly significant, since it shows the drum placed on a table in Inserra's house courtyard next to fresh cabbage that he has just picked from his garden; the scene well illustrates the close relationship between tammurriata music and the rural context in which it developed. Photo by the author.

instrument very similar to the Spanish castanets—essential for the dancers to follow the rhythm, as well as several other percussion instruments, which vary according to each town or area. As for the chanting featured in tammurriata, Gala (1993) defines it *canto a ballo* (dance song), while he defines *tammurriata* dancing as a type of *ballo cantato* (sung dance). While samples of this category can be traced back to Roman times, *canto a ballo* today, at the local festivals, is the product of a long process of development.[12] In folkloric practice, Gala continues, many performers do not recognize the importance of the singing component; the songs are generally viewed as a mnemonic device that helps recall the melody or sometimes as a replacement for musical instruments. But as local scholar Roberto De Simone illustrates in his well-known 1979 book *Canti e tradizioni popolari in Campania*, which offers a detailed analysis of these texts, these songs have their own artistic value and identity aside from their dance counterpart. A tammurriata chant is composed of a long series of hendecasyllabic distiches, which generally describe mythical, narrative, and lyrical themes. Love, both for the woman and for God, death and life, devotion to the Madonna, as well as the peasant's life and labor are some of the songs' main themes.

Tammurriata dancing (fig. 6) usually consists of couple dancing, male-female, male-male, or female-female, and occurs within a circle created by the audience, the drummers, and the chanters. Different geographical areas present different dance movements, but the choreography as a whole maintains a similar structure.

Figure 6. A tammurriata music and dancing circle at the Festa della Madonna dell'Arco in March 2016. The scene also confirms the revitalization of tammurriata among the local youth. Photo courtesy of Luigi Coppola.

While both music playing and chanting featured in tammurriata are there mainly to accompany the dancing (De Simone 1979, 23), both are the expression of individual chanters and musicians trained in the tradition. The drum, in particular, constitutes the central element of tammurriata, and its rhythm shapes both the chanting and the dancing (Gala 1993). In fact, when describing this tradition, performers often prefer the term *ballo sul tamburo* (the dance on the drum) to that of tammurriata, popularized through the 1970s folk music revival thanks to Roberto De Simone and his music group Nuova Compagnia di Canto Popolare (New Folk Singing Group or NCCP).

Developed within the rural areas of the Campania region, tammurriata reflects the local peasant culture through its strong relation between human and geographical spheres, a strong emphasis on the importance of the land and its values—which have earned it the title of "dance of the earth" (Ferraiuolo 2004)—and a close association with both pre-Christian and Catholic rituals, celebrations, and values (Mauro 2004, 212–13). While tarantella, especially Neapolitan tarantella, is usually associated with a refined type of dance from the city of Naples, tammurriata is considered a peasant dance (ibid., 214). These aspects especially deserve our attention, since they are going through major changes within the current revitalization process. Local dancer and educator Pia Vicinanza observes that "tammurriata . . . expresses a distinctive ethnic identity, a much localized sense of geographical and cultural belonging: it is a rite, a feast where once the peasant told the story of his life, of his faith, of his labor in the fields, his love, through the sound of the drum, the singing, and the dance" (Vicinanza 2005, 23). Within the rural world of the Italian South, tammurriata songs are born in the fields as work songs and thus recount the peasants' labor and express their worldview; these songs are then performed "on the drum" within the festival or pilgrimage context (Mauro 2004, 218). This close contact with its rural context, together with its strong "sense of place" (Feld and Basso 1996), is confirmed by tammurriata choreographies: not only in older times did the dancers dance barefoot, but still today their hand gestures while dancing reflect the daily gestures of the peasants, such as seeding and harvesting (Vicinanza 2005, 47). Besides dancing, several other aspects of tammurriata support this pastoral worldview, such as the extensive use of pastoral imagery on the part of the singers or the use of peasant materials like wood and animal skin to build the tammorra drum (Mauro 2004, 216).

Yet another important element to consider when exploring tammurriata relates to its ritual aspects, which are in many ways connected to a pre-Christian cultural framework. Ferraiuolo, for example, describes tammurriata as "a song, a dance, a prayer, a sound, a rhythm, and ecstasy" (2004, 133); in other words, tammurriata has a complex symbolic function beyond strictly musical and choreographic ones. Furthermore, many elements in the tammurriata ritual reflect the religious syncretism typical of the South: tammurriata has consistently intersected with popular medicine and magic, as confirmed by the healing rituals sought by pilgrims at various Madonna sites—the most important of which is the Madonna dell'Arco—as well as by the healing rituals still associated with tammurriata performances today (Dionisio and D'Aquino 2003). All these elements confirm a "religious syncretism derived from pagan rituals and blended with an often imposed Catholicism" (De Simone 1974, 4).

The ritual energy of tammurriata is brilliantly described by Italian scholar Roberto Lamanna: "Old and young, musicians and singers, become one body, replete with passion and vigor, a body that expresses its devotion with tireless energy also thanks to music, the only support and guiding principle for the entire length of the feast. Sound, voice, and steps in every corner of the village, from evening to sunrise, in a continuum that knows neither pause nor fatigue" (2004, 11–12). This description aptly summarizes the ritual essence of a tammurriata performance, and it also seems to suggest (especially to scholars of tammurriata) that this essence has not been lost within the current revival. Even so, this passage does not focus as much on the ways that this ritual is currently translated into new geographical, social, and cultural contexts; I believe that this transformation is central to a study of tammurriata today.

The Italian "Southern Question"

Southern Italy's unique and in some ways problematic sociopolitical and economic situation, along with its linguistic and cultural isolation from the rest of the peninsula, has been at the center of many debates since at least the unification of Italy in 1861 and also one of the major concerns of the postunification government (Dickie 1997, 1999; Verdicchio 1997; Morris 1997); moreover, these debates often reflect and confirm common stereotypes about the South since at least the eighteenth century, particularly through the representation of southern Italy by both Italian and European grand-tour elites (Moe 2002).

The political and social movement that led to the unification of the Italian peninsula in the nineteenth century, also known as Risorgimento, largely contributed to this peculiar sociopolitical and economic situation in the South. After approximately three centuries of Spanish domination in Naples and surrounding areas, the Italian South was under French rule for a good part of the nineteenth century (with the exception of the brief Parthenopean Republic in

1799). In 1815 Ferdinand IV of Bourbon entered Naples, and in 1816 the Kingdom of Naples was established, following the French model, as part of the larger
Kingdom of the Two Sicilies. This new government encountered several moments of resistance, especially in Sicily, where an independent government was
declared in 1848 and then dissolved by the king of Naples. By the time Italian
general Giuseppe Garibaldi's expedition reached Sicily's shores in the spring of
1860, a large revolt was spreading across the island, which ultimately favored
Garibaldi's actions. After Garibaldi entered Naples, the Kingdom of the Two
Sicilies was incorporated into the Kingdom of Italy (Lumley and Morris 1997).

This shift in power created a new historic course for the South and new problems as well. As historian Gabriella Gribaudi puts it, the new government, expression of the entrepreneurial bourgeoisie of the North, considered the South a
barbaric land, a land that had been destroyed by the careless ruling of the Spanish and the Bourbons and needed to be deeply reformed; otherwise the national
project as a whole would not fully take place. Yet this reformation often took place
in the form of an imposition of measures that were not suitable to the particular
socioeconomic structure of the South, such as heavy taxes for the already poverty-
stricken peasant class. In fact, the South was thought of in terms of only what it
lacked: since the national project sought its political model in the central and
northern regions, with their medieval city-states and Renaissance culture and
art, or in the linguistic model of Dante, the South—with its Spanish architecture,
feudal-like land system, and extremely diverse language apparatus—came to
represent a negative model to be eliminated (Gribaudi 1997).

Jane Schneider similarly underlines the importance of analyzing the "force-
ful rhetoric of the North versus South [of Italy]," a rhetoric that she considers a form of "orientalism in one country" (1998, 1, 5).[13] Though technically
the South was not a separate country to colonize, this orientalistic attitude on
the part of the northern elites clearly places Italy within the larger debate over
nineteenth-century Western colonialism and its ideological apparatus. Because
the nineteenth-century national project developed as a political project of the
northern powers, it ultimately "failed" to take root in the South, and the sociopolitical and economic conditions of the South remained a crucial problem in
the minds of both northern rulers and southern intellectuals for many decades.

In his *Quaderni dal carcere* (1948, *Prison Notebooks* [1995]), Italian intellectual
and political thinker Antonio Gramsci (1891–1937) aptly delineated the terms
of this "Southern Question" debate; his reflections on the debate still constitute
an important reference point for scholars of the Italian South today. Gramsci
shared his concern especially over the lack of class solidarity between the proletarian groups of the industrialized North and the peasant groups of the South,

which at the time represented the only two social forces that were "essentially national and bearers of the future" (1995, 47); for Gramsci, solving the Southern Question ultimately meant creating a unified national culture that would be the expression of both groups. This new culture would help defeat what he called the parasitic attitude of the northern industrial powers, which were constantly treating the South as their own colony. However, behind this new political model also lay the need for a new intellectual class, and a new educational policy, that would help liberate the southern people from their own backwardness and lack of civic consciousness. Thus, even as it comes from Gramsci's interest in the future of the southern regions, this image of a parasitic southern population betrays common stereotypes about the South. In fact, Gramsci's vision to solve the Southern Question comprised a large educational project that would help the southern population remove those aspects of their culture that precluded their future within the larger Italian nation.

Since its start, then, the debate over the Southern Question has directly affected the way that Italians perceived southern culture, including its folk culture. Even as Gramsci wrote extensively about southern popular culture and folklore in his *Prison Notebooks* and elsewhere, this interest came from his need to educate the southern populations to be part of a modern Italian culture.[14] Viewed in this light, the gradual dismissal of tarantella music and dance rituals, and of southern folk culture more generally since the 1960s, can also be read within the larger Southern Question debate and as reflecting the way that Italian nationalist discourse has consistently sought to do away with those aspects of southern culture that did not fit within the national model (Bevilacqua 2003; Apolito 2000).

Overall, the socioeconomic conditions of the Italian southern regions have remained problematic until today, as these regions struggle with the highest rates of unemployment in the nation; poor economic, social, and health infrastructures; a strong Mafia system infiltrating both private and public sectors; and local politics mostly based on political patronage (Mignone 1998, 2008). When southern Italians started migrating to the northern industrial triangle of Milan, Turin, and Genoa in the late 1960s and 1970s, during the years of the "economic miracle," the Southern Question became more complex (Mignone 2008), since many southerners now had to cope with the discriminatory attitude of the local population; within this context, the nickname *terrone* (from the Italian word *terra,* or "soil") started becoming a popular way to address southerners, who were often viewed as uncivilized (Mignone 2008, 216–17). This often overt animosity of the northerners, together with the equally strong negative reaction of the southerners, is an inherent part of Italian culture and is ubiquitous in popular culture and the media, since it is often manifested in strong ways, such as during major soccer games. This animosity became particularly evident in the 1990s, since the creation of the nativist Lega Nord (North League) party in the early 1990s. The South's still problematic position within Italian society then became a major topic of debate for both political and cultural groups, especially since Lega Nord leaders took part in Prime Minister Silvio Berlusconi's government in the early 2000s. Lega Nord's discriminatory comments and attitudes toward both southern Italian and foreign immigrants to (northern) Italy—accused of appropriating jobs that should be kept for northerners and of damaging the already poor economic conditions of the country—are common knowledge to Italians and are discussed daily in the Italian media (Cachafeiro 2002). But while for some these represent only the uninformed comments of incompetent politicians, the similarities between Lega Nord's reaction to both internal and foreign immigration and the historical debates on the Southern Question are evident and thus important to acknowledge.

The 1990s also saw an economic recession and the opening of the Italian economy to a liberalized market, which ultimately made things worse for the southern regions, since "liberalization and privatization have resulted in the gradual termination of subsidies to state industry in the South, a drive to reform a welfare state that used disability pensions in the South to disguise long-term unemployment, and winding up of the Fund for the South" (Mignone 1998, 182). The sporadic and often insufficient interventions of the national government have certainly not helped this situation and continue to spur recurring debates in both local and national media.

Antimigration attitudes have taken an even more difficult turn in recent years following the increasing migration influx from northern Africa and the Middle East across the Mediterranean, as reflected by daily debates in the national media (Orizzonti Meridiani 2014; Lombardi-Diop and Romeo 2012); in addition, the current economic stagnation and high rate of unemployment are driving many Italians abroad,[15] but they have also driven again many southerners to the North, especially to the cosmopolitan city of Milan. Given the current high rate of unemployment in the South, the Italian North represents an immediate choice, and moving abroad is often the following step.[16] Within this new context of internal migration, the Southern Question becomes relevant again today, and its legacy is often lurking in both local and national media and scholarly debates; for example, it reemerged during the celebration of the 150th anniversary of Italian unification in 2011. As shown both in the press and on social media, this celebration explicitly reopened the old debate, while also spurring the reemergence of both northern and southern separatist ideas.

Given the troubled past and present of the Italian South, in this book I contend that by exploring the global circulation and current redefinitions of southern Italian folk music and dances, we are able to locate the ways in which southern Italian groups are constantly redefining their local culture and identity in relation to the larger context of Italy—whose national discourse has traditionally linked the North and the South through a colonial, and orientalistic, vision—as well as in relation to Mediterranean, U.S., and international cultural scenes. As I illustrate in the third chapter, Eugenio Bennato's tarantella albums represent an important example in this sense, as they explicitly and consistently engage with the Southern Question debate. At the same time, by moving across different cultural frameworks, such as from the South to the North of Italy and internationally, the revival also necessarily comes to terms with and helps redefine the image of Italian music (and of Italy) both at home and abroad. Thus, the debate over the Southern Question is strictly intertwined with the tarantella folk culture and its current resignifications. Not surprisingly, then, within the contemporary revival of southern Italian folk music, this connection has been restored and brought to the front by several scholars as crucial to a better understanding of southern culture today.[17]

Why Studying Tarantella (and Tammurriata) in the 2010s?

In the 1970s, and again in the 1990s–2010s, southern Italian folk music and dances have been the object of revival, a phenomenon that has become increasingly international—both in Europe and in the United States—and global, via the world music market. The second phase of revival, my focus in this book, shows not only a proliferation of folk music groups and of local, national, and international collaborations, but also the extensive organization of festivals, music and dance workshops, and schools, both in Italy and abroad. While I participated in the revival context in Italy in the late 1990s and early 2000s, my experience with Belloni's tarantella workshop and performance in Hawai'i since 2006 led me to return to the Italian context and study the southern Italian revival as a transnational phenomenon affecting the ways that performers, cultural brokers, and festival participants on both sides of the Atlantic (and the Pacific) perceive these folk traditions today. My initial fieldwork research in the summers of 2007–9 revealed that, like in many other revival contexts, the post-1990s revival has both reclaimed southern Italian folk music and dances and transformed the festival context into a globalized scene, while its music production and distribution have shifted from a folk to a world music framework. Returning to the local festival scene in the summer of 2014, I noticed a rather amplified festival framework, one that lends itself in much more direct ways to touristification and commercialization, while at the same time spurring a renewed interest in discovering and preserving these folk music and dance forms. In his 1991 article "The Global and the Local: Globalization and Ethnicity," Stuart Hall already noted that the ever-growing globalization process had brought forth a reverse localizing effect, as a way to respond to the growing sense of loss of one's identity and sense of belonging. As David Guss also illustrated through his analysis of the politics of festival in the village of Catuaro (Venezuela), traditional forms of expressive behavior have indeed expanded rather than disappeared under the pressure of modernization and globalization. Nevertheless, in looking at festival behaviors, we need to keep constantly in mind that "these forms will always be threatened with appropriation and commodification" (2000, 6). For this reason, one has to be careful in identifying these festivals simply as sites of resistance to globalization trends. In addition, both national and local ideologies tend to privilege certain interpretations of these events as a way to convey a certain image of the local or national culture, or both, let alone to attract local business. On the level of music and dance performance, such dynamics of exoticization have been widely noted in relation to the larger Mediterranean, as suggested by Marta Savigliano's work on tango (1995), and to other world music scenes, such as salsa (Bock and Borland 2011; Borland 2009) and belly dancing (Shay and Sellers-Young 2005). Furthermore, at least in its initial phases, in the 1990s the revival of southern Italian folk music has been occurring on multiple levels: as a resurgence of local traditions, as antihegemonic ways of expression, and as the emergence of a regional perspective encompassing all Mediterranean cultures (Cassano 1996; Bouchard and Ferme 2013). The coexistence of such diverse cultural trends confirms Hall's idea that "the response [to globalization] seems to go in two ways simultaneously. It goes above the nation-state and it goes below it" (Hall 1991, 27), while at the same time testifying to the continued significance of the nationalist model within the current Italian scenario.

More important, this book examines the modalities in which various southern Italian folk music and dance forms have traveled through linguistically and culturally diverse places: from the South of Italy to the whole Italian peninsula—a composite of historically, culturally, and linguistically diverse areas—and from Italy to the United States. This increasingly global trend is especially important to study, since it is contributing to transforming tarantella according to several trajectories: by introducing new song texts, dance styles, and festival costumes; by assigning new spiritual and cultural meanings to these performances; by popularizing a festival format unrelated to Catholic celebrations; and by recovering the pre-Christian aspects of tarantella. Given tarantella's and particularly tammurriata's links to the agricultural cycle and courtship rites and to Catholic celebrations and values, it becomes natural to ask how globalization can affect, and possibly transform, such site-specific and land-based cultural traditions and how the dynamics of revival and of global display—specifically through tourism, translation, and world music venues—operate within this context of revival.

I argue that the transformations inaugurated by the tarantella revival as a whole ultimately contribute to shifting tarantella's core values into new geographical, social, and cultural contexts. This process of decontextualization is particularly relevant to this discussion, because it places the southern Italian folk music revival within the larger debate over the transmission of folk traditions (Briggs and Bauman 1992; Bauman and Briggs 2003). And because the history and development of tarantella, and particularly tammurriata, is closely tied to the religious festivities of the South, it is also important to ask, "How do aesthetic styles associated with the sacred inhabit new, nonsacred contexts, and what does this amalgam produce in the global circulation of sounds and meanings?" (Kapchan 2007, 2).

Moreover, these changes are important as they relate to gender roles in the Italian context. I believe that one of the most significant changes occurring within the current festival scene is women's increasing onstage participation, in contrast to the primarily male roles still displayed in music performances in most traditional festival settings. Translated to the world music scenario, and especially thanks to performers like Alessandra Belloni, this element has contributed to creating a sort of female genealogy for southern Italian folk music and enters into active dialogue with both the feminist perspective and New Age spiritualism (chapter 4). I believe that this is an important aspect of the current reinterpretations of tarantella, but one that has not yet become an object of study among Italian scholars. While studying the tarantism phenomenon from the Apulia region, De Martino, as well as other scholars who followed up on his study, noted the prominent participation of women in these healing ceremonies (De Martino 2005; De Giorgi 1999, 88), but did not develop this element in his analysis. It is within Italian feminist scholarship and thanks to the recent work of ethnomusicologist Tullia Magrini that women's roles in the tarantism ritual have been further explored. According to Magrini, the liberating power of tarantella is strictly connected to the need for a venue for expressing oneself on the part of southern Italian women, who have historically lived within the constraints of patriarchal society and of the Catholic ideological framework (Magrini 1988, 1994). In her essay "The Folk Music Revival and the Culture of Tarantismo in Salento," Italian Canadian folklorist Luisa Del

Giudice also asks, "How does *tarantismo* continue to 'mark' the Salento and the participants in the neo-*tarantismo* movement? What part do women play in this revival?" (2005a, 241). Upon interviewing several dancers, musicians, and folk culture practitioners, as well as personally observing several elements of the local folk culture—including current healing practices and women's close connection with popular religion—Del Giudice concludes that "despite a radically changed socioeconomic milieu, many cultural (as well as some ritual) aspects of *tarantismo* persist and continue to be referenced—sometimes obliquely" (242). Nevertheless, most Italian studies on the Italian revival, let alone of the festival context, have rarely looked at the role of female performers and participants. Given this context, it becomes particularly important to look at how tarantella performance practices are employed outside of the (southern) Italian context and recontextualized within a foreign and globalized scenario, such as the one represented by Belloni's performances. In fact, "Whereas such practices may participate in exotic modes of representation, they may also privilege self-fashioning over conformity to homegrown cultural norms. In this sense, borrowed cultural practices can resist dominant ideologies of personhood and challenge dichotomous notions of cultural difference," especially when it comes to gender dynamics (Bock and Borland 2011, 2).

Finally, it is important to consider the local responses to the ongoing transformation of the tammurriata tradition within the current Italian festival context as well as the larger tarantella music and dance revival globally. For example, my interviewees would often use the term decontextualization (*decontestualizzazione*), which refers to the process of moving a certain cultural tradition out of its original sociopolitical and cultural context (Bauman and Briggs 2003). The use of this term connects the tammurriata festivals directly to the larger debate over the "loss" of traditions and the need to preserve their authenticity—a debate that is common to much folklore studies scholarship. Interestingly enough, the notion of decontextualization shares many similarities with that of "schizophonia"—the disconnect between an original sound and its reproduction—that ethnomusicologist Steven Feld (1994) applies to world music rhythms. While both these frameworks of analysis deal with the changing context of folk music traditions, an analysis in terms of decontextualization, and its kin term *recontextualization*, allows us to focus on the movement across geographical, sociopolitical, cultural, and linguistic borders and from the local to the national level, rather than simply on the loss of authenticity at stake during the process of transformation. In other words, we are able to discuss both what is being lost, canceled, transformed and what is being gained, added, created. In addition, a discussion of the ways that the tammurriata revival has been recontextualized on a global scale will allow us to explore the outcomes of such a movement across national (and national language) borders.

Ultimately, the debates created by the current popularization of tammurriata are in many ways similar to those created by the larger pizzica revival, even as tammurriata presents a different history and culture, as testified by the originality of its rhythm and dance choreographies. By exploring the current transformations within the tammurriata festival context, I therefore hope to create a genealogy that complements the one established for pizzica, a genealogy that illustrates how different notions of tradition, of local identity, and of place are exchanged (and translated) among practitioners, cultural brokers, and tammurriata aficionados from southern Italy to the United States. As a matter of fact, the pizzica music and dance genre is especially well known thanks to its frenetic rhythm and dance steps, which among other things seem to have lent themselves to be more easily adopted by the younger generations.[18] For this reason, most debates and publications, both in Italy and in the United States, have focused on the revival of the Salentine pizzica. Given tammurriata's strong connection to its peasant history and traditional concepts of land, I believe that the global revival of such a place-specific music tradition allows for a deeper understanding of the tarantella revival as a whole and especially of its trans-national movement from a much localized cultural framework to a global one—something that has only recently become of scholarly interest with regard to the larger pizzica revival. On a strictly musical level, I look at how tammurriata music production participates in, and helped shape, both 1970s and post-1990s tarantella revivals, particularly through the work of well-known groups from the Campania region, mainly NCCP, E Zézi, and Eugenio Bennato.

In his introduction to the volume *Ethnicity, Identity, and Music: The Musical Construction of Place,* ethnomusicologist Martin Stokes underlines the importance of studying musical expression in relation to place. He states, in fact, that "music is socially meaningful not entirely but largely because it provides means by which people recognize identities and places, and the boundaries which separate them" (1994, 5). I believe that Stokes's point is crucial to understand the tammurriata music tradition and its geographical variants; these variants represent a way for each local community to preserve its own uniqueness while at the same time relating to different lifestyles in other communities. The meaningfulness of music in relation to place is also evident in the tammurriata tradition, as this tradition is embedded within the peasant culture of southern Italy. Because place can be defined as a space that has become "meaningful" for a certain person or group (Cresswell 2004), an analysis of the revival from a place perspective will allow me to explore not only the loss of the tammurriata's original cultural context and its *"spirito d'a festa"* (spirit or core of the feast), but also the ways that this tradition is being emplaced elsewhere, that is, recontextualized within the geopolitical and cultural scenario of those who get to know the tammurriata as tourists or migrants. But exactly how is this southern music tradition being made meaningful in other parts of Italy? And what are the sociopolitical, cultural, and ethical costs of such a reemplacement?

In analyzing the recontextualization of tammurriata and tarantella performances within a globalized context, it will be useful to remember scholar Deborah Kapchan's definition of performance as a set of "aesthetic practices . . . whose repetitions situate actors in time and space, structuring individual and group identities." Kapchan's definition is crucial to this study, since it clearly illustrates the close relation between performance and identity formation, in the same way that Falassi's definition of festivals highlights their connection with the local group or community. Moreover, this definition shows how repetitions play a central role in any given performance; Kapchan goes as far as saying that "repetitions, whether lines learned, gestures imitated, or discourses reiterated," are what make performances the "generic means of tradition making" (1996, 479). As confirmed by my analysis of the current tammurriata festivals, a strong concern among old-timers and local performers is what they see as the lack of repetition, in the sense of imitating the old-timers and thus learning from them; this lack, they warn, will ultimately create disruption in the tradition-making process and, as a result, the end of the tammurriata tradition.

Southern Italian folk music has similarly reached a wider audience via the world music scene. As the global circulation of local music intensifies, many scholars worldwide deem it important to ask how it affects both local cultures and the global music scene (Frith 2000; Taylor 1997, 2007; Feld 1994, 2000). Since its inception, the notion of world music has had to do with the idea of consuming, and representing, other music cultures, which makes it both an extremely powerful and a complex musical phenomenon (Born and Hesmondhalgh 2000, 26). Anthropologist Steven Feld, for example, has famously stated that "world music participates in shaping a kind of consumer-friendly multiculturalism, one that follows the market logic of expansion and consolidation" (2000, 168). Interestingly enough, these terms are exactly the same as those employed in recent discussions of globalization, in particular its effects on cultural dynamics: "That any and every hybrid or traditional style could so successfully be lumped together by the single market label *world music* signified the commercial triumph of global musical industrialization" (151).

It is precisely in response to the ongoing debate on the globalization of culture that in his seminal article "From Schizofonia to Schismogenesis," Feld also describes world music as a type of "mediated music, commodified grooves, sounds split from sources, consumer products with few if any contextual linkages to the processes, practices, and forms of participation that could give them meaning within local communities" (1994, 259). Here, Feld borrows from Canadian composer and writer Raymond M. Schafer the use of the word *schizofonia*—the disconnect between an original sound and its reproduction—and applies this concept to world music rhythms. Following a common trend within globalization studies, Feld responds to the concerns raised over the globalization of local music by pointing out how local rhythms have been increasingly popularized through global networks; at the same time, he also suggests that the disjunction between these rhythms as they were in their original context and the way they are now being globalized needs to be fully taken into account. What is even more important for this study is that the split between sounds and the community they originate from, as discussed by Feld, not only echoes the critique of globalization and its dislocating effect on peoples and cultures, but also amplifies on a global scale the disconnect between the current revival of the tarantella and the old tarantella festivals in Italy. Yet, Martin Stokes warns, one also needs to be careful not to easily reduce world music to cultural imperialism, since the major music multinationals have been promoting local music, often without being able to completely control it, and much of this local music is still controlled by smaller independent labels (1994, 301). In addition, these multinationals are themselves located in particular places (302), which counters many antiglobalization discourses that look at the global as placeless. As I hope to show in this volume, this tension between a sense of cultural disconnect and at the same time a sense of being in place is clearly emerging from the current globalization of the tarantella phenomenon.

The relation between world music and tourism is another aspect of globalization that is of particular relevance to this study. Tourism, already present in the Italian festival revival, is also closely associated with world music and with the idea that people can enjoy a variety of music cultures without belonging to these cultures. While tourism has existed for centuries, globalization has definitely enhanced it. As Simon Frith writes in his article "The Discourse of World Music," "World music thus remains a form of tourism . . . just as 'world travelers' are still tourists, even if they use local transport and stay in local inns rather than booking package tours and rooms in the national Hilton" (2000, 320). This conjuncture of tourism and world music politics is, I believe, at the core of the current revival of southern Italian folk music in the United States.

An Autoethnographic Perspective

Following the increasing attention to autoethnography within folklore studies in recent years, my study of these festivals starts from my own involvement in the local tammurriata scene and from my own "remembered moments" (Del Giudice 1994, 74). This book presents an autoethnographic component that has largely affected my methodological approach and also spurred me to rethink my own positionality in relation to the tarantella-revival phenomenon. I first became acquainted with tammurriata rhythms and dancing while attending college at the University of Naples and living in my hometown of Gragnano, in the Naples province. Sometime in my third year of college, in 1998–99, it became "cool" for me and my friends to spend our weekend evenings at some old country house watching both old and young people dance to these traditional peasant rhythms, drinking local wine, and eating "peasant" food, such as *pasta e fagioli* (pasta and beans). Our "hanging-out" places seemed to gradually shift from the Irish pub to a more "local" type of entertainment, although this new activity felt equally exotic and in need of discovery. Most of the young people participating in these get-togethers identified themselves with the so-called *alternativi* (literally "alternative," that is, belonging to the counterculture). The same people would also take part in other nonmainstream music events, often hosted by *centri sociali,* social centers where politically progressive groups gather to discuss political issues, prepare for demonstrations as social action, and organize cultural events open to all. Reflecting on these matters years later, I came to realize that by choosing local wine and food over beer and hamburgers, and by singing in the local language at the festivals, we were ultimately looking for an alternative model to globalization in our own domestic roots. Of course, these ideas were not shared by all the *alternativi*, and a lot of the younger participants, including my friends and myself, seemed to choose these events mainly because they were the new fashionable places. For this reason, when I first engaged with festival dancing, sometime around the spring of 2004, most of my friends had already left this scene and considered it not as fashionable as a few years before. In fact, while for many locals the tammurriata festivals were losing their fresh and exotic charm, an increasingly larger group of tourists from all areas of Italy started to flock to these local festivals; in other words, the festivals had increasingly become less local in scope and more national in appeal.

In addition, because of my direct involvement in this revival phenomenon, a large component of my initial fieldwork was possible thanks to my local friendships and acquaintances; through them I was admitted into my informants' houses and drum labs, and I was able to get an insight into what they felt and thought, but this experience also largely altered my initial perception of the phenomenon. Another aspect that emerged right away was my role within the local context. While my first approach to the local festivals dates back to a time when I was still living in the area—I was still a "local"—by the time I started my fieldwork research I found myself justifying my role to the local informants, who often reacted to my questions defensively or assumed that I was not familiar with their social and cultural values. This reminds us, as scholars of folklore, that "the ways in which we choose to represent [our local informants] may in fact be at odds with the ways in which they wish to see themselves, and the two points of views are not always reconcilable" (Magliocco 2006, xxi). More important, I realize that my initial stance toward this phenomenon stemmed from my own self-definition as a local and my own critique of the revival as a form of entertainment for tourists in search of a pristine rural context. But after years removed from the rural context of tammurriata, I have come to rethink my position as I assessed the tammurriata phenomenon and its need to reclaim the importance of the land and its values, as well as the definition of "local" itself, especially as it is often opposed to "global." Similar to the notion of community, the idea of "localness" "permits us to salvage an ideal," thus perpetuating the romanticization of folk culture that has often been debated among folklore scholars (Abrahams 1993, 22). In the same way, my initial definition as a local implicitly put me in a position from which notions of authenticity attached to tarantella emerged strongly. Only by reassessing my own position was I able to look at the revival, particularly the local festival context, beyond the opposition between insiders versus outsiders.

As Augusto Ferraiuolo suggests in his study of Italian American festivals, in "choosing a reflexive approach," one has to face, among other things, "questions of recognizability, issues of emotional distance and excessive proximity, confusions of roles where the dangerous feeling of nostalgia plays[s] a major part" (2009, 108–9). One of the biggest challenges in my fieldwork has been to acknowledge these shifts and make them accessible to my readers in my field-data reports. I also agree that nostalgia can play a crucial role in this type of research, and given my own position, the risk of romanticizing my past and present experience with the local festivals is always lurking. Like Ferraiuolo, I will approach both my own identity as a local-scholar-participant and that of the other participants in terms of "ephemeral identities": in other words, identities that are unfinished and constantly negotiated. In this way, I hope to be able to look at the "multiple identities and belongings" present within the festival space, and outside of them, and to "analyze the dynamic game of entrances, escapes and cultural commuting" (108). At the same time, I will try to look at the local community from a broader perspective and, in particular, as a crucial term of comparison and contrast with other local communities and with the national and global communities as a whole.

Chapter Descriptions

The first chapter offers an overview of the post-1990s tarantella revitalization in Italy along with the debates surrounding it; in addition, I compare the main themes emerging from these debates with those emerging from the 1970s folk music revival and with a special focus on the role of the Southern Question in relation to this revitalization phenomenon.

The second chapter presents my own analysis of the tammurriata festivals in the Campania region and in the northern Italian city of Milan. Based on my firsthand participation, as well as on interviews and site-specific research I have conducted since the summer of 2007, I explore how notions of place and land—main elements in the tammurriata tradition—are being transformed within the current revival to respond to the needs of the new festival participants, often urbanites with little knowledge of the tammurriata's peasant culture. These changes are evident in the introduction of new dance styles and, at least in the core years of the revival in the 1990s, in the combination of traditional elements with urban youth culture. At the same time, I illustrate the new aspects of tammurriata brought forth by the revival, in particular the emergence of (southern) Italian women performers at center stage. These changes are particularly evident when tammurriata moves from the South to the North of Italy, particularly in the large metropolitan center of Milan, where it is usually marketed as "ethnic" music. In Milan where the immigrants from the South, including the Campania region, remain a large component of the population, performing tammurriata and pizzica, or just participating in a related musical event, often becomes a way for southerners to reconnect to traditional cultural practices from their hometowns and villages as well as with other southerners. Campania expatriates, in particular, can find a venue for reconnecting with their own tammurriata heritage away from home.

The third chapter turns the spotlight on song lyrics and musical arrangements as a way to explore the transformation of the tarantella music tradition from the 1970s until today. In particular, I focus on the work of Neapolitan musician Eugenio Bennato and his involvement with the tarantella rhythms within the larger world music context. These examples illustrate how the world music label has not only provided greater access to these local voices but also spurred local debates; these debates echo ethnomusicologists' warnings about the risk of exoticizing local music that is embedded in the world music label. In the final section of the chapter, I explore the ways that this music revival is explicitly contributing both to the discussion of the Southern Question and to the larger debate over the South's position as a postcolonial entity within contemporary Italy and the Mediterranean.

The fourth chapter illustrates how the revival has been exported to the United States by focusing in particular on New York–based artist Alessandra Belloni's tarantella performance and her "Rhythm Is the Cure" workshop. Although Belloni's shows focus mainly on the pizzica rhythm, her tammurriata performance is particularly interesting, since it showcases the artist's extensive adaptation of southern Italian cultural forms for an international audience. I argue that this process of adaptation is very complex, since it enhances an exotic image of Italy as it often emerges in Anglo-American culture, while at the same time adding a New Age woman's perspective to it. I also discuss her reinterpretation of tarantella both within and beyond the Italian American cultural scene. In the second part of the chapter, I illustrate other examples of tarantella music and dance in New York City and elsewhere in the United States since the early twentieth century—these examples often precede or move beyond Belloni's performance model, thus helping us contextualize Belloni's work within the larger Italian American context as well as discuss Belloni's perspective on tarantella in relation to larger issues of representation of (southern) Italian culture for U.S. audiences.

CHAPTER 1

A Brief History
of the Tarantella Revival

Exploring Tarantella through
the Southern Question Debate

As is often the case with folk-revival movements, the changes inaugurated by the post-1990s revival, the focus of my fieldwork research, have not only popularized the tarantella rhythms—especially the pizzica tradition from the Apulia region—but also created tensions, as each individual or group participating in this process holds a specific understanding of what these music and dance traditions mean and how they should be diffused and preserved. While it is not my concern to define what southern Italian folk music and dances should be, in this chapter I seek to reflect on the social and political stakes that have informed the production and transmission of tarantella since the 1990s. I plan to do so by drawing on the terms of these debates, which center on the notions of *authenticity, tradition, identity,* and *place*. In addition, my analysis of these debates suggests that they are important especially because they reflect the ways in which scholars, performers, and cultural brokers negotiate a particular image of the Italian South, an image that often challenges the ones portrayed through popular culture, both throughout the Italian peninsula and in the United States. In the first half of this chapter, I will trace a brief overview of the major dynamics and themes emerging from the post-1990s tarantella revival, as well as its antecedent, the 1970s folk music revival; in the second half, I will analyze the major scholarly arguments surrounding the current tarantella revival, particularly their connection with the Southern Question debate, in order to illustrate the significance of these two revival moments in relation to southern Italian culture today.

1970s: Politically Engaged Italian Folk Music

The "global tarantella" phenomenon represents the tip of the iceberg in a process of revitalization that started in the 1960s and 1970s. The fieldwork research conducted by American folklorist and ethnomusicologist Alan Lomax in Italy in 1954–55 together with Italian ethnomusicologist Diego Carpitella, and the collection of Italian folk-song recordings derived from that experience, largely contributed to the study of Italian folk music in post–World War II Italy. The collection contained about three thousand recordings dated July 1954 through January 1955 and collected for the Columbia World Library project; the material gathered by Lomax and Carpitella in southern Italy was so vast that the two scholars also decided to publish it as a separate disc anthology titled *Southern Italy and the Islands* (Plastino 2008, 47). Both Lomax's avant-garde methodological approach and his observations about Italian folk music spurred a renewed interest in the field and in many ways contributed to the contemporary field of Italian ethnomusicology (18, 31); for example, Lomax noted that "Italian folk music has come down to our time as the most varied, the most antique and very possibly the richest oral tradition in western Europe" (quoted in R. Cohen 2003, 129). In particular, Lomax was interested in exploring and recording for the first time "Italian peasant music" (126), such as tarantella, which "has lived almost without contact with the great streams of Italian fine-art music. It has followed its own course, unknown and neglected, like a great underground river" (127). He also pointed out that a "complete hiatus between folk art and fine art is one of the distinctive features of Italian cultural history" (127), thus suggesting a general lack of interest in oral culture at the time.

Having worked extensively with Lomax, Diego Carpitella was able to realize not only the importance of this work of documentation, but also the need to continue researching oral cultural material that had never been documented before and was about to be covered over or inexorably changed by the increasing urbanization and industrialization of the 1950s (Carpitella 1974, 87). In those same years, other Italian scholars—such as music critic and journalist Roberto Leydi, who had assisted Lomax during his fieldwork trip and later founded a folk-revival group called Almanacco Popolare (Fabbri 2015, 640),[1] and historian and political activist Gianni Bosio, the founder of Istituto Ernesto de Martino— similarly started documenting and studying Italian folk music and also "began to think that popular songs could be made into a less apolitical medium" (Carrera 2001, 330). Indeed, what all these scholars had in common was a more or less explicit commitment to bringing the "life struggles of ordinary 'folk' . . . to the attention of the general public in order that their plight might be ameliorated (and that they might not be forced to emigrate)" (Del Giudice 2009b, 7). Gianni Bosio, for example, created the Istituto Ernesto de Martino in Rome in honor of the anthropologist who famously studied southern Italian folk culture; the institute was committed to "documenting and enriching the counterculture expressed by the rural and working classes" (Carrera 2001, 331).

An important attempt in this direction was also made by the politically engaged group Cantacronache, based in the city of Turin, which was founded in 1958 and included both musicians and major literary figures such as Italo Calvino and Umberto Eco. Soon enough, the group started adding Italian folk songs to their repertoire and also collaborating with Milan-based folklorists Roberto Leydi, Gianni Bosio, and others (Fabbri 2015, 640); this choice was an explicit reaction to the clichéd popular songs that were being increasingly advertised by the media as well as by Festival di Sanremo, a nationally renowned venue for mainstream Italian music (Portelli 2001, 263). In fact, much Italian popular music of the 1950s and early 1960s consisted of "songs that were often pleasant to listen to, and cheerful in tone (with occasional touches of a gentle irony—never permitted to transmute into social comment . . . and most importantly, they were acceptable to the establishment" (Pestelli 2013, 155). In this sense, Cantacronache's phenomenon, with its attention to lyrical quality and social issues, was a "significant break with the existing popular music tradition, always resolutely closed to even the faintest hint of innovation"; thus, its motto of *evadere dall'evasione* (to escape from escapism) pioneered an entire generation of Italian singer-songwriting (153).

Yet Cantacronache's project, with its sophisticated language (Borio 2013, 37), was ultimately "unable to reach a mass audience, partly because of a media boycott and partly because of their own elitism" (Portelli 2001, 263). According to scholar Giovanni Vacca, the real breakthrough came from a new group, Nuovo Canzoniere Italiano, after Cantacronache's dissolution in 1962; as the Istituto Ernesto de Martino's artistic outlet, Nuovo Canzoniere Italiano comprised urban folk and grassroots singer-songwriters such as Giovanna Daffini and trained musician Giovanna Marini (Carrera 2001, 331). The group, which also included Roberto Leydi, was committed to recovering through fieldwork, to studying, and to faithfully reproducing the oral culture of the subaltern classes (Vacca 1999; Bermani 1997; Istituto Ernesto de Martino 1978); they also "produced songs reflecting current political issues" (Borio 2013, 38). Their work thus contributed to a whole new wave of Italian music that was folk inspired and politically engaged; this music did not limit itself to a specific geographical area, but it revalued both the rice-plantation workers' ("mondine") chants from the North and the peasants' songs from the South, as well as Sicilian fishermen's struggles within an increasingly modernized economic structure. In addition, it both recovered old folk material and composed new songs based on old material (Santoro 2009).

It is thus possible to affirm that both Italian and American folk music revivals at the time "sought to . . . promote cultural conservation and advocate for sociopolitical change" (Del Giudice 2009b, 7). This is largely explained by Italy's cultural climate at the time. Italian folk music and culture were in fact being revitalized within a larger cultural movement that branched out to the students' movement and the Italian feminist movement; it also borrowed from 1960s social rights movements in France and the United States and elaborated them within the Italian left-wing framework (Bermani 1997; Borio 2013; Fabbri 2015; Hardt and Virno 2006). Often working within the ideological framework of the Italian Socialist and Communist Parties, many Italian intellectuals saw the revival of Italian folk culture as crucial to moving away from the increasingly capitalistic ways of living and toward Italy's own music roots (Biagi 2004; Hardt and Virno 2006).

As reflected by the presence of the Istituto Ernesto de Martino, at the time Rome was an important center for left-wing intellectuals, a place where they could meet other scholars and performers. This experience would in turn encourage and prepare them to return to their own regional folk material (Santoro 2009). Apulian scholar Rina Durante and Rome-based Giovanna Marini deserve the credit of having spurred the first wave of pizzica revival; following their experience, the groups Nuovo Canzoniere del Salento and Canzoniere Grecanico Salentino initiated a revival movement in the Apulia region. Furthermore, this intellectual movement was not only contemporaneous with but also partly inspired the revitalization of the folk music tradition from the Campania region, including tammurriata, especially thanks to the work of Neapolitan musician and scholar Roberto De Simone and his group Nuova Compagnia di Canto Popolare, who also collaborated with other revivalists in Rome. I will now focus my attention on the 1970s folk music production from Campania as an entry point into some of the major themes emerging from 1970s tarantella folk music.

The folk music production in Campania during the 1970s has been analyzed within the larger Naples Power movement (Plastino 2013), commonly understood as a "complex set of interconnected, often overlapping folk music and popular music activities" occurring within the 1970s music scene in Naples (56). While its fluidity and variety preclude a simplistic and unified analysis, what is clear to most scholars is that this was a period of highly experimental musical forms (58); at least in the 1970s, many of these artists and groups—

such as NCCP, E Zézi, Collettivo Operaio Nacchere Rosse, Gruppo Folk d'Asilia, Gruppo Operaio di Pomigliano d'Arco, Concetta Barra, and Musicanova—were involved in the larger folk music–revival movement.

Founded in 1967, NCCP is certainly one of the most representative voices of the 1970s folk music revival in Campania and throughout Italy and still today an important model for contemporary tarantella-inspired music projects (59). In fact, the band is "appreciated especially for its 'exact' vocal rendition or folk music songs and dance tunes from the Campania region, and for their re-creation of Neapolitan vocal and instrument music from the sixteenth-century and after" (59). Composer, arranger, and ethnomusicologist Roberto De Simone's collaboration with NCCP and his work as a major scholar of tarantella is particularly significant in this context, especially his volume *Canti e tradizioni popolari in Campania* (Songs and folk traditions in Campania [1979]), which provides an extensive work of recording, collection, transcription, and analysis of folk songs from the Campania region. It also presents a first introduction to the historical and ritual context in which these tarantella traditions developed and thrived over time. This study remains the most authoritative account of the folk music culture of the rural area around Naples and of the Campania region as a whole. Neapolitan musician Eugenio Bennato also had a leading role in this context since he was cofounder of NCCP together with Carlo D'Angiò and worked with NCCP on several albums, traveling to music festivals in Italy and Europe. NCCP's masterpieces include both music projects and theater pieces, such as the well-known *La gatta Cenerentola* (Cinderella SheCat, 1976), which is based on literary tales by sixteenth-century Neapolitan writer Giambattista Basile and recounts, in Neapolitan, the story of Cinderella from the perspective of a southern girl living in sixteenth-century Naples. NCCP's version of the story adopts Basile's plot, as well as its many references to the local folk culture, but reframes it within the southern folk music tradition; in doing so, NCCP is able to recover folk melodies, texts, and rhythms overlooked by both the mainstream and foreign-inspired pop music productions.

One of the strategies employed by NCCP in revitalizing the local folk music culture consisted in re-presenting well-known songs from a folk perspective and in historicizing different versions of the same musical form. A famous example is represented by their interpretation of the 1946 Neapolitan song "Tammurriata Nera" (Black tammurriata). The song describes an unusual event—the birth of a dark-skinned child to a local woman—happening during the U.S. Army's occupation of the streets of Naples following Italy's liberation from fascism. An overtly satirical comment on war times and its effects on the moral customs of Naples's citizens, the song makes use of the tammurriata rhythm as a way to express the voice of the people. Already popularized in the 1950s by Neapolitan singer and musician Renato Carosone, the song was rearranged by NCCP in 1973; NCCP's version was so popular as to remain on the "hit parade" list for weeks, and, soon enough, it became the most quoted version of "Tammurriata nera" (Mauro 2004, 212). Unlike most popular versions of the song, NCCP's version makes wide use of both folk instruments, such as the tammorra drum, and more classical instruments, mainly guitar, mandolin (widely employed in *canzone napoletana,* or the Neapolitan song tradition), and violin; in addition, it employs both music and theater elements—the lyrics are dramatized rather than sung. By approaching this song through drama, NCCP's "Tammurriata nera" feels simultaneously closer to the "voice of the people," expressed here in vivid tones, and further from it—the use of dramatic devices derives from De Simone's education and career in theater and is far from the culture of tammurriata. NCCP's project ultimately tried to bring low- and highbrow culture together. This goal was reached in two related ways: by incorporating folk material into the larger repertoire of Italian *canzone d'autore* and theater (Bermani 1997) and by juxtaposing the highbrow culture of the *canzone d'autore* with elements from the oral rural cultures of the South.

NCCP's use of folk materials, particularly tammurriata, is further confirmed by their use of a common tammurriata song template, still performed today at local festivals; the song begins with the line "Bella figliola ca te chiamme Rosa" (You pretty girl called Rosa), as described by De Simone's transcription:

Bella figliola ca te chiamme Rosa	Pretty girl called Rosa
che bellu nomme mammeta t'ha miso	what a pretty name your mum gave you
t'ha miso lu nomme de li rose	she gave you the name of roses
lu meglio sciore ca sta 'mparaviso . . .	the best flower in paradise . . .

These two distiches introduce the audience to the love theme of the song, a courtship song often performed by peasants while they worked in the fields. Now, let's compare this template with the song "Tammurriata," performed by NCCP and first released on the album *Li Sarracini adorano lu sole* (Saracens adore the sun [1974]).[2] The song makes use of tammurriata rhythm and main instruments, while its lyrics employ phrases or whole verses from the traditional tammurriata songs analyzed by De Simone. Here are the first lines of the song:

Bella figliola ca te chiamme Rosa
che bellu nomme mammeta t'ha miso
t'ha miso lu nomme de li rose,
lu meglio sciore ca sta 'mparaviso . . .

Uh aiuto, aiuto lu munno s'è perduto	Help! Help! The world is damned
li monache se vonno maritare . . .	the nuns want to marry . . .
'o tricchitracco 'int' 'a vunnella,	"tricchitracco" under their skirts
'o piglio 'mmano 'o poso 'nterra . . .	I pick it up and put in on the ground . . .

The song reflects the tammurriata tradition through its use of the refrain as well as of the love theme, including the veiled reference to sex. A "classical" effect is reached, however, by NCCP's use of in-studio recording—which, of course, sounds very different from the tammurriata performances at local festivals—and by the polished sound, which reflects the group's extensive musical training and technique.

On the other side of the spectrum from NCCP, the groups Gruppo Operaio E Zézi, Nacchere Rosse, and Gruppo Folk d'Asilia equally contributed to the folk music scene of the Campania region by bringing a politically engaged agenda (Gammella 2009). Within this context, the work of E Zézi is particularly significant not only for its unique music project and its continued role as a counterhegemonic group still today, but also because their music has reached international and global audiences, as I illustrate in the third chapter.[3] The group emerged in 1974, during one of the most critical moments for the workers' movement in the Campania region: harsh working conditions and a series of layoffs inaugurated by the Italian colossus Fiat in the local town of Pomigliano d'Arco. Bringing together workers, the unemployed, and left-wing militants to respond to local and national working-class struggles, the group took its political-artistic program out on the streets. The genesis and development of E Zézi since the 1970s share many similarities with other contemporary revival groups, especially NCCP; however, its politically engaged music and lowbrow approach put it in a special position within the southern Italian folk music–revival scene. In fact, E Zézi's overall project consists of drawing "the folk culture of the area away from the urban middle-class model, as well as using these folk elements as a political instrument in line with the Italian folk music revival" (Vacca 1999, 45). Since its inception, the group has not only privileged forms of expression that were closer to the "people," such as tammurriata rhythm and narratives, but also made the streets and the postindustrial architecture of Naples and elsewhere its main performing sites. Another element confirming their countercultural stance is their consistent use, still today, of the Neapolitan language: their Neapolitan-only website is a brilliant example of an explicitly political use of one of the subaltern languages of the South.

On a strictly musical level, doing politically engaged music geared to the working class and to the "common people" also means using tammurriata rhythms, melodies, and narrative devices to bring the workers back to the preindustrial world that characterized the South until very recently, while at the same time denouncing urban workers' conditions. In so doing, E Zézi is able to counter the rigid and "unnatural" division of labor typical of modern capitalism by drawing on the less rigidly regulated rhythms of rural life, where workers are able to communicate (often through music) while working. The world of the factory is given direct representation in the songs "'A Flobert" (The Flobert),[4] also known as "Sant'Anastasia," from the name of the town where the story is set, and "'A ferriera" (The iron mill). "'A ferriera" recounts the story of a worker who died after falling into a hot cauldron of boiling iron. "'A Flobert," one of the group's most famous songs, recounts the story of a toy factory that exploded in the industrial area of Naples on April 11, 1975, killing twelve workers. The disaster was found to be due to a total lack of safety measures on the part of management.[5] Here E Zézi moves from the traditional structure of the tammurriata texts to that of a narrative song; indeed, the song's opening line, with its explicit reference to the date of the explosion ("Friday, April 11th, in Sant'Anastasia / All of a sudden a noise / I heard and I was so scared") resembles 1970s political ballads employed by folk music revivalists both in England and in the United States (Vacca 1999). This structure is supported by the use of a very slow rhythm and melody evocative of ballads and by the extensive use of the flute. As the story develops, however, "'A Flobert" becomes a more generalized denunciation of the workers' condition:

E chi và 'a faticà	And those who go to work
pur' 'a morte addà affruntà	have to face even death
murimme 'a uno 'a uno	we die one by one
pe' colpa 'e 'sti padrune.	because of these bosses.
A chi ajmma aspettà	What are we waiting for
sti padrune a' cundannà	to condemn our bosses
ca ce fanno faticà	who make us work
cu 'o pericolo 'e schiattà.	with the danger of kicking the bucket.

The repeated use of *we* in these verses implies not only a group identity and a common destiny as workers, but also the collective identity of the people. Both songs, in fact, present a strong choral quality that helps represent the voice to the community in a way that echoes the "Tammurriata nera" song discussed above. But in order to employ tammurriata as a form of political intervention, E Zézi also had to challenge and modify the tammurriata tradition from a ritualistic and thus ahistorical musical form to one that would express contingent historical facts. The Italian South lacks the tradition of social or workers' songs that can be found in the North as well as in other countries; therefore, to create a politically engaged tammurriata, E Zézi had to transform a strongly religious tradition into a secular one, unlike NCCP, whose music production intended to preserve the cultural values embedded in the rural world of the tammurriata. So, in the first phase of its music production, E Zézi would often borrow from traditional tammurriata chants and repurpose them according to their own needs; over time, however, they have come to create an entirely new repertoire. This repertoire is rather varied, ranging from the song-slogan, as in the song "Pose e sorde" (Leave the money), to the social ballad and several examples of tammurriata. More often than not, however, these elements are brought into a mix of cabaret, stand-up comedy, and social protest moments.

Even this brief overview of the 1970s folk music revival in Campania shows that a major concern over what makes "authentic" southern music and what makes a "folk" tradition was at stake within the 1970s revival. From its start, NCCP was committed to educating its audience to the authentic folk music tradition of Naples and of the Campania region. In the liner notes of their 1971 debut album, NCCP maps out its aesthetic goal in terms of "researching those means of communication that are genuinely of the people." "The interest in extinct folk-song forms," NCCP continues, "aims at re-proposing their primitive spirit, which in our view reveals characteristics in both lyrics and music that are just as valid and effective today" (quoted in Plastino 2013, 59). The notions of genuineness and primitiveness mark a clear commitment to narrating the "folk" (Bendix 1997), while also reflecting the central role of "the people" within Italian socialist ideology. However, NCCP's idea about what it meant to play folk music was ultimately different from E Zézi's. Within the highly politicized cultural climate of the 1970s, NCCP's music was also said to have "sugarcoated [Campania's folk songs]" and "made them palatable to any taste" (quoted in Plastino 2013, 59), thus offering an ultimately conservative endeavor. This debate over the social and cultural values to attach to this music echoes current debates within the tarantella festival context and also anticipates key questions concerning the post-1990s tarantella music production, especially as it is labeled as world music.

The Post-1990s Revival

The second wave of Italian folk music revival has spread throughout Italy since the 1990s and has featured an unprecedented popularity of tarantella, particularly its pizzica variety from the Apulia region. According to Italian scholar Gianni Pizza, 1994 was a crucial year in this sense, since it saw the reappearance on the Italian bookshelves of Ernesto De Martino's book *La terra del rimorso* after decades of forgetfulness (Pizza 2015, 68). This was followed by the production of several texts by local scholars, who started rediscovering the importance of tarantism in relation to southern Italian ethnology and folklore studies. This renewed interest in studying tarantism in Apulia is important to note here because it went hand in hand with the increasing popularization of the pizzica festivals and of a new music production, since many of these scholars were also artists and performers who actively participated in the festival context and contributed to the music scene (75). This can be read as yet another reason for the current popularity of Apulian pizzica compared to other southern Italian folk rhythms.[6]

The increasing popular attraction to these rhythms since the 1990s is reflected by the extensive organization of both local and nationwide festivals, courses, and workshops. The most important example of this phenomenon is the annual Notte della Taranta (Night of the Taranta) festival, a festival held in the town of Melpignano in the Apulia region, the land of pizzica, since 1998 and devoted to southern Italian rhythms. Following its large success, the festival has contributed to popularizing pizzica both nationally and internationally, while also boosting tourism in the region. Over time the festival's scope has become increasingly international, thanks to the presence of many artists from around the world, including artists from world music, rock, and pop music scenes. Besides hosting various Italian and international folk music performers, the 2014 edition, for example, featured as special guests artist Bombino, who presented his reinterpretation of a well-known pizzica classic, the song "Lu rusciu te lu mare," as well as American and Grammy Award–winning percussionist Glen Velez, together with well-known Italian pop singers Roberto Vecchioni and Antonella Ruggieri.[7]

This national and international visibility is further confirmed by the fact that the festival, now lasting an entire week, is recorded and transmitted live and can be streamed on the festival's website. Besides becoming a symbol of the post-1990s revival phenomenon, the festival has also become a hot topic of debate among local practitioners and scholars, who have often complained about its increasing touristification and the consequent commercialization of pizzica and tarantella more generally (Pizza 2002, 2004). As a result of these tensions, in the summer of 2015 cofounder Sergio Blasi decided to leave the Fondazione della Notte della Taranta—the foundation in charge of organizing the festival—since, as he wrote in the southern newspaper *Corriere del Mezzogiorno,* the dynamics of spectacularization seem to have largely replaced what Blasi and others saw as the inspiration behind the festival, "to show with pride what was long considered something to be ashamed of." He also reminds, however, that the festival has been successful, insofar as it has "demonstrated how cultural events and the encounter with other musical cultures . . . can become economic growth and contribute to guaranteeing a better future for this land" (Mandese 2015).

Even beyond this major music event, it is possible to discern an increasing presence of tarantella music and dance at local festivals, food fairs, and various other cultural events throughout Italy, and especially in the major cities of Rome, Milan, Turin, and Bologna—places that have no direct cultural connection with tarantella but host many southern migrants in search of work and often create their own folk music groups to reconnect to their roots. Indeed, tarantella, and pizzica in particular, has become not only a major touristic attraction to Italy's southern regions—as reflected by the popularity of youth summer trips to the Apulian region—but also a cultural and social attraction for both old and young urbanites living in Italy's major urban centers, as confirmed by the ubiquity of posters and Facebook events advertising both local and national tarantella events.

These festival dynamics are in turn echoed by the proliferation of folk music groups and of album production, ranging from self-production and distribution at the local level to national and international distribution via the world music label. In fact, tarantella music production since the 1990s is vast and features several major groups, from Canzoniere Grecanico Salentino to Eugenio Bennato, Officina Zoé, Arakne Mediterranea, and Aramiré, whose work has become known both nationally and in some cases also internationally. Within this context, it is particularly important to note the production and nationwide marketing of the multivolume music collection titled *Pizzica la taranta* (Bite the taranta or The taranta bites), which was first released in 2012 and collects some of the most important names in the pizzica revival. This album production, in its fifth year as of July 2016, represents an important step in the larger process of massification of tarantella music, since it was distributed by Milan-based Arnoldo Mondadori Editore through popular Italian magazines such as *TV Sorrisi e Canzoni* and *Chi* and can be purchased through major Italian bookstores like Feltrinelli and Mondadori as well as via Amazon. This type of distribution grants pizzica, and tarantella more generally, unprecedented attention within the Italian mainstream music scene. And to get a sense of how mainstream tarantella can become, one can have a quick look at some of the major Italian wedding websites, such as http://www.matrimonio.it, which now provide pizzica and tarantella suggestions for a wedding's musical arrangements. Whereas in the 1970s the production of folk music remained of interest mostly to left-wing students and intellectuals, this wider reception contributes to an increasingly large audience for tarantella, but also spurs many to ask whether the social value of this folk music, as conceived by 1970s artists, has being watered down or even replaced by a purely commercial music phenomenon.

This larger reception of tarantella since the 1990s has also been marked by an opening up of the local music scene to regional, national, and international music frameworks; transregional music collaborations are evident in the work of Neoplitan Eugenio Bennato—and his Taranta Power movement (chapter 3)—and of Daniele Sepe. Sepe released two albums during the hot years of the tarantella revival, *Vite Perdite* (1993) and *Viaggi fuori dai paraggi* (1996); in particular, the song "La tarantella del Gargano" (Gargano's tarantella)[8] offers a contemporary rendering of tarantella that, it is safe to say, largely contributed to the 1990s neotarantism phenomenon among young generations in Campania and among young left-wing intellectuals. Another example comes from NCCP's 2005 album, *Candelora,* which contains an homage song to the pizzica revival titled "'A vita è 'na taranta" (Life is a taranta); following a well-known pizzica song format, the song reflects NCCP's participation within the larger pizzica revival. Moreover, this attempt to move beyond the geographical boundaries of pizzica and tammurriata has often led these artists to an interest in similar folk sounds from other parts of Europe and the Mediterranean, such as Balkan music in Sepe's case. These examples also show that this new wave of interest in tarantella presents both local and international aspects. Indeed, the tarantella revival, as shaped by the larger world music market, confirms the copresence of tarantella music with Romani or gypsy music—and in later years also with other types of ethnic music from Europe, Africa, the Middle East, and Latin America—which has received increasing attention within the Italian music scene since the 1990s (Silverman 2012), as also suggested by the popularity in Italy of both Serbian filmmaker Emir Kusturica's films about Romani culture as well as musician and composer Goran Bregovic's Balkan music performances. In addition, textual choices and music arrangements on the part of current southern Italian folk musicians often include a blend of Mediterranean, African, Balkan, and other Eastern European sounds. A significant example is the song "Tammurriata dell'est" (Eastern tammurriata) by Neapolitan musician Raiz, the leader of the hip-hop group Almamagretta. The song employs the gypsy sounds of the Balkans and remixes them into a tammurriata narrative sung in Neapolitan. In this sense, the tarantella revival also shares many elements with other subcultural sounds developed in Italy since the early 1990s, such as Italian hip-hop, rap, and ragamuffin (Gala 2002).

Further, this revitalization of southern Italian folk music, particularly tarantella, has spurred several musicians to rework these folk sounds into contemporary musical forms, as the revival movement stimulates the creativity of many young musicians. An interesting example of this type of musical mélange is the album *Rockammorra* (2009) by Neapolitan musician Joe Petrosino. In the album, Petrosino juxtaposes rock sounds and instruments with the tammurriata rhythm as well as with Neapolitan folklore. The result is a unique combination of traditional and modern sounds confirming the many possibilities of reviving southern folk music today beyond the mere revitalization of traditional melodies and sounds. A particularly interesting piece is represented by the song "Vesuvius" (2009), whose title recalls a well-known song by E Zézi, "Vesuvio" (1996), which I will also discuss in the third chapter. The video of the "Vesuvius" song opens up with a black-and-white view of a mountain scene, from which it is possible to view the city of Naples and Mount Vesuvius, the dormant volcano famous for having caused the destruction of Pompeii in AD 79. The camera then moves to a close-up shot of Nando Citarella—a southern drummer who is well known throughout Italy and internationally—showing him in the act of playing the tammorra drum and singing a tammurriata-style narrative about the volcano. Two female dancers follow a typical tammurriata choreography, while Petrosino adds the rock sound of his bass to this bucolic scene. Although known mostly in the region, this piece presents a unique combination of old and new ways of practicing southern Italian folk music.

Finally, the wide-ranging aspects of this music include various and diverse reinterpretations and echoes of both pizzica and tammurriata within other music genres. Several critics have already noted the many intersections between this folk music revival and Italian hip-hop music of the 1990s (Plastino 1996). As the revival increasingly transforms into a nationwide touristic and commercial phenomenon, several well-known artists, both from the South and other Italian regions, have paid homage to tarantella, ranging from Rome-based singer-songwriter Mannarino to classical composer Ludovico Einaudi, while also reflecting on the cultural significance and ambiguities of this revival phenomenon.

Singer-songwriter and musician Vinicio Capossela vividly described the craze for southern Italian folk music in his 1996 hit song, "Il ballo di San Vito" (St. Vito's dance). San Vito dei Normanni is a small town in the Apulia region that is famous for a particular type of pizzica, usually called the "pizzica di San Vito" (St. Vitus's pizzica). Tuned to the pizzica rhythm, the song opens with a typical festival scene that well illustrates the close relation between the sacred, the secular, and the touristic within the current tarantella festival context:

Salsicce fegatini	Sausages chicken liver
viscere alla brace	grilled intestines

| e fiaccole danzanti . . . | and dancing lanterns . . . |
| sul dorso della chiesa fiammeggiante | on the back of a blazing church |

In the second stanza, instead, Capossela introduces the theme of the land, central to southern Italian folk music, as well as the role of the South in relation to the Italian nationalist project and to a "Mediterranean imagination":

terra arsa e rossa	scorched, red land
terra di sud, terra di sud . . .	southern land, southern land . . .
e il continente se ne infischia . . .	and the continent doesn't care . . .
e qui soffia il vento d'Africa. . . .	and here an African wind blows. . . .

The singer's voice then moves on to what is at stake today in the reinvention of tarantism and its music rituals:

Vecchi e giovani pizzicati . . .	The bitten, old and young . . .
dalla taranta, dalla taranta	by the taranta, by the taranta
dalla tarantolata	by the tarantolata[9]
cerchio che chiude, cerchio che apre	a circle that closes, a circle that opens
cerchio che stringe, cerchio che spinge	a circle that presses, that pushes
cerchio che abbraccia e poi ti scaccia . . .	a circle that hugs and then pushes you away

This song carries powerful lyrics: note, in particular, the musical effect of the rhyme, and the repetition of certain words and phrases, which re-creates the obsessive quality of the spider-dance rhythm. Both the lyrics and the captivating pizzica rhythm have made this song into a big hit among tarantella aficionados.

Another hit song, "Vieni a ballare in Puglia" (Come and dance in Apulia), released in 2008 by Apulian rapper Caparezza, invited reflection on the current revival and in particular on its often acritical celebration on the part of local scholars. The much darker tone of this song clearly reflects how eight years from Capossela's own hit song, the positive energy associated with the 1990s pizzica revival had been replaced by an increasing awareness of the effects of commercialization. The song skillfully employs the tarantella fast beat and uses it as a basis for a rap song of protest. The Salento area, where the tarantella revival is now particularly strong, has one of the least developed shores in the South and is also a main port for migrants and refugees from the Mediterranean. As both the song lyrics and the vivid images featured in the song video suggest, pollution, high rates of unemployment, Mafia, poor working conditions, and illegal immigration are some of the main issues in this region, all covered up by the inviting and exotic image of Apulia offered by tourist marketing. The narrator ironically concludes:

O Puglia Puglia mia tu Puglia mia	Oh Apulia, my Apulia
Ti porto sempre nel cuore quando vado via	I always carry you in my heart when I leave
E poi penso che potrei morire senza te	and then I think I could die without you
E poi penso che potrei morire anche con te.	and then I think I could die with you as well.

By using the upbeat rhythm of tarantella, and by juxtaposing it with images portraying the harsh reality of Apulia, the author seems to suggest that the celebratory version of tarantella that attracts tourists from other regions of Italy and from abroad can even become detrimental to the future of the region. The video makes this aspect very clear by showing skeletons everywhere on the beach, photographed by tourists. From this perspective, the tarantella revival becomes a coperpetrator of the agony of the locals. Therefore, the song also denounces the hypocrisy behind the tourist's view of Apulia; as the author puts it, "Tourist, you dance and sing while I count the dead people of this land." In addition, the song critiques the local politics of culture, which often use the tarantella revival as an excuse to draw funds from the European Union directly into the pockets of local political groups (Pizza 2004).

As Caparezza's example illustrates, the post-1990s revival has also encouraged the production of feature films, documentaries, and music videos inspired by the tarantella rhythms and its history. Major examples that are well known to tarantella aficionados in Italy are director Edoardo Winspeare's films *Pizzicata* (Bitten [1996]) and *Life Blood* (original title *Sangue vivo* [2000]), both films produced during the core years of the pizzica revival; these films have particularly contributed to the popularization of the pizzica revival and to a renewed understanding of tarantism today (Laviosa 2010, 2011). Set in 1943 in the Salento area, *Pizzicata* looks at pizzica from the perspective of an Italian-American pilot, Tony, whose plane falls near a local farmhouse and who is rescued by the owners' family, which event eventually results in his falling in love with one of the owners' daughters. The film shows Tony's introduction to the rural life of southern Italy, including its folk dances, particularly the local pizzica. The film *Sangue vivo,* on the other hand, takes the same title as a popular album by the Salentine group Officina Zoè, one of the most representative pizzica albums within the current revival and also the film's soundtrack. Set in the Apulia region, the film's main interest lies in the fact that the main characters, a group of tarantella players, are played by actual tarantella performers such as the film's well-known protagonist Pino Zimba, a Salentine drummer and among the major promoters of the post-1990s pizzica revival. As reflected through the protagonist's life vicissitudes, pizzica music does play an important role in the film, not only as a hope for a better future for southern Italians (who like Zimba in the film in many cases have picked up their drums to make a living for lack of a more stable job) but also as a ritual that can still help southern Italians exorcise their owns fears and problems. In this sense, the film can be read within a larger revitalization movement that sees several, especially from the Salento region, as proponents of tarantella's therapeutic role within the contemporary social formation of the Italian South (Nacci 2001, 2004).

This reenactment of the tarantism ritual is often present in music videos from the revival, as suggested by Salentine group Alla Bua's video released for the song "Lu rusciu te lu mare" (The sound of the sea). The video, presented at the nationally renowned Giffoni Film Festival in 2002, shows a little girl dressed in white (one of the main symbolic colors of tarantism) and trapped within a cubic space; as the band starts playing, the girl starts squirming and then gradually moving faster and faster, her figure resembling a spider, according to the tarantism myth. As the pizzica rhythm gets faster, the girl liberates herself and looks outside of her cubicle, while female dancers appear dancing frantically in the fields to the rhythm of pizzica.

Similar to tarantella music production, echoes of the post-1990s tarantella revival are to be increasingly found throughout Italian and Italian American cinema. For example, the 2008 Italian film *Nuovomondo* (released in the United States under the title *The Golden Door*), which recounts the story of a southern Italian family migrating to the United States at the turn of the twentieth century, contains a powerful performance scene featuring singing as well as tammorra and tamburello drumming. While trapped on the long and exhausting transatlantic journey to New York City, migrants get together for a moment of respite through music; they fetch drums and violins they brought with them and engage in a powerful tarantella performance. As it shows the importance of tarantella music for southern migrants to the United States, this scene well reflects the film's overall goal of portraying folk culture as an integral part of the Italian American experience (Del Giudice 2009b; Sciorra 2011), contrary to previous representations of Italian American culture. Within the Italian American context, it is also important to remember the 1995 film *Tarantella*, the story of an Italian American girl who embraces her ethnic roots, of which dancing is a major component. Finally, several southern Italian groups have made it onto the American screen. Neapolitan group Spakka Neapolis 55's

2000 album, *Aneme perze—Lost Souls,* which I discuss in the third chapter, was featured in *The Sopranos* TV series, while Milan-based band Domo Emigrantes's music was featured in the recent Italian Canadian comedy *Mangiacake* (2015).

With respect to the folk-song tradition from the Campania region, the musical film *Passione,* released in 2010 and directed by Italian American actor, director, and producer John Turturro, stands out for its fresh perspective on the southern Italian city of Naples and its world-renowned music culture, a perspective achieved by portraying Naples not only as the city of the internationally renowned Neapolitan song tradition, but also as an important hub of musical and cultural influences, including tammurriata. This directing choice clearly reflects a growing international visibility of southern Italian folk music and dances, but also Turturro's reinterpretation of southern Italian folk music within a transnational and world music framework. Such a reinterpretation is evident from the group Spakka Neapolis 55's performance of the song "Vesuvio" in the introductory scene. Even as it presents an homage to the current southern Italian folk music revival, the film juxtaposes Spakka Neapolis 55's performance with images of flamenco dancing. In order to present a global image of Neapolitan music, here the director has evidently opted for a globally familiar image of folk dancing from the Mediterranean; in doing so, he not only reinterprets Neapolitan music according to Mediterranean, global, and diasporic perspectives but also creates a new product that is more suitable for the world music market. Thus, while reflecting a recontextualization of tarantella within a transnational and global framework, these examples also suggest the need to reflect on the social and cultural significance of the post-1990s revival moment, especially on the issues of representation and commercialization that emerge from this cultural movement.

Scholarship on the Tarantella Revival

Since its start, the scholarship surrounding the post-1990s tarantella revival, particularly the pizzica revival, has had several goals: to challenge the image of tarantella (and of the South) commonly reflected through the internationally renowned Neapolitan tarantella dance and recover the complex history and ritual aspects of tarantella, to push for an understanding of tarantella in relation to the peculiar history of the Italian South and its related Southern Question debate, to understand the role of tarantella today as a nonreligious social phenomenon, and to explore the revival phenomenon in relation to local (and national) politics of culture. In the next few sections, I will look at each of these interpretations and at their related debates, since they echo similar debates surrounding the tammurriata revival (chapter 2), the world music marketing of tarantella by musician Eugenio Bennato (chapter 3), and the recontextualization of tarantella rhythms for U.S. and international audiences by New York–based artist Alessandra Belloni (chapter 4).

Scholars of the post-1990s tarantella revival have striven to recover the sociocultural import of tarantella by reconnecting tarantella to the peculiar cultural and religious context of the Italian South. For example, Eugenio Bennato (2001), one of the leading voices of both 1970s and 1990s tarantella revivals, writes that the internationally renowned Neapolitan tarantella consists of an overpolished and stereotyped tarantella choreography; this international image of tarantella thus reflects a stereotypical image of the city of Naples, and of Italy in general, in the eyes of foreigners, by reducing the extremely diverse scenario of southern Italian folk dance to a single choreography. In addition, according to Bennato, Neapolitan tarantella "conveys an image that has no relation with the ritual energy of the places it is mostly associated with: mainly Salento, the Gargano area, the whole Calabria region and so on" (87). Thus, recovering the cultural complexity of tarantella also means reclaiming the ritual energy embedded in its rhythms and moving away from the simplifying notion of tarantella as a dance for entertainment purposes. This is indeed an important trend within the post-1990s revival, since it is also echoed by the work of Alessandra Belloni in New York and elsewhere in the United States since the 1970s.

Another way to reclaim the sociocultural import of tarantella is by rediscovering the significance of De Martino's study of tarantism, as well as Gramsci's ideas about Italian popular culture. De Martino's book *The Land of Remorse* was the first to illustrate tarantella music and dance rituals in relation to the larger sociopolitical and cultural context of southern Italy. According to De Martino, by understanding the phenomenon of tarantism, we are able to make sense of the troubled history of southern Italy and of its vexed relation with the industrial North (Saunders 1993). For example, the particular psychological condition of the *tarantati* is also illustrated by De Martino's use of the term *rimorso* (remorse), which in Italian has the double meaning of a literal "second bite" and of remorse in the usual sense. In the first case, *remorse* refers to the recurring nature of the syndrome, while in the second De Martino borrows from Levi-Strauss to describe southern Italy's "wretched past that returns and regurgitates and oppresses with its regurgitation" (De Martino 2005, xxi). Viewed in this light, the "land of remorse" is not only Apulia, the region where most tarantism cases have concentrated over time, but also southern Italy as a whole. Furthermore, De Martino provides historical evidence for comparisons between southern Italy and other "primitive" societies such as India and the "New World." The phrase *Italian India,* used to refer to the Italian South and first circulated in the mid-sixteenth century among Jesuits in Naples, brilliantly summarizes the condition of the South within the Italian peninsula. In response to such a history, De Martino explains, his vocation soon came to be that of writing as a way to better understand the Southern Question and to help the South through its process of "rebirth and emancipation" (6).

Understanding the folk culture of these areas is crucial for De Martino, as it was for Antonio Gramsci before him, to address the larger problem of the southern condition. Indeed, both Gramsci and De Martino wrote about the folk culture of the South, and they both were convinced that by studying the culture of the working classes, one could better understand these groups and therefore help them move beyond their marginalized condition. Improving the living conditions and the educational level of these subaltern groups would in turn help construct a stronger national culture and fill the cultural gap between ruling and marginalized groups in Italian society. According to this view, folklore was essentially a form of barbarism that contributed to the marginalization of the lower classes. At the same time, both De Martino's study of tarantism and Gramsci's reflections on Italian folk culture reveal an understanding of Italian folk culture as crucial to shed light on the social, cultural, and religious history of southern Italy. In addition, Gramsci's attempt to understand the culture of subaltern groups also works as a model for contemporary Italian scholars who are studying the resurgence of popular culture among young generations of Italians. In fact, Gramsci's idea that popular culture can function as an anti-hegemonic form of expression is common to several students of the revival, writing both during the 1970s and again in the 1990s.

Inspired by De Martino's analysis of tarantism, since the 1990s the Italian scholarship on the revival has been devoted primarily to pizzica music and dance from the Salento area and the Apulia region more generally and has often insisted on the continued significance of tarantism rituals within the current sociopolitical and cultural structure of southern Italy.[10] Italian scholars Vincenzo Santoro and Sergio Torsello explain that "forty years after De Martino's study, the scene has completely changed. The plan to guide Mezzogiorno[11] toward 'modernity' through industrialization, which was at the center of the debates on the Southern Question, is now finally being put aside, leaving behind a stream of social and environmental damage. . . . Nevertheless, like never before, a general interest in [tarantism]—a phenomenon that had been relegated to the margins of modernity as symbol of ignorance, suffering, and of the 'bad past' that cyclically returns—is growing and expanding" (2002, 5–6). Fifty years after De Martino's famous study, therefore, a significant difference in the perception of the tarantella tradition concerns the passage from a negative view of tarantism that is reflected throughout De Martino's ethnographic work to the celebratory tone of today's festivals. By the 1990s, the tourist slogan read something like this: "Come to the land of tarantism. . . . [C]ome to know the Salento area, which has tarantism in its blood" (Apolito 2000, 141). In other words, far from being symbols of ignorance, such folk practices as tarantella have now moved to the front stage of modernity, and from this new position they are able to question the very ideology of modernity, which had cast them into the margins of mainstream culture. Together with the commodification of tarantism to promote local business and tourism, this celebration of tarantella has contributed to make Salento, and southern Italy more generally, the land of celebration rather than a land of remorse. As a result, the main task for local and global scholars is not so much to study or recover tarantism rituals, but rather to understand how the "current repositories of tarantism culture and its young neophytes perceive this form of expression, judged shameful until a few decades ago" (Bevilacqua 2003, 385). For Salvatore Bevilacqua, therefore, the main issue at stake within the current "neotarantismo" phenomenon is an "appropriation of tarantism rituals" (390), which follows three main trajectories: first, toward an affirmation of local identities from the South or the social identities of the (southern) Italian youth, or both; second, toward a use of tarantism myths for specific political and cultural purposes; and third, toward a use of these myths for specifically commercial purposes. A closer look at each of these trajectories will offer a better understanding of this complex revival phenomenon.

In his volume *Il pensiero meridiano* (1996, 2005), Italian philosopher Franco Cassano illustrates a view common to many Italian students of the revival in the 1990s and early 2000s, especially those writing from the Salento area.[12] These scholars consider the liberating potential of tarantella as crucial to the construction of antihegemonic local and regional identities that are shared by a large population throughout the Mediterranean and that contest the homogenizing effects of both globalization and nationalism. This view is reflected by what Cassano calls "il pensiero meridiano" (Meridian or southern thought), an alternative to the Think-Global slogan, arguably shaped by the hegemonic position of the most powerful countries. But the local identities (re)affirmed through the folk music revival are not fixed; instead, they are the product of a long series of political and cultural changes often linked to the ever-growing migration of workers from the northern coasts of Africa and other parts of the Mediterranean. Thus, the need to understand, and recover, one's identity as a southern Italian seems due, especially in the Salento's case, to the growing role of the area as the center for Mediterranean migration and therefore to the need to understand its changing identity. Santoro and Torsello further describe the current "pizzica movement" as a "phenomenon typical of 'modernity,' but that exists both 'within' and 'in spite of' the paradigms of modernity" (2002, 9). "In a land marked by a century-old inclination to syncretism," they explain, "pizzica, with its geographical and cultural background, presents itself as an 'identity marker' in the proper sense. But the identity expressed by pizzica is open, hybrid, and welcoming; it bears the dynamic quality of dance, and constantly looks for a time, space, and ways to relate to the 'other'" (9–10). The importance of the current tarantella movement, therefore, consists in its affirmation of a local identity that exists within a larger globalized structure and that is constantly in dialogue with the larger Mediterranean culture through migration. This particular reading is, however, felt to be controversial by some: as anthropologist Gianni Pizza points out, the main risk embedded in such a position consists of essentializing the South, as well as the Mediterranean, through the image of the "Meridian thought," and thus perpetuating the same ideological mechanisms involved in the creation of the Southern Question. In his letter to Santoro and Torsello in the volume quoted above, Pizza comments: "Mediterraneo, as well as South and North, are material, intellectual and sentimental products that can be felt as pre-existing and natural only through the enforcement of ideological structures" (2002, 53). Further insisting on the ambiguity of such a position, Pizza concludes: "It is for this reason that I don't believe that 'the Meridian thought' represents the right critical answer to the strategies of hegemonic power. . . . [T]he stereotyping of certain practices should not be fought with the practice of stereotypes" (55).

A different framework for understanding the social history and significance of the current folk music revival is provided by that of "neotarantism." Rome-based radio journalist Anna Nacci, conductor, since 1999, of the radio show *Tarantula rubra* (Red tarantula) that is entirely devoted to southern Italian folk music, first introduced the word *neotarantismo* to label this latest wave of the southern folk music revival (Nacci 2001). Nacci's active participation in the revival debate, through her radio show and the organization of several conferences and publications on the matter, attests to the spreading of the revival to both the Italian capital and the whole Italian peninsula since the 1990s. In her introduction to the volume *Tarantismo e neotarantismo,* the result of a major conference on the revival held in Rome in 2001, Nacci defines the revival as "a movement without geographical or cultural barriers, an expression of joy, of new ways of communicating that is different from the ones forced upon us from above, of new forms of catharsis and liberation" (2001, 23–24). On the one hand, the *neotarantismo* label shows a reduction of the revival, which is occurring in different forms in several Italian regions, to the pizzica revival spread from the Apulia region. On the other hand, Nacci's definition of *neotarantismo* confirms an inaccurate reinterpretation of the historical tarantism phenomenon as something positive and thus very different from the phenomenon described by De Martino (Pizza 2015, 79). More important, in Nacci's view, the current revival of southern Italian folk music is connected not so much to the specific social and cultural history of southern Italy, but rather to a more general need for alternative ways of expression among young generations of Italians coming from every part of the peninsula. In other words, Nacci looks at the revival mainly as a postmodern cultural movement, thus implicitly dismissing the cultural specificity of tarantella. At the same time, she is also able to trace similarities between today's mainstream forms of expression, such as fast food and Anglo-American rock/pop—products of a globalized, metropolitan Italy—and the claustrophobic, patriarchal Catholic structure discovered by De Martino in the most remote, rural areas of the South.

While Nacci's view of the revival can certainly help make sense of the increasing participation of younger people in the local festivals, including the *tammurriata* festivals from the Campania region, I believe that the relation between the revival and the historical, sociopolitical, and cultural context of southern Italy cannot be overlooked. Not surprisingly, several scholars have challenged Nacci's use of the term *neotarantismo* for its historical inaccuracy, since it seems to suggest the continued presence of tarantism practices today, even as tarantism in the proper sense cannot be found anymore.

Further developing Nacci's interpretation of the revival, Salvatore Bevilacqua critiques the use of the term *neotarantismo* and also points out that the need to dance tarantella on the part of the younger generations has nothing to do with tarantism and trance in their proper sense; rather, it becomes an "antidote to boredom, a negative result of cultural homogenization." In this sense, Bevilacqua accepts Nacci's view of the revival as an important social phenomenon in contemporary Italy; however, he also states that "even as they borrow from the cultural heritage of the older generations, the Italian youth perceives the 'spider dance' differently, and mainly as a choice; in doing so, they are counteracting the pressure of cultural uniformity, rather than paying homage to the values of the [*tarantella*] tradition" (2003, 392). Nacci and Bevilacqua are not alone here; several scholars believe that the current recovering of tarantism music rituals reflects the need for an alternative cultural model to the one developed through globalization. For example, French anthropologist George Lapassade has worked extensively on tarantism; in particular, he has developed Gilbert Rouget's ideas on music and trance (1985) and applied them to the Italian context. The originality of Lapassade's theory consists in recovering the trance element that is associated with tarantism and in projecting it onto the post-1990s folk music scene; he explains that by reaching the state of trance, young generations are not only able to reach an altered state of mind, but can also create new ways of communicating with each other, while also expressing their rejection of hegemonic cultural expressions.

Trance therefore becomes a powerful antidote to increasingly globalized ways of living, in Italy and elsewhere, and can help return to more "authentic" ways of feeling and communicating with each other. In Lapassade's view, southern Italian folk music, and tarantella in particular, plays a role very similar to that of electronic music and other subcultural music expressions within the current globalized world order, while the tarantella festival context shares many elements with rave parties and other alternative music spaces. The main problem with Lapassade's reading of the revival is that he applies the notion of trance to the current festival scene, a cultural context that does not feature elements of trance in its proper sense. Lapassade is aware that today's tarantella festivals often reflect a "moda giovanile" (a youth fashion) (Lapassade 2001, 34), and thus a very different phenomenon from tarantism practices; however, even if these festivals don't stimulate actual trance, Lapassade seems to suggest, their meaning cannot be simply dismissed as a trend or commercial product, since they remain important moments to reconnect with one's own local identity. This last aspect, which Lapassade calls "etnicizzazione" (a process of "ethnicization" or reethnicizing [34]), clearly resembles Franco Cassano's idea of a "Meridian thought." Gianni Pizza also identifies Lapassade's book *Intervista al Tarantismo* (Interview with tarantism) as crucial to the translation of the discourse of tarantism into a rhetoric of "salentinità" or salentine-ness (2015, 78).

Finally, an element shared by both Lapassade's and Nacci's readings of the revival is the explicit use of the term *anti-egemonico* (antihegemonic). This term visibly reflects an Italian left-wing perspective on Italian anthropology via Gramsci's lesson. However, especially in Nacci's and Lapassade's cases, it remains unclear to what extent such forms of cultural expression as the tarantella festivals can perform an antihegemonic function in the actual practice of being (southern) Italian citizens. When reading the work of Lapassade and other scholars of the revival, one often has the impression that the antihegemonic quality of tarantella remains an overused slogan rather than a concrete and achievable goal.

To conclude, as Torsello suggests, a common limit to most studies on the post-1990s tarantella revival has to do with their tendency to construct an overly positive notion of tarantism and of its spider dance. Another problem relates to their tendency to essentialize the revival as typically Salentine, and therefore to dismiss other folk-culture phenomena within the larger southern Italian context. At the Quarant'anni dopo De Martino conference held in Galatina (Apulia) in 2000, several scholars of De Martino's work had already warned against the risk of generalization and historical inaccuracy behind the current revitalization of tarantella. In particular, Paolo Apolito mentions two main forms of reduction: the "psychological" and the "folkloristic" (2000, 143); the first reduces the tarantism phenomenon to its medical and psychic aspects, in the same way as the pre–De Martino studies, and the second, and opposite, one dismisses this specific social phenomenon as simply a "folkloristic tradition" (138). He also warns that once tarantism becomes synonymous with southern "folklore," according to the layman use of the term, its appropriation for touristic advertisement is already in place. He further suggests that what is lost in the current reinterpretation of tarantism is the human aspect of the phenomenon: many revivalists seem to have completely forgotten the many oral histories of suffering on the part of tarantati, as reported both by De Martino in Apulia and later by his colleague Annabella Rossi in the Campania region. At the same time, Apolito continues, the reappropriation of tarantism rituals on the part of Salentine people does carry profound meanings within the current sociopolitical context of southern Italy. This return to tarantism in fact shows how "this time it is the Apulian people, and in particular its educated, critical, and post-modernist urban section, who lay a claim to tarantism as a positive, noble, and deep symbol of their own history and difference" (145). This act of reclamation ultimately implies the redefinition of the South as a part of a larger Mediterranean and postcolonial context.

The Politics of Tradition

The scholarship on the revival has often brought to the foreground the politics of place at work in the festival context, especially in relation to tourist advertisements. Gianni Pizza, for example, has argued that local politicians, cultural brokers, and scholars all employ the history of tarantism to support their own politics of culture; in other words, "'tarantism' is now a complex field of cultural production. Observing 'tarantism' today means coming to terms with a complex interweaving of various practices of writing, art, cinema, philosophical reflection, academic anthropology and cultural politics put into play by local institutions" (2004, 200). Pizza's words echo those of Sergio Torsello, who notes that only twenty years after the first folk revival, the study of "musica popolare" (folk music) in Italy has ceased to be an "oggetto" (object) of study and has become a "progetto" (project), in the sense that it is consciously employed by local cultural brokers and tourist agencies to promote an exciting image of their land and culture. To further illustrate this point, Pizza brings in the example of La Notte della Taranta festival. Over the years, the festival has become the most renowned event within the southern Italian folk music scene, and it is attended every year by hundreds of people, mostly young, from all parts of Italy and abroad. Such a huge popularity has, however, elicited varying responses among cultural brokers, scholars, and musicians; the last group, especially, has complained about the increasing commodification of the festival by local politicians who seek to upgrade the touristic image of the area. For example, a major point of debate among local practitioners has been the inclusion in the festival program of nonlocal nationally and internationally known musicians who are not directly connected to tarantella but are experts "of that 'ethnic' music which has had so much success in the global market of reinvented traditions" (216). It is clear from these words that the world music brand is not always accepted as a positive change for southern Italian folk music; on the contrary, it is seen as a way of giving in to the market logic and thus to employ traditional music as yet another consumer item rather than as a way to preserve local traditions. In addition, the festival has attracted much criticism for having monopolized huge sums of public funds coming from the European Union. It is important to note that Pizza's criticism is not an isolated case; instead, it reflects the opinions of several scholars, performers, and locals who have been appalled by the vast changes brought to the pizzica tradition by this international festival format and who have circulated their ideas mostly on the Internet. On his widely accessible personal website, local student of tarantella Vincenzo Santoro (2015), for example, has written extensively on the problematic revival of pizzica.

While the criticism mentioned above focuses on the commercialization of tarantella festivals and music production, Giuseppe Gala has complained about the extent of the current reinterpretations of tarantella, and pizzica in particular, in relation to dance choreographies. He explains that "toward the ethno-musical event one tends to have an attitude of imitation, distinction or innovation, while in the case of the ethno-choreutic event every act of interpretation is somehow considered legitimate" (2002, 138). Having developed later than the music revival, the revival of southern Italian folk dance since the 1990s has in fact "reinvented several ways of dancing that have no direct connection with their traditional forms and are not based on a constructive dialogue with older generations; instead, these forms come from nowhere and are simply the product of someone's personal creation" (133). Such transformations, Gala explains, include the creation *ex novo* of several categories

of pizzica dance performances, such as the "pizzica de core," the "slow pizzica," the "trance pizzica," the "energico-pizzica," and the "techno-pizzica."
What these forms have in common is a highly choreographic quality and a
close bodily interaction between the dancers, both elements absent within
the traditional peasant culture; however, this fact alone does not account for
Gala's negative reaction, since these forms can be seen as an expansion of
the genres that inspired them. It is important to note that Gala acknowledges
the legitimacy of creative interpretation from a strictly artistic perspective
but also points out that, at least in the case of the pizzica revival, these new
dance forms ultimately lack the "collective memory" that is at the center of
every tradition and allows it to live on (133). This disconnect from the history
and traditional values of tarantella is ultimately part of a larger process of
decontextualization, a process that is often associated with the globalization
of folklore and oral culture in other contexts as well. Likewise, Pizza argues
that "the transformation of tarantism into a positive symbol, freed of its connection to suffering, is ultimately possible only because the symbol has been
totally decontextualized, reified, and projected onto an ill-defined universal
dimension" (2004, 205). While these changes to the tarantella traditions are
to be expected within the currently globalized context, both Gala's and Pizza's
words remind us that it is important to recognize and understand both the
process that led to these changes and their consequences, especially when
these changes have to do with both local and national politics of culture. For
example, Pizza warns that evident differences remain between ancient tarantism practices and what he defines as "a 'popular dance' with an indefinite
trance meaning"; in other words, the *neopizzica* (new pizzica) promoted by the
post-1990s revival is at risk of watering down tarantella's unique history and
cultural values (201).

   Yet another example of the politics of culture associated with the tarantella
revival relates to tourist advertisements. In the case of the pizzica revival, for
example, Bevilacqua argues that "the promotion of Salentine culture . . . aims
at seducing this new 'type' of tourist who defines himself in opposition to mass
tourism and as being in search of a sense of otherness in the 'authentic' land of
pizzica" (2003, 400). He also argues that this type of advertisement ultimately
falls within a "successful 'ethno-touristic formula'" (393). As it employs tarantella's core values to sell a particular image of the Apulia region and of the
South more generally, ethnotourism is therefore problematic, especially since
the image of the South conveyed by tourist advertisements contributes to per-
petuate stereotypes of exoticism related to the Italian South, as reflected by the
Southern Question debate. At the same time, Bevilacqua reminds the skeptics

of current tarantella performances that the revival is also spurring great musi-cal creativity on the part of the local performers, while also contributing to the social affirmation of the South (393).

These debates become significant especially when one considers that tour-ist development in these regions since the 1960s has failed to improve their economic conditions, since it lacked a stable, sustainable, and socially equi-table project. The more recent calls for modernization have spurred the further development of tourist infrastructures, which has only made more evident the continued dependence of these regions on external factors and socioeconomic powers. As Cassano puts it, "We have modernized by putting everything up for sale . . . by prostituting our land and environment, public spaces and institu-tions" (1996, 6). Who benefits then from the local marketing of tarantella? And how are the benefits shared?

More important, the tourist image of the South offered by the tarantella revival is not too different from the colonial image of the South: they both em-phasize the otherness, the exotic quality of Southern culture. The current revival of tarantella in the Apulia region has attracted more capital to the region and helped younger generations of locals reconnect to their cultural roots; on the other hand, it has also accelerated the touristic flux to the region, thus ironi-cally perpetuating rather than challenging the outsider's view of this region. Indeed, these conflicting aspects make for a rather complex cultural project that is worth exploring in more detail, especially since they reflect similar debates surrounding the tammurriata festival revival in the Campania region.

CHAPTER 2

Exporting Southern Italian Festivals from South to North

The Post-1990s Tammurriata Revival

According to local musician, dancer, and cultural broker Giuseppe Dionisio, "attention, passion, and respect" (attenzione, passione, e rispetto) are the main principles to bear in mind when it comes to folk traditions.[1] Commenting on his thirty-year engagement with the revitalization of tammurriata festivals in his hometown of Scafati (in the Salerno province of the Campania region), Dionisio asserts that only by cherishing these values can we truly reclaim and promote our own local traditions. Because learning to appreciate and respect local cultures is a central concern to folklorists, following Dionisio's exhortation this chapter will not only examine the renewed interest in tammurriata (both locally and nationally) in the late 2000s and early 2010s—as well as the changes brought by it to the festival scene—but also analyze the responses to these changes on the part of tammurriata performers, participants, and cultural brokers, responses that often echo Dionisio's comment above. My goal in this chapter is to juxtapose these responses, which often reveal a concern over the ethical implications of popularizing and commercializing tammurriata, with a reflection on the dynamics of resignification of tammurriata, as they contribute to renewing tammurriata according to changing cultural trends. I will therefore explore this revitalization movement both in the Campania region and in the major northern city of Milan, while also mapping out the shifting meanings that different groups assign to tammurriata as it travels from rural to urban, from local to national, and from southern to northern Italian music scenes. This transformation is even more striking if one considers tammurriata's strong link to the rural and religious culture of the South (see the Introduction). I argue that rather than being simply lost, tammurriata's rural and religious worldview is reemplaced within an urbanized and globalized cultural context and accordingly replaced by different cultural, celebratory, and aesthetic norms. At the same time, I also propose an analysis of this phenomenon that is both aware of the local tensions created by this process of transformation and attentive to, and respectful of, local voices and their worldview. Even as, like all traditions, tammurriata is constantly being redefined and re-created in the present (Bendix 1989, 132), to fully appreciate tammurriata today it is important to know where it comes from and how it got there. As local drummer Raffaele Inserra puts it in Neapolitan, "you have to know where you come from to understand where you're going" (tu aje da sapé 'a ronne vieni e po' saje addó vaje).[2]

Because festivals display the ways that a community "perceives itself and the way it wishes to present itself to outsiders" (Magliocco 2006, 5), changes in the festival settings and dynamics have an important impact on the group who organizes the festivals, and the effects of these changes go beyond the festival time, reaching into the daily lives of the village or town. To those who regularly attend the calendrical festivals in Campania, it is evident that the tammurriata's festival space is gradually shifting from a rural and rooted setting to an urban and global one. This growth has, on the one hand, allowed tammurriata to be known outside of its original locations and to compete with the pizzica festivals for tourist revenues and European Union funds; on the other hand, the older festival sites are becoming increasingly commercialized, and this has often led to the negative reaction of the locals, who feel deprived of what Inserra calls "the essence or soul of the feast" ('o spirito d' 'a festa). Different perceptions of what a tammurriata feast should look like have in turn generated heated debates among local performers and cultural brokers—debates that entail different ideas of how to best use the festival space. These politics of place ultimately illustrate not only how different views of tammurriata are being affirmed and exchanged, but also that the very notion of local culture and its values, and thus of southern Italian local identity, is being debated. Therefore, changes in both the festival space and the festival dynamics in Campania, as well as their export to the northern Italian city of Milan, help us understand how different groups familiar with tammurriata performances and festivals—performers, cultural brokers, marketers, and visitors—perceive their own local culture (and their own place) and how they decide to represent it within a larger context of global consumerism and tourism.

Dynamics of Popularization in the Tammurriata Festival Space

My initial study of the tammurriata festival space concentrated on the calendrical festivals occurring in the rural areas around the major cities of Naples and Salerno in the Campania region, particularly the festivals that I am familiar with through direct participation in the late 1990s–early 2000s and fieldwork research during the period 2007–10.[3] Figure 7 shows the calendrical and religious festival locations mentioned in this book, such as Pagani, Scafati, Lettere, Nocera Superiore, and Maiori. The town of Gragnano, my hometown, is where several of my interviewees also reside, including drummer Raffaele Inserra. Table 1 shows the dates, names, and locations of these festivals. This list is by no means complete, since there are many religious events featuring tammurriata throughout the region.

All the festivals reported above share several elements of a local *festa* (celebration): they all follow the Catholic celebration calendar (from Christmas to Easter) and the Marian cycle, a series of seasonal celebrations devoted to the Virgin Mary, while also reflecting the agricultural cycle, from planting to harvest.

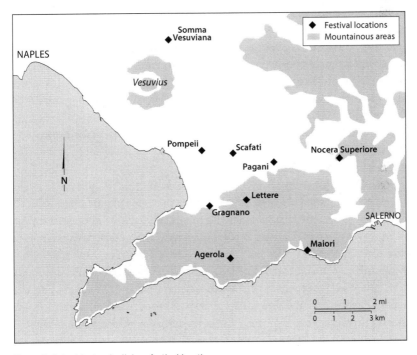

Figure 7. Calendrical and religious festival locations.

Table 1. Calendrical and religious festivals mentioned

Date	Religious Event	Location	Name
March–April	Second Easter Sunday	Pagani (Salerno)	Festa della Madonna delle Galline
May–June	Ascension	Scafati (Salerno)	Festa della Madonna dei Bagni
May–June	Pentecost	Maiori (Salerno)	Festa della Madonna dell'Avvocata
July 16	Madonna del Carmine	Episcopio, Sarno (Salerno)	Festa della Madonna del Carmine
July 26	St. Anne	Lettere (Naples)	Festa di Sant'Anna
August 14	Madonna di Materdomini	Nocera Superiore (Salerno)	Festa della Madonna di Materdomini

At the same time, several elements indicate the slow but steady transformation of these festivals into global-scale events, especially for those organized in more urbanized areas. Both my yearly trips to these festivals in the late 1990s–early 2000s and my fieldwork trips in 2007–10 have immediately drawn attention to the increasing popularization of these festivals, especially the larger ones celebrating Madonna delle Galline, Madonna di Materdomini, and Madonna dei Bagni. This process of touristification has been largely sustained by the local city governments' efforts to draw in an ever-larger number of visitors through an intensive publicity campaign and the help of local sponsors, since these festivals, like many other Mediterranean festivals, have "become a new potential source of profit and have been valorized as genuine cultural events" (Fournier 2008, 4). At the same time, it has also been embraced by local performers and cultural brokers who realize the economic and social potential of advertising one's own culture (Boissevain 2008).

While this phenomenon has certainly helped many locals like me to rediscover the local tammurriata traditions of their own villages and towns (Cohen 1988), it has also spurred an increasing commercialization of these festivals. Writing in 1999, dance ethnographer Giuseppe Gala, who conducted on-site recordings in the area from 1981 to 1995, had already shared his concern that "the current state of the traditional feast is going through evident transformation: trends and forms of participation are changing and the act of living the feast is increasingly conforming to the dominant consumerist model" (1999a, 8). As one visits these locations on festival days, the public area adjacent the Madonna's church, usually devoted to musicians and dancers as well as to food and craft sales, has both visibly expanded but also become a marketing point not

Figure 8. A drum practioner and vendor at the Festa di Sant'Anna in Lettere on July 26, 2014. Photo by the author.

only for tammurriata instruments, books, and CDs, often sold by the performers themselves, but also for tourist merchandise, such as traditional ceramics from the well-known Amalfi Coast and other touristic items that bear no direct link to tammurriata.

In addition, the church square features a large stage where several tammurriata groups or *paranze* are invited to perform for several nights;[4] in turn, the replacing of spontaneous music and dancing circles with staged concerts affects the audience's perception of tammurriata and transforms tammurriata into an urban and spectacle-oriented type of festival. The introduction of a concert program has expanded the time of festivity, since now the city offers tammurriata concerts for several nights, and the groups included in the program vary from local *paranze* to nationally renowned artists. The reaction of local performers and audiences is often very eloquent. At the 2010 Madonna dei Bagni festival, many had left the center of the church square and had formed dancing circles around its perimeter, where they could enjoy music and dance almost undisturbed by the music onstage, a variety of tarantella that is unconnected to tammurriata and was performed by a group visiting from a different geographical area.

The large number of visitors to the town of Pagani for the Madonna delle Galline festival—hundreds of them already in my early visits and also evident from numerous audience videos now available on YouTube—has encouraged the implementation of a new festival infrastructure; the 2009 festival brochure, for example, enlightened future visitors on the new traffic and parking regulations, strict police surveillance throughout the town, bus-tour facilities for people coming from other areas, child-care units, and even tourist guide and interpreting services. These elements are clear signs that the Pagani festival has become a source of profit for the local authorities (Fournier 2008, 2), especially given the high rate of unemployment throughout the region. The use of interpreting services also suggests the increasing presence of foreign tourists, thus revealing a shift in scope from a much localized context to a global one. In 2003 a wrought-iron monument of a hand holding a *tammorra* drum has been placed at the entrance to the city center to invite visitors to Pagani. The monument represents a clear example of "staged authenticity" (MacCannell 1999), in that it reflects the city government's effort to claim the city of Pagani as a leading place in the preservation of tammurriata.

The presence of tourists from other parts of Italy and even from abroad further confirms the kind of global dynamics at work in the local festivals. Several artists and aficionados whom I met and interviewed in Milan, especially those originally from Campania such as Rosa Maurelli, Francesca Di Ieso, Armando Illario, and Valeria Lista, have talked about their yearly trips to the southern festivals, including the tammurriata festivals I discuss here.[5] Over the years, I have often run into local friends now living and working in Rome or Milan

Figure 9. The tammorra monument in the town of Pagani. Photo by the author.

and visiting the festivals on their way back home for the weekend or summer holidays. But while returning immigrants represent an important component of the festival audience similar to other contests of folk revival (Barwick 2012), the scope of these festivals is much larger, since "the strong interest in [this] folk culture has brought to the feast aficionados that are outside the local communities, thus giving rise to a new form of folk tourism" (Gala 1999a, 8). At the Festa della Madonna di Materdomini on August 14, 2008, I met Eleonora, a young dancer from the Salento area—the core area of the current pizzica phenomenon—who had been touring tammurriata festivals for several years. When I asked Eleonora about the reason for such an ongoing interest, she answered that, as someone who grew up dancing pizzica, getting to know tammurriata is a sort of natural next step, especially since tammurriata is now becoming as well known as pizzica everywhere in Italy. As a southern Italian and a dance lover, Eleonora thinks it is important to familiarize herself with a music tradition that is also from the South. As many young people from Naples and the entire Campania region pay their annual visits to the summer pizzica festivals, Eleonora's tour to tammurriata festivals might also be a reaction to the larger pizzica tourism phenomenon, a way for Salentine locals to find fresh turf away from the overtouristified pizzica festivals. In any case, these folk music trips certainly testify to the current transformation of southern Italian festivals into tourist destinations. Because Eleonora is quite familiar with southern Italian folk music and dances, her case is in many ways different from that of the typical "global traveler" who "neither expects nor seeks authentic festivals" (MacLeod 2006, 229); nevertheless, her and her friends' presence at the festival confirms tammurriata's gradual shift to an increasingly globalized music scene, following the pizzica example.

Like many other expressions of folk culture, these festivals have indeed expanded rather than disappeared under the pressure of modernization and globalization (Guss 2000; Boissevain 1992), even if it is often in the form of commodification. In fact, in many cases the current process of touristification has become "a spur to recover these [festival] aspects, since they offer an unexpected fame to the last dancers and singers from the tradition" (Gala 1999a, 8). During his concert at the Agerola World Festival on July 19, 2014, in the small town on Agerola by the Amalfi Coast, renowned local performer Marcello Colasurdo, a longtime component of the music group E Zézi, repeatedly invoked the old-timers' essential role in keeping the tradition alive and even invited singer Giovanni Del Sorbo, also known as zi Giannino (Uncle Giannino), to perform on the stage with him, thus confirming the singer's status as a *portatore della tradizione* (tradition bearer).

Figure 10. Nationally and internationally renowned tammurriata performer Marcello Colasurdo (right) on the stage with old-timer zi Giannino (left) at the Agerola World Festival on July 19, 2014. Photo by the author.

While the major music scenes and performers see an increased popularity, however, touristification can sometimes also mean the replacement of communal forms of gathering and socialization with more generalized forms of spectacle. The tammurriata scene at the Sant'Anna festival, one of the most well-known pilgrimage sites for local devotees and therefore also for tammurriata performers, is slowly disappearing, according to several visitors and performers I talked to in the summer of 2014.[6] On July 26, 2014, at ten at night, I arrived at the dancing ground, a small park near the Sant'Anna church, and to my surprise it was empty, unlike my last time at the festival in 2010, when it was full starting in the early evening; I then ran into a group of locals from the nearby town of Casola, who were disappointed since there was no dancing and confirmed the general impression that this dancing ground is slowly dying out. By eleven thirty, zi Giannino arrived and started singing together with a young local drummer; slowly, a small dancing circle formed around them, surrounded by an audience of about thirty people. Even so, and even considering that this tammurriata ground has always been much smaller than the Pagani or Bagni festival grounds, the change was evident from the scene I had witnessed only a few years earlier. Among the reasons for this change, some noted the fact that on that same night several tammurriata concerts and events were to take place in different towns, some hosting major performers from the area. In this sense, the expansion of tammurriata performances beyond the festival calendar runs the risk of putting aside the older festivals, which have traditionally worked as yearly gatherings for the local communities as well as for performers from different villages and towns in the area; as Inserra puts it, "At the [old] feast, it felt like a community, like a family" (Era 'nu clan, 'na famiglia, 'int' 'a festa).

The increasing diversification of the groups that participate in these events can become equally problematic when it creates friction among the festival participants. Within the close-knit environment of Sant'Anna in July 2008, I spotted a small group of *alternativi* playing and dancing pizzica. Although a minority compared to tammurriata practitioners, the group's activity was significant, not only because their attire (a mix of gypsy and hippie styles that can be traced back to the 1970s student movement in Italy and signals one's refusal of mainstream culture) reflected a very different cultural framework than tammurriata's, but especially since several musicians and visitors started complaining, more or less loudly, about their performance; this remonstration ultimately led the group to retreat to a less crowded area. Challenging the images of cohesive unity and shared values that social scientists have often attributed to the notion of festival (Falassi 1987, 2), different groups seemed to perceive the event and participate in it in very different ways. Tammurriata practitioners evidently perceived the pizzica group's activity as interfering with the main interest of the participants, and thus as a form of disrespect toward what they consider as the "true essence" of the Sant'Anna celebration. This willingness to assign tammurriata an official role as the only authorized performance within the Sant'Anna celebration space ultimately reflects a concern over the authenticity of tammurriata—a concern that arises whenever a certain tradition goes through a process of change, caused by either external or internal factors; until then the truth-value of that tradition is not necessarily weighed against its authenticity (Briggs 1996). At the same time, the incident also suggests that the *alternativi* group held an outsider's view of tammurriata and their desire to consume a "spectacle" (MacLeod 2006) that they were not closely related to; in fact, given tammurriata's strong sense of place, performing pizzica on a tammurriata performance site suggests a detachment from both traditions. Inserra's reaction to this type of attitude is very eloquent: "You see this youth, they just care about coming to the party with a bottle of wine. . . . [T]hey think that that's the party. . . . [T]hey're *fricchettoni* [hippies]. . . . They could go to an *agriturismo* [holiday farm] to do the same thing."[7] From his perspective, this renewed interest in tammurriata on the part of many young people consists in a merely touristic curiosity and thus lacks the spirit of communal belonging that is embedded in the local tammurriata feasts he is accustomed to. For Dionisio, who has taught seminars on tammurriata's cultural heritage in the local public schools, the cultural exchange with pizzica is more than welcome, but it needs to be done "without getting too far from the cultural specificity [of the local feasts]" (senza allontanarsi troppo dalla specificità culturale [delle feste locali]). That is to say, you do not dance pizzica on a tammurriata festival ground, since it is ultimately a form of disrespect toward the local participants as well as the other performers.

Shifting Time, Space, and Aesthetics of Tammurriata

These changing festival dynamics reach beyond the festival space, as several tammurriata events, from small-scale parties to large festivals, are being organized outside the religious festival calendar as well as the rural context in which tammurriata developed.[8] These events largely contribute to turning tammurriata into a spectacle to consume, as opposed to a communal event to participate in, especially since many of these events take place in the summer, a high tourist season for Campania's seaside locations and an important vacation moment for returning locals. A major example is represented by the Notte della Tammorra (Night of Tammorra) festival, occurring since 2000 in the summer within Naples's metropolitan area and hosting some of the major voices of the current folk music and dance scene; additionally, by 2016 several Night of the Tammorra events have proliferated throughout the Campania region. This type of festival privileges a stage format; it is explicitly conceived for both locals and tourists and features not only tammurriata but also pizzica, tarantella, and many other forms of folk music.[9] In July 2008, I witnessed another, and more complex, example of change within the tammurriata festival context, the Festival Internazionale di Musica Etnica, organized by Ethnos—a cultural association established in 1995 in the city of Torre del Greco (Napoli)—and featuring tammurriata, pizzica, and tarantella in the same performance space as other Mediterranean and North African, Balkan, Middle Eastern, and Caribbean sounds. As artistic director

Gigi Di Luca explains in the festival program booklet, by including southern Italian voices, Ethnos is "going back to [our] origins to remain faithful to the real meaning of the word 'ethnic.'" In a global context, where cross-cultural migration is increasing, the word *ethnic* can be read as a general term for being rooted in a certain place, as well as for being part of the subaltern cultures of the South. To confirm this perspective, the fifth and last day of the 2008 festival was entitled Le Terre del Rimorso (the Lands of Remorse). Entirely devoted to southern Italian folk rhythms, it included free dance and music workshops, a conference, and a concert featuring artists from several southern regions. This last event called for continuity between the current conditions of the South and those described by Ernesto De Martino in his 1959 trip. It also seemed to encourage the audience to envision a closer, and more educative, relation between the lands of pizzica and tammurriata.

In some cases, however, a more touristified festival structure has been willingly adopted by performing groups coming from the tradition. The Festa della Tammorra, held in the town of Somma Vesuviana, has developed with the collaboration of the local cultural association La Pertica, whose members are tammurriata practitioners eager to share their skills and passion for the *tammorra* with locals and outsiders. As Luca Iovine, the youngest member and musician, explained to me in June 2009, Somma Vesuviana has a long tradition of tammurriata, and every year performing groups from all over the Naples area have flocked to this town to participate in tammurriata circles. Iovine learned to drum when he was a little boy thanks to his uncle, who is widely recognized as a leading drummer in the area and who initiated Iovine into the art of the *tammorra*. Thanks to Iovine, the association established its own website, as well as both MySpace and Facebook pages, which helped place this event within a much wider context than the religious feasts, while also attracting a different audience typology: not just the religious festival devotees but people in search of entertainment. When I visited their office on June 2, 2009, I was struck by the welcoming atmosphere: once in the office, Iovine and other members showed me through their tammorra studio, where I could also look at photos of the festival's previous editions. When I told them that I was accompanied by some of my "American professors" (professori americani), they immediately invited us all to celebrate with local wine and then also invited us to dance. While this convivial attitude is typical of tammurriata performances, which have always represented moments of general celebration for the local communities, Iovine and his fellow performers seemed very much aware of their official role as *portatori della tradizione* (tradition bearers) and also eager to sell their image (and hopefully their drums!) to a foreign audience. As is often the case with folk cultures, in moving from local to global spheres, this tammurriata group has deliberately transformed their community-bound rituals into "public," that is, tourist-bound, performances, thus responding to the new global configuration "in a way which is simultaneously traditional and modern" (Siikala 2000, 71). In doing so, they have ceased being simply local performers and become "entrepreneurs" (Boissevain 2008, 27).

The organization of tammurriata dancing and instrument workshops has especially helped expand tammurriata's time frame to year-round, while also allowing students to learn tammurriata beyond the festival grounds. The recently published *Tammurrianti: Metodo pratico per tammorra e tamburello* (2012), for example, offers a way for drum aficionados to learn at home with the use of a DVD and an attached instructional book. The passage from communal festival learning to private, and paid, workshops is an especially important one in terms of commodification dynamics, especially when it comes to dancing, since not only do students prolong the pleasure of dancing beyond the spatial and geographical limits of the festivals, but they also use the religious festival or a band's concert to practice steps learned in a workshop. At the July 7, 2014, concert by the group Le Ninfe della Tammorra on Salerno city's beach walk, I met a group of about thirty eager students who had been taking a tammurriata course and had come to the concert hoping to be able to dance. Having learned in a class does not preclude the dance experience; however, it certainly modifies it in some ways, especially given the classes' focus on the technical aspects of dancing such as choreography, elements that are absent from the traditional context of the rural festivals.

This new learning context has undoubtedly contributed to the creation of a new dance aesthetics that is now visible on the festival ground and is very far from the rural world of tammurriata. As Gianni Pizza (2004) already notes for the pizzica revival, it is easy to identify this new style of dancing, usually privileged by the younger generations and those who have taken a class: the dancers' hand gestures and steps tend to be faster, more choreographic, and more explicitly sexualized, thus moving apart from the Catholic-peasant tradition of southern Italy. Several locals I talked to, or danced with, in the summer of 2014 voiced their awareness that this *danza globale* (global dance) is very far from the tradition, while at the same time recognizing that this way of dancing is a natural product of changing times and social codes.[10] Local practitioners are also aware of this discrepancy, and they often strive to negotiate between innovation and respect for the tradition. Tiziana Torelli, a steady participant in the local festivals who first took a tammurriata course with local practitioner Ugo Maiorano in 2009, has also taught tammurriata.[11] As a young dancer,

Torelli's approach to tammurriata teaching reveals her willingness to help pass on the tradition while also respecting its cultural uniqueness and specificity. She teaches mostly the Nocerino-Sarnese style common in her area (near the towns of Scafati, Angri, Nocera, and Sarno) and that she is mostly familiar with, and, more important, she invites to her class major singers and drummers in the area so that the students can enter into direct contact with the voices of the tradition. Instead of using a particular choreography, she teaches only the basic steps, thus leaving a certain degree of improvisation, which is part of dancing tammurriata in a festival context. Torelli's main idea, as confirmed by several dancers and performers I talked to on the dancing ground, is that "you need to 'live' the dance" (il ballo si vive), and in order to do that you need to learn it on the festival grounds and possibly from the old-timers; going to classes helps mostly the rehearsing and improving of certain steps. This idea ultimately echoes Dionisio's exhortation that for the tradition to move forward, we first need to "reeducate the youth to the importance of the tradition and its values" (rieducare i giovani all'importanza della traditione e dei suoi valori), thus moving beyond the simplistic teaching of dancing steps and toward the teaching of a particular worldview. Curiously enough, this renewed attention toward the core values of the tradition sometimes goes as far as leading to a negative attitude toward any form of adulteration, while at the same time still buying into dynamics of commercialization linked to workshop learning. When Le Ninfe della Tammorra started playing their original takes on classic tammurriata songs, some among the group of students I was interacting with stopped dancing because, as they explained to me, they were not able to recognize those rhythms as traditional and didn't feel comfortable dancing to them.[12]

Finally, dynamics of desacralization at work in the religious festival context are evident in the way that younger festival participants approach these festivals as well as other religious aspects of tammurriata. On May 29, 2007, I participated for the first time in the Festa della Madonna dell'Avvocata in honor of Mary Advocate; the festival takes place by a small church on a mountaintop near the small town of Maiori, on the Amalfi Coast. When my friends and I finally arrived at the top of the mountain, to our surprise we spotted a large number of people assembled on that impervious hill and spread out over the surrounding valleys, as if they represented, in fact, an entire town. In front of us, the procession with the Madonna statue had just begun; many people, of different ages and social groups, accompanied the procession, singing and praying. However, not everyone in the festival space was engaged in the procession; only the ones standing within the walls of the church space were. All the others outside seemed engaged in other activities: some of the younger ones were forming their own music and dance circles and performing both tammurriata and pizzica, some were barbecuing or just hanging out, and some seemed to be there to watch everybody else. Given the peculiar history and geography of this festival site, considered by many one of the most "authentic" sites of the tammurriata tradition, these signs of popularization and desacralization become even more striking. While the "playful" aspect of the celebration has increased, the ritual aspect, connected to the Catholic religion, has certainly lost is centrality within the current festival context, just like in other European contexts of revival (Boissevain 2008, 24). In his influential 1979 book, *Canti e tradizioni popolari in Campania*, Roberto De Simone had already complained about what he saw as a "loss of devotion" among the younger generations participating in tammurriata rituals; it is much harder, however, to measure this "loss of devotion" and to decide to what degree the local festivals are becoming secularized.

It is also important to remember that the coexistence of the sacred and the secular is inherent to the history of the festival (Falassi 1987, 3), and in any case, the secular roots of tammurriata are evident throughout its history, which is intertwined with Greek and Roman pagan rituals (Mauro 2004, 213). At the same time, the obvious spatial separation between the sacred and the secular evident within this festival site represented, in a nutshell, the current phenomenon of revival, in which certain performances "may still be linked to seasonal and religious cycles, but detachment from these cycles—be it, for instance, . . . a lack of common belief systems—gives more credit to other cycles, such as those of commerce, politics and tourism" (Lüdtke 2009, 169). The attitude of those outside the church perimeter spurred the negative reaction of my trip compan-

Figure 11. Music playing and singing inside the church to honor the local Madonna at the Festa della Madonna dei Bagni in Scafati (Salerno) in May 2016. The photo shows emerging tammurriata singer Biago De Prisco (*center*) leading a chant of invocation to the Madonna. Photo courtesy of Luigi Coppola.

Figure 12. A crowded Madonna procession during the Festa della Madonna dei Bagni in May 2015; the photo shows the strong presence of young participants and also of recording devices, which testify to the strong interest in this event among both local and nonlocal participants. Photo courtesy of Luigi Coppola.

ions, all locals, who felt that visitors, even if they are not religious, should pay more respect to the Madonna procession, the main component of the religious celebration while we were there. Far from being lost, however, the importance of the Avvocata as a religious feast remains strong for many in today's celebration. Even though there is only one old, rugged mountain path leading to the church, and the hiking trip to the top takes about five hours, among the participants there were people of all ages, and some of the older people had come with a helicopter arranged by the police. This example shows that the religious aspect of this festival is still important to some of the groups involved. Indeed, while younger people are generally less or not at all interested in the religious element, many other locals, including some of the performers I have encountered on the festival grounds, patronize both religious and secular aspects of the festival.

In this sense, touristification does not necessarily preclude the sharing of beliefs and values that also occurs among many participants on the festival ground, since both the procession and the Mass in honor of the Madonna are inherent parts of the attendees' tour, as confirmed by the still large number of visitors to the church not only in Maiori but also at the Pagani and Bagni festivals. Nonetheless, the meanings that different groups assign to these celebrations vary individually as well as from group to group (Noyes 1995, 449), and a simplistic distinction between locals and tourists is not enough to account for these complex celebration dynamics.[13]

Reinventing the "Spirito d' 'a Festa"

The dynamics of popularization and resignification of tammurriata certainly contribute to "inventing" a new, urbanized festive tradition (Hobsbawm and Ranger 1992) with global ramifications. Not only have time, space, and aesthetics of tammurriata transformed, but the groups involved have also changed. Given the increasing urbanization of the tammurriata areas since at least the 1960s, many local performers are in fact living and working in the same geographical areas in which tammurriata developed but within increasingly urbanized settings, even as they reclaim the importance of knowing and respecting the peasant world of tammurriata: Raffaele Inserra works as a clerk in a local mall, but he still cultivates his father's piece of land on the weekends and holidays; the life experience of Pia Vicinanza, a young dancer and teacher of tammurriata I met in 2009, is completely removed from the rural culture of tammurriata; Giuseppe Dionisio worked for a local health center before he retired; Ugo Maiorano is also an office employee; an important exception is represented by well-known local drummer and tammorra maker (tammorraro) Antonio Matrone, known as 'O Lione, or "the Lion," for his red complexion, whose lifestyle is still very much part of the rural world expressed by tammurriata. 'O Lione learned to drum from the old-timers in his area, known as *agro nocerino-sarnese* in the Salerno province; for him, learning tammurriata was never limited to learning the rhythm of the drum, but it entailed learning about the peasant's lifestyle, which is in turn strictly connected to the drum's cycle. For example, from October to January, "one prepares the instruments, gathering the best type of wood, tanning the skin, then the first drumming moments (Saint Anthony on January 17 and Fat Tuesday), and then the spring and summer with their big festivals and the long vigils of the pilgrims" (Mauro 2004, 216–17). Nevertheless, many of those who are now considered expert practitioners of tammurriata in the area are often living in urbanized centers. While some of them are still connected to the rural past through their family history, they often have white-collar jobs; therefore, they are not immediately close to the peasant world of tammurriata. Even when they do spend time on the farm, because of extensive mechanization their approach to the rural life of tammurriata chanted in the local folk songs is naturally different from that of the few old-timers remaining. The same goes for many festival participants from the younger generation, like myself, who are attracted to the rural festivals from more urbanized areas.

These changes in the social composition of the festivals are also evident in the presence of subcultural youth groups. Especially in its core years (late 1990s–

mid 2000s), the increased popularity of tammurriata has indeed attracted a large number of young people in search of nonmainstream entertainment, similarly to Anna Nacci's description (2001) of the pizzica phenomenon; this aspect is evident from the dress code of these, mostly young, participants— which usually includes long, colorful, flowing skirts and ethnic accessories for the girls, a style that was already very popular during the 1970s folk revival and reminds one of the American hippie style. As a result, tammurriata events, both the religious festivals and the recently "invented" ones, have often assumed the characteristics of a big social event, in which young participants participate next to the old-timers, often visibly eager to learn from them (fig. 14). My festival participation in the summer 2014 made clear that, even when the participants belong to elder or more mainstream groups, they still do wear what have become the typical festival costumes, mostly long gypsy-style skirts for women but also resembling tarantella peasant costumes (fig. 15). In this regard, the popularity of tammurriata contributes to defining new ways of communication, self-expression, and group-identity formation among several generations (Nacci 2001, 2004).

Figure 13. Young women's dress code at the Festa della Madonna di Materdomini on August 14, 2008. Photo by the author.

Figure 14. A young festival participant asking old-timer and virtuosa Anna Rosanova (zi Nannina) to show him how to play the drum. The fact that he is holding a wine bottle shows his participation both in the rural festival context and in the *alternativi*'s subculture. Photo by the author.

Figure 15. Tammurriata festival costumes among older generations at the Festa della Madonna del Carmine in Episcopio (Sarno) on July 16, 2014. Photo by the author.

As shown in the images, the tammurriata trend has also changed over the years, as youth groups find new forms of subcultural entertainment; among my old group of local friends, most have stopped going because, as Andrea Iozzino puts it, "it is not fashionable anymore" (nun se porta cchiù; literally, this phrase means "it is no longer worn").[14] In the meantime, new groups are attracted to the festivals, especially through the many dancing schools in the area:[15] at the Agerola World Festival on July 19, 2014, for the first time I joined the dancing circle together with a group of dancing aficionados in their forties, fifties, and sixties, none of whom looked or acted like the *alternativi* I used to find at the festivals in the late 1990s, and most of whom had taken some sort of dance class. For many in this group, tammurriata seems to have become an alternative to salsa, tango, or ballroom dance, since it offers another way of spending leisure time. This element is evident especially in the way that these participants often act on the dancing ground; for example, even if the 2014 Agerola World Festival featured many samples of local cuisine, and even if eating, drinking, and dancing usually go hand by hand at local *festas,* my dancing partners did not eat anything since their purpose at the festival was mainly dancing, and, as a result, they treated the dancing ground as a sort of gym. In addition, because these participants are older, their social background is very different from that of *alternativi*—most of them are professionals or retired professionals; this new social makeup speaks of a process of gentrification of the festivals that one would not associate with tammurriata in the late 1990s. According to my dancing partner that night, Luigi Coppola, who has been touring most tammurriata festivals and parties in the area since 2011, it is still possible to spot *alternativi* groups at the festivals but usually at the bigger and more touristified festivals like the ones in Pagani, Bagni, or Materdomini; their presence is rare at less popular festivals and small local events.[16]

Several scholars of pizzica have noted that the current recovering of tarantism music rituals in Italy reflects the need for an alternative cultural model to the one developed through globalization, the need to counteract the "pressure of cultural uniformity" (Bevilacqua 2003, 392). While the late 1990s–early 2000s tammurriata festivals may have equally contributed to relocating younger generations of southerners within an increasingly globalized Italian society, as tammurriata festivals become middle class, it becomes natural to ask to what extent this is a natural process occurring in folk revival movements (Ivanova-Nyberg 2014).

Yet as a social phenomenon, tammurriata has at least the potential to take on new social and cultural meanings, as confirmed by several performers' participation in social protests, such as workers' strikes or community protests against the Terra dei Fuochi (Land of Fires) phenomenon.[17] A major concern for the local communities still today, the waste-management problem in Campania, strictly connected to the power of the local Mafia, is central not only to many cultural debates in the area—called the Land of Fires precisely because of this problem—but also to several cultural and artistic projects. The video *Tammurriata d'a munnezza* (Rubbish tammurriata) was uploaded to YouTube in 2010, during a period of strong protests against a local dumping site; the song and video were put together by a group of local artists on behalf of the protest communities in the towns of Boscoreale, Trecase, Boscotrecase, and Terzigno. During his concert at the Agerola World Festival on July 19, 2014, performer Marcello Colasurdo also reminded the audience that the value of the land, central to the tammurriata tradition, can really live on today only if the local population makes a collective effort to fight for the future of their land, such as by raising their voice about the Land of Fires problem. As a left-wing performer-activist, Colasurdo has constantly employed tammurriata as a vehicle of social protest, participating, for example, in the workers' strike at the Fiat factory in Pomigliano D'Arco in the summer of 2014 and many other occasions of social protest.

For local anthropologist Augusto Ferraiuolo, it is possible to pinpoint a specific moment for the recovering of tammurriata as a vehicle of social protest—the twentieth G7 summit opened at the Royal Palace in Piazza Plebiscito, Naples, on July 8, 1994. That date is important because it coincides with the release of the album *Cantanapoli antifascista* by antiestablishment hip-hop group 99 Posse, an album featuring a strong political message partly spurred by the G7 meeting.

As Ferraiuolo (2015) points out, the song "Sant'Antonio, Sant'Antonio, 'o nemico r' 'o demonio" (Saint Anthony, Saint Anthony, the devil fighter), which employs the tammurriata rhythm and style, clearly shows how the group "dragged the tammurriata out of the churchyard, the usual scenario of this kind of performance, and drove it into the proletarian ghettos of Naples." In a rhetorical move that echoes the work of E Zézi from the 1970s, 99 Posse in fact associates the devil with the local police, which played a major role in sending off, often violently, local protesters during the G7 meeting.[18]

Furthermore, the current festivals often provide new perspectives on social codes and behaviors, thus forming "privileged arenas of cultural creativity" (Picard and Robinson 2006, 14). Because musical events are "traditionally a privileged venue for the public construction and representation of individual gender identity, as well as of the relational models between genders within particular communities" (Magrini 2003, 5), it is possible to assert that the new style of dancing tammurriata that is visible on the festival ground in fact reinterprets the tammurriata tradition according to contemporary socialization and gender codes. The way that the old-timers dance tammurriata is indeed very different from the way of the younger generations, which offers a much closer bodily interaction between the dancers; this difference is viewed by some as disruptive of the old festival spirit, since supposedly some old-timers feel intimidated by the youth's way of dancing, as Inserra told me. While I have never witnessed this type of situation in person, it is easy to see how the current way of dancing reflects contemporary gender codes, which are certainly less rigid than they used to be within the rural world of tammurriata. For some practitioners, this less rigid dancing code is also problematic because it is more sexualized, as noted by Inserra; however, some of them embrace the claim that tammurriata has always contained a strong erotic component, especially when it was used for courtship purposes, as Rosa Maurelli pointed out; the potentially disruptive role of tammurriata as a form of social gathering with a sensual component is confirmed by my grandmother's stories of a local priest who used to go around and smash *tammorra* drums every time he ran into a gathering. In this sense, the claim that the younger generation has introduced sexuality into the dance ultimately reflects the current politics of tradition, which tend to impute a socially and formally conservative character to the "authentic" tammurriata of the past after the fact and thus to overlook the elements of disruption that have always been present at tammurriata gatherings. A major plus of the current festival scene consists in having brought these issues to the forefront of cultural debate and therefore created a site for discussion over the role of gender in tammurriata.

Scholars have already noted women's roles as drummers in ancient times, as well as tarantella as a carnivalesque moment that allowed women, as well as gay men, to dance, drum, and break free from the restraining orders of patriarchal society (De Simone 1982). Because the sacred and the profane have always been part of the religiosity of the South, the old-timers, closer to the rural world of tammurriata in which women and men worked together in the fields during the day and played and danced at night, testify to the strength of this tradition. However, the increasingly urbanized post–World War II context and the popularization of Italian pop music through television and other media seem to have discouraged many women from my mother's generation not only from dancing the local folk music but also from singing and drumming. For some, making music and dancing were even considered inappropriate for respectable women; according to my grandmother, only some women in the area where she lived felt free to do it, the ones living in the *curtigli* (courtyards) or from the streets, while as a good Catholic she would never venture into such contexts. Within the current festival context, therefore, it is not rare to find older women dancing and drumming next to younger people; however, what I find particularly innovative is the increasing participation of female musicians onstage. Undeniably, while women have always participated in the festivals as dancers or singers (Lamanna 2004; Dionisio and D'Aquino 2003), their role as drummers on center stage grants them new visibility locally and also globally via visual and social media recording. And because the drum is the central element of the tammurriata, by establishing themselves among the skilled drummers in the local context, women can thus establish themselves as major voices in the tammurriata tradition. A look at the local festivals shows that women extensively participate in the dancing circle. However, female drummers are still more rare to find than male drummers; one of the reasons is allegedly the fact that the drum is very heavy and needs a strong hand. As musician Valeria Lista, from the Milan-based, all-female music group puts it, "Women have often the problem of how they appear, so they have to be beautiful in any case. Perhaps it is for this reason that women usually play only instruments that allow a more poised physical posture, such as the flute, the violin, the piano, and naturally, the voice. . . . As for the dancing, the idea is very similar: one expects women to dance, because the female body that swings in a sexy way is a value within our aesthetic system."[19]

These observations have been confirmed by several women I have met in this context. Raffaella Coppola, for example, has been both playing the drum and dancing tammurriata since at least the early 2000s, and she has also been performing with several local groups at both local and national festivals and concerts. However, when she works with the local musicians, it is taken for granted that she will dance for them but won't play the drum, because, she says, it is implied that that drum is for the male performers, who supposedly are the ones with enough physical strength to play the drum for hours. When you do get to play the drum, Coppola explains, it is in the form of a favor, and it usually happens offstage. On the other hand, when she performs with her group, MusicaStoria, whose members are younger musicians from several parts of Italy, Coppola's drum skills are fully recognized. But even within such a male-chauvinist scenario, young drummers like Coppola can look up to older role models; in fact, here and there at the festivals, it is possible to spot older women joining the musicians' circle to sing or accompany the songs with castanets or, more rarely, to drum. At the same time, as Coppola also points out, they are usually left off the stage or out of the music circle.[20]

Figure 16 shows why Anna Rosanova, known as zi Nannina (Aunty Nannina), is becoming a well-known drum virtuosa within the current festival context, thanks to the effort of younger aficionados and scholars of tammurriata. Local filmmaker Salvatore Raiola, author of two recent documentaries on tam-

Figure 16. Zi Nannina drumming at the 2008 Festa di Materdomini. Photo by the author.

murriata, features zi Nannina as one of the major voices of the tammurriata tradition.[21] At Materdomini on August 14, 2008, I could personally testify to her role in this context: near the main tammurriata circle was zi Nannina with her drum, playing on her own. All around her, there was a group of young dancers who listened attentively and in some cases even recorded her performance with their camera or mobile phone; every time the woman finished a song, they would encourage her to play more. In a matter of minutes, the woman was able to attract an audience, all praising the quality and style of her performance. I found this moment to be very interesting, not only because it showed the possibility of a constructive dialogue between the older generation and the younger, but also because it seemed to grant an official role to the female performer, entrusted by the younger generations to pass on what she had learned. The use of recording devices seemed to confirm this moment of entrustment by adding an authoritative quality to it. The presence of female performers is much more evident when one steps outside the local feast scene—even just a quick Web search shows the increasing presence of female-only groups featuring tammurriata even in the Campania region, such as the group Le Ninfe della Tammorra from the Salerno area. The group features four main female members comprising voice, tammorra and tambourines, accordion, and guitar; tammorra drums appear extensively in their shows and contribute to creating both traditional tunes and a juxtaposition of jazz and folk. Midway through their concert on Salerno's boardwalk on July 7, 2014, the group performed an Avvocata style of tammurriata—which requires a circle with several drums—together with local drummer 'O Lione. The drum-only performance accompanied by such a well-known male drummer helped legitimize the group's position toward the local tradition bearers and also illustrated an increased visibility of female drummers at center stage, thus testifying to the extent of the changes that are occurring within the tammurriata tradition in Campania.

The all-female group Moriarmoniche, based in Milan but with southern roots, is equally committed to playing Italian folk music that is *popolare al femminile* (folk from a woman's perspective), and they do so by privileging, for example, female workers' songs from both the South and the North of Italy; by focusing on the image and history of strong southern women, such as female brigands from the nineteenth century; and by popularizing folk songs by often unrecognized southern female folk musicians such as Sicilian Rosa Balistreri (1927–90).

These dynamics are especially important because they ultimately illustrate the social potential of the tammurriata revival from a woman's perspective. Yet another recent example is provided by Campania-based frame-drum artist Valentina Ferraiuolo, whose southern Italian folk music group, Malmaritate, has helped organize a series of educational workshops both in Italian schools and abroad on occasion of the International Day for the Elimination of Vio-

Figure 17. Le Ninfe della Tammorra drumming on the stage together with well-known performer 'O Lione. Photo by the author.

Figures 18–19. (Top) Female drummer performing together with several male drummers at the Festa della Madonna dei Bagni in May 2015; (Bottom) a young female drummer at the Festa della Madonna dell'Arco in March 2016. Photos courtesy of Luigi Coppola.

lence against Women on November 25, 2015; this initiative carried the slogan *La pelle del tamburo è l'unica che puoi percuotere* (The drum's skin is the only one you can beat). Malmaritate's repertoire similarly explores women's struggles both historically and contemporarily. One can only hope to find more examples like this one within the local festival scene.

Exploring Tammurriata in Milan

My acquaintance with tammurriata performances in Milan started one evening in June 2007 when I attended the Sud Sud Festival; the festival was held in a suburban farmhouse known as Cascina Monluè, which for many years hosted nonmainstream and world music events. That night was revelatory not only because I witnessed tammurriata dancing in Milan for the first time, but also because I first met the drummer Raffaele Inserra, who had been invited to play onstage and also conduct a drumming workshop. Meeting one of the major names associated with tammurriata in my area (and one with whom I share a surname!) at a festival in Milan gave me a good sense of how far tammurriata has moved from its original context over the years. Since then my yearly participation in summer music and dance events in Milan, every time I visited my brother and friends, has confirmed the still strong presence of tarantella rhythms, including tammurriata, in Milan as of 2014. It also confirmed that the changes in celebration and performance dynamics illustrated so far are more evident, and complex, when tammurriata is transplanted to a metropolitan center like Milan's, since there it gets reframed within the more popular and commercialized pizzica revival. It also loses the geographical, social, and, to some extent, cultural specificity that comes from its association with the rural life in the South, its language, and its customs.

In a large urban context like Milan's, performing groups consist of college graduates and young professionals coming from the South in search of white-collar jobs, blue-collar southern migrants who came to Milan in the 1960s and 1970s, northerners who are fascinated with southern rhythms but are not very familiar with southern culture, and second- or third-generation southerners who were born and raised in Milan and therefore are familiar with southern culture through their family connections and annual summer vacations in the South. At the same time, tarantella's, and particularly tammurriata's, rural origins and values are often explicitly invoked by performers as a way both to legitimize themselves in the eyes of an urban audience and to educate Milan's audience about the uniqueness of the tammurriata tradition. For example, the biography blurb of the music group Canto Antico, whose members first brought tammurriata and pizzica to Milan in the late 1990s, states: "The members of Canto Antico are descendants of the farmers around the Mt. Vesuvius. Before they went to town to study as musicians (even their profession now) and [sic] they lived part of their lives working on the field, as is common in this community."[22] The "staging" of peasantry at work in this description reflects the ways that "peasantry has become cultural capital to market" (Silverman 2012, 250), thus confirming Milan's tammurriata performances as fully part of the world music market. Indeed, while the religious element seems to have completely disappeared within Milan's cosmopolitan and secularized context, the rural world of tammurriata, as well as of tarantella more generally, seems to fit well within the larger movement toward sustainability evident in Milan since at least the early 2000s. The Expo Milano 2015's theme, "Feeding the Planet, Energy for Life," has generally encouraged sustainability-related cultural programs in the city, and within this climate it is important to note the promotion and in some cases the reopening of *cascine* (old farmhouses) as public spaces to use for recreational purposes as well as for cultural events. As confirmed by many event posters and Facebook advertising, this bucolic context fits well with folk music performance, tarantella included.

In addition to this staging of peasantry, within this new cosmopolitan frame-work, tammurriata's place-specific quality, strictly connected as it is to the lo-cal feast or town, is reframed within a more general sense of social interaction and gathering. Not only has the time of celebration moved outside the local calendar—and often in concomitance with various secular celebrations such as International Women's Day and New Year's Eve—but the space of performance has also changed, as it ranges from clubs and restaurants to various community spaces aimed at promoting social and cultural values that are either specific to Milan's context (such as community awareness, sustainability, and environ-mental issues) or have to do with broader social and political causes, such as political refugees, poverty, disability, and so forth.

Because pizzica is more popular than tammurriata when one moves out of the southern context, the frequency of tammurriata performances in Milan depends on the audience's taste as well as on the musician's ability to recognize and exploit the audience's inclination to create a good show, as explained by several of my interviewees.[23] Much more so than for Campania performances, here marketing and taste thus become crucial factors in creating a tammurriata performance. Furthermore, since tammurriata performances are here labeled under the generic term *traditional tammurriata*, tammurriata loses the central role it holds in the Campania festivals, while its melodic, stylistic, and cultural com-plexity also risks going unnoticed. At the July 5, 2014, Festa per Metromondo, many groups from the current tarantella scene in Milan performed to fund-raise on behalf of Arci Metromondo; together with Canto Antico's Movimenti association, the Arci Metromondo association has in fact largely contributed to promoting tarantella and training many young musicians in Milan since the late 1990s.[24] On this occasion, the preponderance of Salentine pizzica in Milan's context, and of the recently discovered tarantella from the Calabria region, was evident from the performance choices of each group. For this reason, when Canto Antico's singer and drummer Armando Illario intoned a *fronna* type of tammurriata song (a type of song that is very specific to the tammurriata feast circle in Campania) to pay homage to Arci Metromondo, the effect felt almost exotic, since it was completely different from all the other songs in the night's repertoire.[25]

Since pizzica and tammurriata are usually performed together—as the example above shows—tammurriata's roots from the Campania region are usually de-emphasized in favor of a broader southern identity, as confirmed by event advertising employing the phrase *musiche e danze del sud* (southern music and dances). There are a few but notable exceptions, mainly the work done by Canto Antico Movimenti since 1999 to educate its audiences to the cultural specificity of tammurriata by organizing concerts and events featuring performers from Campania, as well as collaborating with these performers on the organization of courses and workshops. Nevertheless, as suggested by Canto Antico's singer, dancer, and drummer Francesca Di Ieso in our interview, the label *musiche e danze del sud* remains a constant marketing choice in a context in which the more easily recognizable, and imitable, pizzica rhythm and steps serve to attract the audience's attention to other forms of tarantella that are less known or harder to comprehend, such as tammurriata's complex choreography.

On the one hand, this reframing as "southern music" creates an expectation of otherness and exoticism that the northern audience recognizes as historically part of southern Italian culture—especially since the South remains one of the main summer vacation destinations within the national borders; on the other hand, it provides an inclusive label in which many southerners working in Milan can recognize themselves. In addition, this categorization assigns a spot to tammurriata and pizzica next to several other folk and ethnic music cultures from the Mediterranean and the world, as often evident by concert and workshop advertisement. In this sense, it allows for a fruitful dialogue with other subcultural sounds or, as Di Ieso puts it, "the many possible Souths" (i molti sud possibili). The work of the group Domo Emigrantes, for example, combines sounds and rhythms from several folk cultures from the Italian South, the Mediterranean, and the Middle East to convey the sense of common Mediterranean roots.[26]

Even so, commercialization remains a constant element in Milan's tarantella scene. Classes and shows of pizzica and tammurriata dances—easier to consume as a tourist attraction than playing or singing—are often featured in the same space as belly dancing, salsa, and other global rhythms, there to attract the global tourist who is often not knowledgeable or interested in the culture behind the dance. A noteworthy example is the pairing of tarantella concerts with *aperitivo* (Italian for "happy hour") nights, which helps rebrand tarantella as yet another evening and weekend entertainment for both young and older urbanites in search of something new and exotic. In this sense, tammurriata has officially "moved toward a cosmopolitan, elite aesthetic" (Borland 2009, 473), which lies very far from the peasant aesthetic with which it is associated within its local cultural framework. At the Sud Sud Festival in June 2007, a tammurriata group was playing onstage while several, mostly young, people danced. While some dancers had clearly participated in a dance workshop, others were very likely improvising due to lack of specific dance knowledge; their steps in fact represented a type of "global folk dance," a mix of flamenco, tarantella, and gypsy dance steps that little resembled tammurriata. Needless to say, this perception of southern Italian dances as "other" in the same way as belly dancing or salsa often goes beyond the musicians' intent: as Domo Emigrantes performed the song "Spagna" (Spain)—an homage to a pan-Mediterranean sound—during their Peperoncino (Chili Pepper) Sud Festival appearance on June 7, 2014, several dancers naturally switched from southern Italian steps to salsa, among the most popular forms of ethnic dancing in Italy.

A few elements remain similar to tammurriata festivals in Campania, at least those of the 1990s—the emergence of tammurriata and pizzica as types of subcultural music attracting a small group of participants, mostly students, left-wing intellectuals, and in any case those in search of more non-mainstream cultural and music events. Indeed, this aspect seems to be even amplified in Milan performances, especially since this type of event is largely promoted by the Arci association[27] and its many *circoli* (clubs). The long-term association between Arci and the Italian Left confirms the importance of both tarantella and other types of folk music in Milan as *cultura di contestazione* (counterculture) (Lombardi-Satriani 1974), as it did during the 1970s folk music revival. From this perspective, it is important to note the emergence of the Tarantella Clandestina (clandestine tarantella) movement, whose name explicitly references an underground and counterhegemonic type of music, following the Mazurka Clandestina movement that is now spreading throughout the Italian peninsula. Tarantella Clandestina consists of performing in public spaces, such as major squares or outside government buildings, without any sort of permission or organization other than word-of-mouth advertising. This advertising happens through the Amici Pizzicati (Bitten Friends) Facebook page, which gathers most tarantella aficionados in Milan.[28] Performer and promoter Armando Soldano explains that, since the city government has tried in many ways to limit performance spaces in Milan, starting with the closing of Cascina Monluè in 2009, the

Figure 20. Armando Soldano (*left*) and Antonio Ricci (*center*) playing the tammorra drum and the accordion, respectively, in front of Centro Sociale Autogestito in Milan on July 12, 2014. Photo by the author.

Tarantella Clandestina movement intends to occupy the city's public space as a way to keep music free from the government's control.[29] At the performance I attended on July 12, 2014, an underground tone was added by the setting—a Centro Sociale.

The explicitly political tone of these "clandestine" performances is echoed by the work of the group Malapizzica (Bad pizzica), which regularly performs in prisons or other "tough" settings, while also participating in many events aimed at raising social consciousness. From a working-class background, group member Rosa Maurelli remembers that her first performance was in the 1990s during an occupation to protest a homestead eviction; Malapizzica's performances have always followed a distinct political and social agenda—they even campaigned for the left-leaning Partito Democratico and its mayoral candidate Michele Pisapia during the city's 2011 elections.

While it is true that most emerging groups in Milan are not necessarily engaged socially or politically, the often explicit political tone of these performances confirms that in the passage from South to North, many elements are lost but new ones are also gained. And while it is also true that, at least music-wise, many of the emerging groups limit themselves to perform what they consider "traditional" versions of pizzica and tammurriata without necessarily creating a new repertoire, there are those who strive to innovate, such as Canto Antico's recent project *South Beat*, which I illustrate below.

Reimagining the South in Milan

Reframing tammurriata, and tarantella more generally, for a Milanese audience is not an easy task, not only because of the complex dynamics of performance discussed above, but also because of the cliché usually associated with tarantella, and southern culture more generally, a cliché that is well established within the national context. According to Neapolitan practitioner Antonio Ricci, until the 1980s, when he first started to perform tarantella in Milan, Milanese audiences were most familiar with northern Italian and southern European folk music, while the only image of tarantella within this music scene consisted of the imitative and stereotypical Neapolitan tarantella; thus, for musicians like Ricci or Di Ieso, it became important to "popularize a culture that in reality is a photography of a piece of Italy that does not exist in the books, in the official history, to try and destroy that holographic image; [that music] is something else, there is a poetic, there is a story, a [social] function, a ritual" (Di Ieso).[30] In fact, since the beginning, the biggest challenge for Canto Antico, as the main cultural promoter of tarantella in Milan, has been to "narrate a different, plausible south that is not nostalgic, that is not a cliché, and that is also an alternative Italian music project" (Di Ieso).[31] One way to do this was by showing that tarantella is actually part of a larger and complex cultural context, "a world made in a certain way . . . a particular way of relating to each other. . . . spent around the table on Sundays."[32] Therefore, besides the strictly musical aspect, over the years their events have featured various cultural activities related to southern culture, including, for example, food-making workshops. In spite of all these efforts, however, the general attitude of the audience seems to be that of idealizing tarantella and the world it comes from: "You play a pizzica for them and they get all excited, they can't even imagine that that is the tip of the iceberg of a complex world that is full of contradictions, sometimes of terrible things."[33] This seems to be especially true for the younger generations, Di Ieso continues, who are completely removed from the rural world of tarantella, yet they take on the peasant dress code typical of the current festivals as a way to nostalgically reclaim a lost world that according to them is supposed to be *bello* (beautiful). They ultimately seem to fit the description of the postmodern tourist in search of an authentic, organic place that is still purer and less polluted than their own (Urry 1990). According to Di Ieso, this attitude is particularly problematic because it "removes all the aspects [of that world] that are bothersome" (toglie tutti gli aspetti che danno fastidio), including the difficult roles of southern women living within traditional peasant societies of the South. Thus, this nostalgic look at tarantella is a missed opportunity, especially as it fails to propose "a critical reflection on the real role of [southern] women" (una riflessione sul reale ruolo della donna).

This is very important to note because, on the one hand, the current popularity of tarantella has brought on more visibility to female performers both in the South and in larger urban centers like Milan's; on the other hand, the idealized image of tarantella that is being popularized within this urbanized context does not help northern audiences to better understand the social context of tarantella. The main problem, at least according to Canto Antico, is the fact that many people attending tarantella events in Milan are looking mostly for moments of socialization and not necessarily for opportunities to learn about the music's culture; thus, they fail to take home a larger picture of what it means to be from or live in the South. For this reason, while several performers from the South invoke the Southern Question as a way to reclaim their cultural pride in a northern city, these performance dynamics ultimately "do not affect Milan's cultural context" (non vanno a incidere sul territorio di Milano).

Nevertheless, while the transformation of tammurriata and pizzica into yet another form of entertainment for northern urbanites has certainly reduced the social and cultural potential of these performances, performing or consuming the music's culture also helps many southerners living in Milan to relocate within a globalized context of migration (Stokes 1994). Indeed, in a city like Milan, where the immigrants from the South remain a large component of the population, performing tarantella or just participating in a related music event often becomes a way for southerners to practice cultural traditions from their hometowns and villages and to reconnect with other southerners. One could get a quick glimpse of this type of dynamics at the June 18, 2009, concert by the folk-inspired Apulian group Sud Sound System: as soon as the group started performing the famous hit "Le radici ca tieni" (The roots you have), a hip-hop remixing of Apulian pizzica sung in the local language, the entire audience, at least several hundred people, started singing along, in the local language. Moments like this one have revealed to me the importance of doing southern Italian (folk) music today in the city of Milan. The experience of my brother, my cousins, and their friends as immigrants in this city, as well as my experience as a participant-observer, has over the past few years confirmed this importance. In this sense, the city of Milan works as a powerful "ethnoscape," that is, a "landscape of persons who constitute the shifting world in which we live: tourists, immigrants, refugees, exiles, guestworkers and other moving groups" (Appadurai 1996, 33). The tarantella performances occurring within this ethnoscape thus play an important role, as they help both performers and audiences, both southern Italian and foreign immigrants, express, share, negotiate, and perform their own ethnic identities within a globalized urban space.

On June 19, 2009, I went with my brother to a pizzica night at Arci's Scighera circle in Milan's Isola quarter, where I had the opportunity to meet I Briganti (Brigands), one of the earliest groups to perform southern Italian folk music in Milan, starting in the late 1990s. We immediately made friends with the group's singer and drummer Gianpiero Caruso, from the Naples area, who learned tammurriata drumming and singing at the same festivals I participated in in the late 1990s and therefore is very familiar with that festival context. Once he found a job in Milan, Caruso looked for a way to continue playing tammurriata; soon enough he found himself playing with I Briganti as well as other local music groups. On that night, Caruso invited my brother to join him in a typical "Bella Figliola" tammurriata song, since we also were "di giù" (from down south) and therefore closer to that music culture than his Milanese audience.[34] Indeed, both our common experience at the southern festivals and my brother's role as a Campanian immigrant to Milan, like so many others from our generation, immediately established a special rapport with the group.

Since that night, I have had the opportunity to meet several Milan-based musicians from Campania and elsewhere in the South and to discover that for most of them, just like for Caruso, making or listening to southern music has been a way to reconnect to their own home culture. Rosa Maurelli, who plays tammorra, tamburello, and *chitarra battente* (beating guitar) in the group Malapizzica, moved from the town of San Giuseppe Vesuviano (near Naples) to Milan with her family as a child in 1970, a period of strong migration from the South. Maurelli clearly remembers the trauma of migration, her mother crying all the time, and the shock of finding oneself, all of a sudden, in a big city, a completely different world with a lot of rules, where children were not free to play like they used to back home. This experience has shaped her life in many ways and has certainly influenced her choice to play southern music, "because it is always something that you have inside . . . and you'd like it to come out" (perchè è sempre una cosa che tu hai dentro . . . e vorresti che uscisse fuori). Maurelli remembers her grandmother playing tammorra and the whole family (seven children) to be "very much into the [tammurriata] tradition" (molto dentro alla tradizione); she also remembers going to the religious festivals in her hometown as a child accompanied by her older brother. But helping this southern voice to emerge also allows the encounter with other southern roots; for example, Maurelli mentions that foreign immigrants from Africa and the Mediterranean often participate in her group's shows in Milan, and they often comment on the similarities with their own musical and cultural roots, such as the central role of the drum and the fast and almost obsessive rhythms of tarantella. She feels that this is an important moment of cultural exchange that is in some ways possible thanks to this folk music.

The experience of living and working in Milan is, of course, very different for recent immigrants like Francesca Di Ieso and Armando Illario (of Canto Antico), who, like many others from the current generation, have moved to Milan as adults with a college degree and in search of white-collar jobs. As both musicians and cultural promoters, the members of Canto Antico are well aware of the cultural significance of bringing southern music to Milan; as a group, doing southern music for them means to both "live" and "transmit" to others their own sense of belonging (appartenenza). And this idea is the basis for their South Beat [sic] music project, according to Illario; in fact, as Di Ieso stated, "The Southern beat is the sense of belonging that we bring with us and stays inside; however, it does not look back with nostalgia but it goes, it moves towards other beats."[35] On a strictly musical level, she continued, this is possible only if one is able to "translate the complexity that is intrinsic to the tammurriata performances of zi Giannino [and others]" (tradurre la complessità intrinsica alla tammurriata di zi giannino) into a language that works for younger southerners like them, living in an urbanized and globalized context such as Milan. The project includes a juxtaposition of sounds from the southern Italian folk music tradition with elements of electronic music—an effort that has been praised as an example of music that moves beyond the simplistic mimicking of well-known tarantella rhythms (Murizzi 2014).

As their group name suggests, the music of Domo Emigrantes (Migrants from Home) deals with the notions of migration and both personal and community roots: not only are the group's main founders either first- or second-generation southerners living in the northern town of Lodi and the metropolitan center of Milan, but their songs, especially those included in their second and newest album, titled *Kolymbetra* (2015), often contain a reflection on southern

Figure 21. Domo Emigrantes at the Peperoncino Sud Festival in Milan on June 7, 2014. The photo shows Kurdish group member Ashti Abdo in Middle Eastern attire and playing the southern Italian frame drum. Photo by the author.

Italian culture as part of the larger Mediterranean crossroad and therefore a hybrid culture by definition (Renna). At the center of this cross-cultural exchange stands Sicily and its rhythms, featured extensively in their songs. The importance of migration as a central theme to the group's repertoire is confirmed by their advertising campaign, which often includes photos of an old train or a Sicilian *carretto,* an old-style painted cart.

The idea of cross-cultural exchange within a larger southern perspective has become particularly significant for the group, since Ashti Abdo (known as Salam), a young Kurdish refugee who arrived in Milan in 2006, started playing with them. At first Abdo joined the group by playing his *saz* (*tambiur* in Kurdish), a string instrument common among Kurdish communities; then he learned the southern Italian *tamburello* frame drum and started to play and sing Sicilian tarantella as well as Apulian pizzica, while also becoming familiar with other southern Italian instruments, such as the Sicilian *marranzano* (jaw's harp). However, very soon Abdo found his own playing style using these southern Italian instruments. In the meantime, the group started to play and sing a few Kurdish songs, thus creating a rather unique example of cultural exchange within the tarantella context in Milan. For Abdo, the exchange with tarantella makes a lot of sense, since both southern Italian and Kurdish songs often center on the theme of the land, not just the love for the land but especially "the longing for or the loss of one's homeland" (*la mancanza della patria*). Considering how much Kurdish communities have lost, or been dispossessed of, in terms of their cultural heritage, including access to their language, he proudly states that "for Kurdish people, it is a form of success that an Italian sings [in Kurdish] in a chorus with a Kurd" (per i kurdi anche è un successo che un italiano fa il coro con un kurdo). A particularly exciting moment for the group happened during a concert in Arcore (on the outskirts of Milan), where at the end of their concert a jam session was improvised with a group of musicians from Togo—on that occasion, Domo Emigrantes performed a Calabrian-style tarantella and were accompanied by *jembe* (a West African drum) and guitars, thus giving rise to this "musical sharing . . . even from the audience, a real blending of traditions" (c'è stata questa condivisione musicale ma anche da parte del pubblico, un miscuglio di tradizioni). This group's experience, along with their personal and artistic relationship with Abdo, is very promising within the larger context of foreign migration to Italy; however, as both Abdo and Renna admit, it is very rare to see foreign immigrants at tarantella shows, not only because this continues to be a niche type of music, but also because most foreigners probably do not yet feel part of Italian communities.

As these examples illustrate, in popularizing tammurriata for Milanese audiences, southern performers and scholars have had to deal with, and respond to, common clichéd images of the South. As the next two chapters illustrate, similar dynamics are at play not only in tarantella music production within the world music market, but also in tarantella performances in the United States. This fact in turn reflects the importance of the tarantella revival as a whole in conveying a certain image of the South and therefore its direct contribution to the Southern Question debate. As they respond to previous and stereotypical representations of the South, tammurriata performances outside of the Campania context largely contribute to reinventing tammurriata according to new social and cultural dynamics. While these changes are already at work in the local context, the higher degree of change in the Milanese context is strictly linked to the dynamics of living and performing in a metropole. In this sense, these changes reflect dynamics of globalization—especially in the sense of a detachment from local cultural values—that are evident in the marketing of tarantella for the world music market as well as in the export of tarantella to the United States.

In the following section I discuss some of the major local responses to these changes while also reflecting on the cultural and moral stakes at play in the reinvention of tammurriata performances for national and global audiences.

The Politics of Tammurriata

In this chapter, I have attempted to illustrate the dynamics of revitalization within the tammurriata context, as well as the current tammurriata festival dynamics in all their complexity, while also looking at some of the local responses to this phenomenon of revitalization. The current process of popularization and commercialization of tammurriata has certainly sparked much criticism among local scholars and aficionados. Among the most eloquent responses is Roberto De Simone's; even during the 1970s revival, the well-known Neapolitan student of Campania's folk music responded to the increasing secularization of the local festivals by reminding that "only devotion, that interior feeling that is connected to the myth, is able to give rise to the musical expression and to determine its collective role in the community. . . . This devotion is defined by the community as the emotional component that determines the 'need for' the chant and the music, as well as their social role" (1979, 9). It thus becomes natural for someone as firmly rooted in the religious tradition of tammurriata as De Simone to ask nonbeliever performers and participants the reason for their performance. As I suggested earlier in this chapter, I believe that this question is misleading, since it looks at the current revival only in terms of what it lacks without asking what new perspective it brings to the tammurriata context. At the same time, De Simone's words, and the secularization process he discusses, do raise important questions regarding a possible lack of "attention" and "respect," as Dionisio stated, toward the religious aspects of tammurriata on the part of festival participants today.

Writing again in 2005, during the current revival, De Simone noted that the extremely standardized dance steps and performance styles that are visible at the current festivals suggest a difference between the "unaware" repetition of urban performances and the interactive repetition of forms and contents that originate within the ritual framework. This observation echoes Gala's own preoccupation with the pizzica festival dynamics and the emergence of a new style of dancing that is highly codified. As I have discussed above, this is indeed still a common preoccupation among local performers today, especially as they compare the local festivals with tammurriata dancing elsewhere in Italy; as my interviews with Milan-based performers, such the group Canto Antico, reveal, this is a risk especially when such localized forms like tammurriata are exported outside of their original context. Upon observing the recent setting of tammurriata festivals, Gala also commented, "For the time being . . . it is not possible to perceive in the original context a more general/larger interest in the old dances; the local youth who has assimilated the ethnochoreutic language directly from the old timers come from a family custom to dancing and singing. Only a new collective awareness in the places where these dances belong, can guarantee the continuation of the tradition; instead, today the temptation is to transform the remaining elements of the tradition into a spectacle and commodity to export" (1999a, 8). Following Gala's words, then, one is tempted to say that the tammurriata tradition is in fact dead. Yet both the major performers I interviewed at the Campania festivals and even some of the ones based in Milan are very much aware of this risk and work hard to address it in their everyday interactions with tammurriata aficionados, including Di Ieso, Torelli, and Inserra. The idea of "paying attention," according to Dionisio, to the essence of tammurriata is in fact one of the emerging issues within the current festival context, one that performers, scholars, and cultural brokers both locally and nationally are purposefully addressing.

In addition, according to De Simone, the pedagogical moments of the *festa* seem to be lost, since today many performers learn at workshops and schools. "A traditional festival," De Simone continues, "combines celebratory and didactic elements, and here the role of the maestro, through his own examples and authority, makes it possible for the tradition to continue" (quoted in Vincenzo Santoro 2015). As the ritual function of the festivals disappears, concludes De Simone, the whole process of "socialization," expressed by tammurriata music rituals and rites of passage, seems to disappear as well. This is a crucial factor to keep in mind, one that several local performers today associate with tammurriata. However, De Simone's interpretation does not take into account the fact that a similar process of imitation based on repetition can be at work within a tammurriata workshop and that its socialization aspect is particularly evident if the teacher is also a local practitioner aware of the complexities of tammurriata, such as Dionisio, Vicinanza, or Torelli.

Given this complexity, I believe that to fully comprehend the current recontextualization of tammurriata, it is neither valuable nor enough to search for, and identify, the "authentic" tammurriata tradition. Because "traditions are always defined in the present . . . the actors doing the defining are not concerned about whether scholars [or locals] will perceive a given festival or piece of art as genuine or spurious but whether the manifestation will accomplish for them what they intend to accomplish" (Bendix 1989, 132). The 1999 documentary film

Tam-Tam Tammorra, by local filmmaker Salvatore Raiola, reports an interview with local performer Marcello Colasurdo, who also confirms the need to look at tammurriata as alive and in continuous change. On the one hand, Colasurdo explains, urban development has evidently taken over (*usurpata*) the rural world in which tammurriata developed; on the other hand, tammurriata's folk tradition continues to live on within an industrialized and urbanized world. Their interview location—under a highway bridge by a graffiti wall—further corroborates this perspective.

Local performer Ugo Maiorano and his Paranza dell'Agro (Paranza or music group from the Agro-Nocerino Sarnese area), for example, explicitly employ the tammurriata tradition for new purposes—their July 16, 2014, show in honor of the Madonna del Carmine in Episcopio (Sarno), in the Salerno province, featured a mix of tammurriata songs usually performed at the religious festivals and a variety of mainstream Neapolitan music, such as the world-renowned "Tammurriata nera" (Black tammurriata), which attracts a larger audience, including those who are not familiar with the tammurriata folk tradition. This repertoire choice was striking, since the show was held outside the church, which usually hosts more traditional tammurriata rhythms. Increasing this estrangement effect was the show's opening, which featured a pizzica song by Eugenio Bennato (see chapter 3) and two dancers, dressed in typical pizzica costumes and choreographing a *pizzica de core* (courtship pizzica). This artistic choice can obviously be explained in terms of audience demand, but at least to my understanding, Majorano is also well versed in and aware of the importance of the tammurriata tradition and its values, and he is widely respected in the local scene. In other words, going back to the tradition for Majorano often means to reinvent it (Magliocco 2006, 105), and because he is one of the major voices of the local tammurriata tradition, he can afford to do that. This example seems to suggest that for one's tammurriata performance to be accepted, what ultimately matters is how the performer positions him- or herself within the tradition, whether he or she is able to show his or her attention to, passion, and respect for the tradition, while at the same time contributing toward reinventing that tradition every day.

The views expressed by De Simone and Gala above are actually common to practitioners in many other folk revival settings and to the folklore studies tradition both in the United States and internationally (Bendix 1997). In fact, the need to determine whether a certain tradition is or remains authentic is strictly connected to local, national, and global politics of culture and to the socioeconomic and political interests of those groups who invest in the authenticity or inauthenticity of that particular tradition. In the case of tammurriata, being defined as an "official" representative of the tradition also means ensuring one's own group, town, or political affiliation plus the support of the local authorities and, as the tradition becomes popular on a global scale, of national and European agencies as well. In other words, because southern Italian folk music has now become very popular both nationally and internationally, it has spurred local actors to interrogate the authenticity of other revitalized tammurriata performances and to designate their local performances as the "most traditional" ones.

It is not surprising, then, that throughout my time at the tammurriata festivals in Campania, most local performers, participants, and scholars tended to talk about the tammurriata tradition in the present tense, thus assigning tammurriata never-changing and mythical qualities. In other words, what they tell us is an "idealized" version of the tradition (Magliocco 2006, 60). This element is important to note since they all share an awareness that festivals are changing and that the tradition is changing with them. Behind this contradictory attitude lie idealized expectations of what traditions are supposed to be or represent; as the revival phenomenon receives wider attention, the politics of heritage making seem to dictate an official representation of tammurriata, even as the actual festival dynamics tell a different story. Therefore, by keeping tammurriata in the never-changing present, they are not only actively assigning tammurriata the role of local cultural heritage, whereby heritage works as "a mode of cultural production in the present that has recourse to the past" (Kirshenblatt-Gimblett 1998, 7), but also offering a rigid representation of the local culture.

In addition, whenever I approached the locals for an interview on the current festival dynamics, I was constantly told that I had to go and talk to the old-timers because they were the only ones who retained the truth about tammurriata, the only ones who knew what tammurriata "really" is. Whenever I explained that I was particularly interested in the current transformations of the festival context, their reactions seemed to suggest that I was wasting my time, since the current festival context offers only an impure and distorted version of tammurriata. This attitude is evident even in the current scholarship on tammurriata. In their book on the tammurriata tradition in Pagani, Dionisio and D'Aquino state that today, "the protagonist of the feast is still the old timer, the 'contadino' (peasant) and his/her worldview, especially the 'contadino-tammorraro' (peasant-drummer)" (2003, 17), whose example is imitated by the younger musicians and also observed and admired by the audience outside the *cerchio* (circle) of performers. But as I discussed above, the social composition of the local performers has changed drastically just in the last generation. Furthermore, following a common feeling among tammurriata aficionados, Vicinanza also states, "There is no school to learn the folk dances, but only initiation from and imitation of the old-timers, the only source of knowledge for those who don't want to contribute to a fake and corrupted version of folk culture" (2005, 19–20). Yet this is from someone who has been teaching tammurriata in the local schools for several years.

While, on the one hand, this attitude reveals a deep respect for the older generations of performers, on the other hand, it also reflects the need to defend oneself from criticism and ensure that one is "on the safe side." It is not difficult to imagine, however, how this need to do things right will be replaced by other needs and understandings of tammurriata, as this tradition moves away from the circle of the local performers and audience. In other words, the concern over practicing a certain version of tammurriata that is respectful of the old-timers' teachings makes sense within the framework of the local festivals, but it is not enough to explain the dynamics of recontextualization of tammurriata outside this framework.

Thus, while the local concern over the current revitalization of tammurriata testifies to the importance of looking at tammurriata as something more than a set of choreographies and drum patterns, it also betrays the ambiguity of any folklore project that tries to establish the true or authentic values of a certain tradition. Moreover, these scholars' observations on tammurriata ultimately suggest a willingness to define themselves as authentic representatives of the tradition and to put down other performers or scholars. In his harsh criticism of today's tammurriata performances, De Simone, for example, does not seem to take into account his own role as an urbanized scholar who visited the local festivals in the 1970s and whose perspective on tammurriata might have been as romanticized as that of other scholars at the time (Biagi 2004). Vicinanza's educational project on the local schools regarding the historical and cultural specificity of tammurriata represents a very laudable effort. Yet their position is not much different from that of other young urbanites without a deep knowledge of the peasant world of tammurriata, a world that they are now discovering for the first time through the revival. For all these reasons, this renewed effort to revitalize the peasant values of tammurriata represents a rather complex project and carries with it similar feelings of nostalgia for the "folk" and the "popular" as the ones displayed by the 1970s revival movement (ibid.). Therefore, the attempt to define the most authentic version of tammurriata and the most genuine way of performing this music remains ironic, to say the least. Inserra's skeptical attitude toward these young urbanites is equally problematic, since in the past few years he has accepted many invitations to participate in folk music festivals all over Italy as well as in several European countries; his group was also featured by the 2007 Sud Sud Festival at Cascina Monluè. In addition, because his advertised image is that of a major tammurriata player in Italy today, he has also become an icon for the globalized version of tammurriata that is popular outside Naples. Inserra's role within the current revival is thus a complex one and symbolizes the many intersections between local traditions and global markets.

Nevertheless, both competing notions of tammurriata existing within the current revival and the touristic version of tammurriata brought to audiences outside the local context remain important points on which to reflect. Neapolitan singer Marcello Colasurdo, who has famously performed tammurriata both within and outside the local context as well as nationally and internationally, describes this duality in the following terms: "It is exactly there, from the old timers that I learn new tammurriata texts, that is, the traditional ones, which have been passed on orally and vary according to each geographical area. What you sing on the festival site you don't sing on the stage: real tammurriata is danced, played, and sung at the local *festa*, for hours and hours, without a microphone. It is there that you can measure everyone's performing skills: musicians, singers, and dancers" (Mauro 2004, 219). Thus, while tammurriata has the potential to be recontextualized and enriched with new meanings outside of the local context, the importance of understanding the traditional festival context lies in the particular role that this context retains in relation to tammurriata's performance dynamics.

This effort to educate new acolytes, both local and nonlocal, to the essence of a tammurriata performance on the part of local practitioners was evident in Raffaele Inserra's tammurriata workshop held at Arci's Scighera circle in Milan on January 9, 2010. Indeed, that experience made very clear to me the competing notions of tammurriata emerging from its recontextualization in such a global city as Milan. Inserra's teaching method and workshop organization—a mix of improvised historical accounts, personal anecdotes about his own experience with drum playing, and an explicit critique of the current revival and its watered-down tammurriata version—did not respond to the workshop format. Moreover, the tammurriata dance performance included in the workshop, an example of Pimontese from Inserra's home area and my own,[36] did not seem to attract much interest from the participants, since it lacked the highly choreographed and faster dance steps associated with tammurriata performances from other Campania locations; the Milan-based friend I was dancing with complained, for example, about this version being too slow and boring. In the cosmopolitan context of Milan, where different performance cultures compete for the spotlight, Inserra's workshop had set itself up for failure. However, from the perspective of a southerner whose ideas are firmly rooted in the rural culture of South, this workshop became a way to educate Milan's middle-class urbanites about tammurriata music culture and consequently southern culture. On this occasion, I couldn't but admire Inserra's effort to remind his audience that before learning to drum, sing, or dance tammurriata, it is important to learn, and respect, the cultural framework it comes from, even when this cultural framework does not carry the same degree of sex appeal as the more popular pizzica performances. This is also a strong reminder that, in the handing over of traditional knowledge from one generation or group to another, "the receiver must respect, but the giver must let go. The constraint is thus mutual, as is the room for maneuver" (Noyes 2009, 249).

CHAPTER 3

Images of the Italian South within and beyond World Music

Eugenio Bennato's Taranta Power Movement

The festival context discussed in the previous chapter offers direct testimony to the current changes in terms of dance choreographies, costumes, and festival dynamics while also confirming that many of the current debates surrounding tarantella focus on the notions of authenticity, tradition, and place. The tarantella songs' lyrical content and musical arrangements that I discuss in this chapter confirm the resilience of these debates on the level of music production and distribution, as tarantella music is marketed as world music. In fact, this music offers an often explicit commentary on the ongoing tarantella phenomenon. In addition, since music "plays an important role in the narrativization of place" (Whiteley, Bennett, and Hawkins 2005, 2), this song production is important especially because it narrates the sociopolitical and cultural context in which this music and dance tradition has developed and transformed over time—particularly the Southern Question debate—while also affecting the way that southern Italians perceive the history of their own place. In particular, in this chapter I focus on the dynamics of resignification of the tarantella genre since the late 1990s by looking at production, distribution, and marketing of new tarantella songs, particularly through the work of musician Eugenio Bennato and its representation of the Italian South. As confirmed by my own personal experience as a festivalgoer in the late 1990s–early 2000s, Bennato's albums and concert tours have touched many tarantella aficionados throughout Italy as well as the rest of Europe, Canada, and the United States, thus largely contributing to popularizing a new wave of tarantella music. This global visibility not only testifies to Bennato's popularity within the world music scene, but also exemplifies the dynamics of global circulation of tarantella since the late 1990s. During the 1970s folk music revival, which signaled Bennato's debut, his music featured tarantella from the Campania region and songs written in the Neapolitan language, while also discussing the Italian Southern Question; his late 1990s–early 2000s music production, instead, focuses on pizzica and other tarantella subgenres from several southern regions and makes use of various southern languages as well as Italian, English, French, and Arabic. It also reimagines the South from a pan-Mediterranean perspective by drawing on both North African sounds and cross-cultural themes. This example shows the complexity of the 1990s–2000s tarantella phenomenon: on the one hand, it provides a space for narrating the still difficult role of the Italian South today within the larger Mediterranean context; on the other hand, it offers music that is more accessible and often less place and culture specific, and therefore ready to be consumed by a wider audience who speaks standard-Italian and foreign languages but probably not the southern languages of tarantella. It also opens up to foreign audiences that will likely not be familiar with, or understand, the sociopolitical import of Bennato's songs. In this sense, Bennato's overall music project involving tarantella allows him to "choose[s] between the local or the particular, the global or the popular, or enter[s] into, a non-localized place where mediation occurs, whether in the form of assimilation, syncretism or fusion" (Motherway 2013, 5). I argue that, as Bennato's tarantella project adapts to these global dynamics, its perspective on the Italian South changes accordingly, thus clearly illustrating the different roles that tarantella has taken on within the Italian folk music scene over time. While in his 1970s albums, tarantella was mostly looked at as a form of counterculture, Bennato's post-1990s albums continue to represent it as a counterhegemonic force through the choice of a pan-Mediterranean perspective and by employing tarantella to challenge the exotic image usually associated with the South in tourist discourse. At the same time, these more recent albums often present an overly positive celebration of tarantella, and of southern identity, which leaves in the background the negative aspects connected to its troubled history and sociocultural milieu, as several scholars have already noted for the neotarantism phenomenon. To further add to the complexity of Bennato's tarantella project, I will discuss his latest album, *Questione Meridionale* (Southern Question [2011]), and the ways that it announces a return to a historical perspective on tarantella, while at the same time opening up to the Italian American diaspora and thus to a transnational vision of Italian folk culture.

Musicanova

Eugenio Bennato's forty-year involvement with southern Italian folk music is indeed essential to fully understanding the genealogy and current development of the revival. After cofounding NCCP in 1967 and working with the group for a few years, in 1976 Bennato founded the group Musicanova (New music), which ensured him success on both local and national scenes. Among the factors contributing to this decision was Bennato's encounter in 1976 with minstrel Andrea Sacco and his use of *chitarra battente* to "replicate the many rhythmic variations of folkloric dances"; since the start, then, Musicanova's goal was "no longer only the preservation of folkloric traditions but also their recreations" (Bouchard and Ferme 2013, 110).

This group featured Bennato and D'Angiò as musicians and composers, Neapolitan singer and guitarist Teresa De Sio, and percussionist Toni Esposito. The last two members have become well known in Naples's contemporary music scene and also represent, together with Bennato, integral voices of the larger "Naples Power" movement—a fluid musical movement started in the 1970s that included both folk and rock sounds and brought about "novel performing attitudes, different compositional approaches, and revolutionary sonic productions" (Plastino 2013, 58).

From 1977 through 1980, Musicanova released five albums; the most well known is probably *Brigante se more* (One dies brigand), released in 1980. Musicanova's music project consisted of a conscious and well-informed reinterpretation of southern Italian folk music. The project certainly "marked a real shift in Neapolitan folk revival in so far as it included some Naples Power sounds and pointed towards a different approach to folk music, by leaving more space for singers and performers to improvise and by not strictly adhering to traditional conventions" (64). The result was a type of music that especially pleased young audiences represented by the 1970s student movement and left-wing intellectuals, since it reflected a "radicalization of Bennato's objectives and musical sonority" (Bouchard and Ferme 2013, 110), but it often encountered the criticism of folklore scholars, including De Simone. Defending himself from such criticism, Bennato declares that the group's intention was "to explore a new and autonomous activity of musical composition, although it would still be linked to the style and aesthetics that the traditional masters had illustrated and taught us" (Bennato 2010, 16). This vision is explicitly announced in the album *Musicanova* (1978). The song "Pizzica minore" (Minor pizzica) in particular borrows the captivating, wild rhythm of tarantella and makes use of the Neapolitan language. It also employs both traditional instruments, such as *tamburello* and *chitarra battente*, and more highbrow sounds, such as the violin, in a manner that is similar to NCCP's style; however, both the heavier presence of folk instruments and the use of a ballad-like structure resonating with the folk tradition from the hill towns of Basilicata and Puglia set the album apart from NCCP's project and also reflect the album's main theme, brigandism, a phenomenon that is typical from those regions (Bouchard and Ferme 2013, 110). The song's opening underlines the band's music agenda through its direct reference to a "new music," which also makes the song a sort of manifesto of Bennato's group:

Io l'aggio sentuta è 'na musica nova . . .	and I have heard it, it's a new music . . .
senza sante nè padrune . . .	without subordinates nor bosses,
a la festa 'e tutte quante,	at the party thrown for everybody
senza diavule senza sante.	Without devils or saints.

This music project is new because it seeks to appeal to "everybody" and everyday people as a way to move beyond class boundaries, according to the logic of a music made for the "folk." It is also new because it reflects the 1970s folk revival's refusal of mainstream music genres—ranging from the Italian pop genre to the Beatles model—and toward "a completely different path," that is, "towards the countryside, in search of folk music or of the oral tradition that is still made today, and to the libraries, in search of that music that is not sung anymore" (Bennato and D'Angiò 1987, 64). This agenda clearly reflects the similarities between Bennato's Musicanova project and NCCP's project as described in the first chapter; however, Musicanova's focus on "improvisation, composition, alternative uses of folk instruments, instrumental tunes, pop song structures, genre crossing" (Plastino 2013, 64) strikingly contrasted NCCP's notion of an accurate rendering of folk-song repertoires. Furthermore, what Bennato's project had in common with such groups as E Zézi and Nacchere Rosse was a political commitment that often explicitly emerged from its song lyrics. This in turn reminds us that musical authorings of space produce not one but a series of competing local narratives (Whiteley, Bennett, and Hawkins 2005, 3). For Bennato, this commitment meant not only reclaiming and appreciating local music, but also narrating the Italian South, as I illustrate in the next section. This work ultimately helped establish the basis for Bennato's tarantella project from the 1970s until today.

Counternarratives of the South

Music texts are "creatively combined with local knowledges and sensibilities in ways that tell particular stories about the local, and impose collectively defined meanings and significance on space" (ibid.). As a case in point, some of the most common images of the South, and of Naples in particular—both in Italy and abroad—are touristic and holographic ones since they have been "collectively imposed" through the internationally renowned *canzone napoletana* genre (Bennato 2010). Working within the Naples Power movement, several Neapolitan artists from the 1970s and 1980s shared their concern over this representation and sought to move away from it. Thus, Naples Power became "an indispensable move away from the 'reactionary' Neapolitan song productions of the 1960s, against an older and powerful musical hegemony" (Plastino 2013, 58). An interesting example is represented by the song "Nuie simme d' 'o Sud" (We are from the South), performed by Pietra Montecorvino (Eugenio Bennato's professional partner since *Musicanova*) and featured in the 1983 Naples-based comedy *F.F.S.S.: Che mi hai portato a fare sopra Posillipo se non mi vuoi più bene,* a locally well-known example of Neapolitan comedy. The lyrics of this song summarize the stereotypes associated with Naples, and the South more generally, while also reappropriating these images and reclaiming them as part of southern Italian identity in typical postcolonial fashion:

> South
> South
> we are from the South
> we are short and black
> we are good at singing
> but we work too
> . . . we come from the South
> and we walk
> please give us time to get here
> because we're from the South.
> The sun
> the sea
> the blue sky
> the mandolin and the putipù[1]
> tomato for ragù [meat sauce]
> pizza and mozzarella
> a mother's heart and tarantella
> pasta to eat
> and a little voice for singing
> it's true or perhaps not?
> Give us a break
> because we are from the South.[2]

While it acknowledges and reclaims the stereotype, however, the song fails to propose an alternative image for the city. In fact, the long-standing tradition of *canzone napoletana* seems to have locked the image of Naples and the South into a holographic picture from which not even southerners know how to disentangle (Fabbri 2001).

The 1970s folk music revival in Campania reflected a strong commitment to creating an alternative narrative of the South to the one provided by pop culture both in Italy and abroad. The very act of broadcasting local folk music, written and performed in Neapolitan, to the entire Italian peninsula represented a great step toward educating national audiences about the linguistic, musical, and cultural richness of the South. In particular, by presenting a product that was not immediately recognizable as pop culture, but employed the folk material and linguistic specificity of Naples, NCCP was trying to push a rather innovative image of Neapolitan music and of the city itself. In commenting on NCCP's attitude on the stage—a self-presentation closer to that of classical musicians than to popular singers—Fausta Vetere, one of the group's veteran voices, explains: "We came from Naples, and about Naples people knew only the classical songs: a stereotypical and holographic image that was being exported abroad as well"; "we wanted to avoid the usual cliché 'pizza and mandolin,'" she adds (Manzotti 2005). In this sense, NCCP's project was explicitly challenging the popular image of Naples's music as limited to the Neapolitan music genre and devoid of a folk or oral tradition. On the other hand, E Zézi's and Nacchere Rosse's commitment to narrating the poor working conditions in the South worked as another brilliant example of a counterhistory of the South, since it ultimately brought to light the difficult relation between the Turin-based national structure of Fiat and its southern branches as well as what the southern workers felt was a lack of interest toward their future on the part of Fiat headquarters (Vacca 1999; Gammella 2009).

Particularly relevant to this discussion is Eugenio Bennato's Musicanova project, since it consciously enters the debate over the Southern Question and seeks to renarrate the South from a southern perspective, thus providing Italian audiences with an explicit counterhistory of the South and accordingly of the history of Italy as a nation. De Simone's historical research on folk material of the Campania region provided a great starting point in this new direction; in NCCP's first album, *Cicerenella* (1972), NCCP recovered and made popular the folk song "Canto dei Sanfedisti" (Sanfedisti's Chant), which recounts the preunification South through the eyes of the followers of the Bourbon regime.[3] Bennato's 1980 album, *Brigante se more,* takes NCCP's example to the next step by presenting new songs that focus on the history of southern Italian brigands, especially those groups who rebelled against the power of the northern nationalist army in 1860s, during the process of occupation of the South under the Savoy control. An example of what historian Hobsbawm calls a "social bandit," the southern Italian brigand typically antagonized the local government and often had the favor of the local population. The 1860s brigands, in particular, "saw themselves as the people's champions against the gentry and the 'foreigners,'" or the northern forces. Indeed, these bandits represented heroes to the eyes of southern peasants, "for whom the 'years of the brigands' are among the few parts of history which are alive and real because, unlike the kings and wars, they belong to them" (1959, 21). Bennato's reclaiming of the brigands' history thus needs to be read within the larger context of the Southern Question and the peculiar history of the Italian unification.

The song "Brigante se more" (One dies brigand) perhaps remains Bennato's most famous song, often still sung among Neapolitans at friendly gatherings today. Several other songs in the album are also devoted to the brigand theme, from "Vulesse addeventare nu brigante" (I would like to become a brigand) to "Il brigante Carmine Rocco" (The brigand Carmine Rocco, the story of a well-known historical figure) to "Il cammino del brigante" (The brigand's path). "Brigante se more," written in March 1979, is particularly relevant first of all for its popularity; as Bennato himself recalls, the song is "one of the most popular folksongs in the last decades of Italian music" (2010, 31). Second, the song signals an important moment of awareness regarding the history of the South, since the history of southern resistance to northern occupation has been either ignored or minimized by official historical records (19). Written in Neapolitan, the song was composed by Bennato and D'Angiò for the 1980 TV series *L'eredità della priora* (The priory's inheritance), which described the turbulent revolts following the Savoia's conquest of the southern regions in the 1860. A look at the opening lines will give a sense of its powerful lyrics:

Amme pusate chitarre e tammure	We have put down guitars and drums
pecchè sta musica s'ha da cagnà	Because this music has to change
simme brigant' e facimme paura	We are brigands and we are scary
e ca schiuppetta vulimme cantà	and with the rifle we want to sing
e ca schiuppetta vulimme cantà	and with the rifle we want to sing

Narrated through the voice of the brigands, the song describes their fight in vivid color. Here Bennato's goal is to employ a language that is "free and impetuous like the guerilla soldiers it writes about, passionate and immediate" (34). More important, in this song the rifle takes the place of the drums, because this new historical contingency requires "new music." As the strong tone of

this song testifies, for Bennato "brigandism assumes . . . if not a positive con-
notation then at least the function of social and political response against the
injustices perpetrated by northern politicians and their armies on the weakest
social groups in the South" (Bouchard and Ferme 2013, 111). As Bennato points
out, the musical form adopted in this album is in itself a direct response to the
colonial ideology of the northern powers that viewed southerners as "those of
the primitive tarantella . . . of the love songs that can't harm anybody . . . and
now as *brigands,* a biased and derogatory label" (2010, 70). Leaving aside the
harmless musical instruments of tarantella, now the brigands decide to become
as scary as others portray them to be. The following stanza further centers on
the main issues at stake in brigandism: the question of landownership—"We
don't care about the Bourbon King / the land is ours and shouldn't be touched"
(nun ce ne fott' do' re burbone / 'a terra è 'a nosta e nun s'ha da tuccà)—and the
peculiar position of the South in this time period, caught between the Bourbon
regime and the northern powers. In turn, the following section vividly describes
the North-South relationship at the time:

Chi ha vist' 'o lupo e s' è mise paur'	Those who saw the wolf were scared
nun sape buon qual' è 'a verità	they don't know the truth
'o ver' lupo ca magna e creature	the real wolf who eats the babies
è 'o piemuntese c'avimm' 'a caccià	is the Piemontese that we need to
	send away

The Savoia family from the northern region of Piemonte represented a major political power at the time and was mainly responsible for the military occupation
of the South in 1860. By comparing the Piemontese (Savoia) people to wolves,
the song takes a very strong position on Italian nationalism and the North-
South relationship. By bringing back to light this peculiar period of southern
Italian history, then, Bennato makes the Southern Question an explicit object
of discussion on the folk music stage. In this way, he is able to enter the larger
scene of politically engaged folklore within the 1970s folk music revival and to
support the folk music model created by E Zézi through the use of historical
argument. In reflecting back on this stage of his career, Bennato writes that this
way of doing southern folk music was a great way for his group of Neapolitan
musicians to "win back" the national music scene, since from that moment on,
"at summer camps and on the beaches all over Italy, you could hear tambourines
and acoustic guitars together with Gucci, Edoardo Bennato, and Bob Dylan, and
the youth sang villanelle and tammurriate . . . and the youth from Veneto and Li-
guria would learn the Southern languages" (Bennato and D'Angiò 1987, 70–71).

The song's structure, with its ballad-like narrative tone and the repetitions of the last distich twice at the end of every stanza, inserts this song within the larger corpus of 1970s political or social songs (Bermani 1997). The final distich is particularly interesting in this sense, since it borrows the rhetoric of Italian nationalist activism—both during the anti-Austrian campaign of the 1850s and the Italian resistance to fascism and Nazism in the 1940s—and adapts it to the southern Italian perspective:

Omm' se nasce brigante se more	As men we are born but as brigands we die
ma fin' all'ultim' avimm' 'a sparà	but until the end we need to shoot
e si murimme menate nu fiore	and if we die throw a flower [on our grave]
e 'na bestemmia pe' 'sta libertà.	and a curse for this freedom.

While the heroism of the narrator reflects the nationalist fights of the Italian partisans, the last verse, "and a curse for this freedom," not only laments the immense loss caused by this fight, but also refuses the nationalist cause and its alleged fight for freedom. As Bennato comments, the curse is directed not at freedom in general, but at "this freedom that is announced and imposed on us by the winners, to this false freedom promised by Garibaldi, Cavour and the Savoia, to this freedom . . . in whose name other agendas are covered and the genocide takes place" (2010, 36).

In 1999 the song appeared in the film *They called them . . . Brigands* (*Li chiamarono . . . briganti!*) by Neapolitan director Pasquale Squitieri, which narrated the life of Carmine Crocco, a well-known brigand who fought against the northern Italian army in the 1860s. The version of the song used by Squitieri was, however, performed by the group Musicastoria and presented an important textual difference with Bennato's version. The last line, "and a curse for this freedom," was changed to "and a prayer for this freedom," thus stressing the brigands' honor and patriotic values rather than the controversial aspects of Italy's nationalist campaign. The spirit of the film, released during the boom of the second folk music revival, confirms the existence of a growing revisionist movement among southern Italian intellectuals. Such a movement has also affected the reception of the "Brigante se more" song on the part of the current generations; as Bennato explains in his book *Brigante se more: Viaggio nella musica del Sud* (One dies brigand: An exploration of southern music [2010]), today's main sources on brigandage treat "Brigante se more" as a song from the Risorgimento period, later revised by Bennato. Yet Bennato continues to claim that he himself composed the song in 1979. According to Bennato, such a revisionist approach ultimately confirms the continued importance of the Southern Question debate today as well as the ideological framework within which the folk music revival has been taking place. The very publication of Bennato's book in 2010 needs to be read in relation to the 150-year anniversary of the unification of Italy, in 2011, which reignited old debates on the problematic role of the Italian South still existing today, especially given continued discriminatory attitudes toward southerners on the part of the northern political party Lega Nord.

Also featured in *Brigands* is another song composed in Neapolitan by Bennato, "Vulesse addeventare nu brigante" (I would like to become a brigand). The song's structure, with its recurring phrase "vulesse addeventare" (I would like to become), reveals the influence of the *villanella* structure on Bennato's style.[4] Among the numerous *villanelle* discovered by NCCP in the 1970s is the one called "Vurria addiventare"—in Neapolitan the term *vurria* and *vulesse* are synonyms—where the speaker imagines taking the shape of different objects, such as a plant, a mirror, and a shoe, so that he is able to get closer to his beloved. While NCCP's version adopts the slow rhythm and harp melody typical of sixteenth-century *villanelle,* Bennato's version turns the *villanella* structure into a fast and loud tarantella that is both captivating for the contemporary audience and also suitable for addressing the heated Southern Question debate. The themes of rebellion and southern patriotism already appear in the first stanza:

Vulesse addeventare suricillo	I would like to become a little mouse
pe' li rusecare sti catene	to gnaw at these chains
ca m'astrigneno lu pede	that squeeze my foot
e ca me fanno schiavo.	and make me a slave.

While the first three stanzas follow an animal persona pattern—the protagonist is a mouse, a dove, and a swordfish, respectively—in the fourth stanza, the narrating voice imagines himself to be a tammorra that can wake up the citizens (and probably the audience) to social-political awareness through the captivating rhythm of the instrument:

Vulesse addeventare 'na tammorra	I would like to become a tammorra
pe' scetare a tutta chella gente	to wake up all those people
ca nun ha capito niente	who have not understood anything
e ce sta' a guardare.	And that are here to watch us.

The reference to the tammorra drum in this song—and of its standard Italian counterpart, tamburo, in the previous song—creates a metatextual reference that seems to suggest, once again, a direct connection between the stereotypical tarantella image associated with the South and the orientalistic view of the colonizing

North. As the song continues, the listener gathers enough elements to visualize its context—the brigands' war and its protagonists. The final stanza expresses the narrator's wish to live his life as a brigand: lonely, rough, and honorable.

Vulesse addeventare nu brigante	I would like to become a brigand
ca po' sta sulo a la montagna scura	who can live alone on the dark mountain
pe' te fa' sempe paura	so he can always scare you
fino a quanno more.	until [the day] he dies.

The heroic tone of this ending reiterates the celebration of brigandage and confirms Bennato's counterhistorical intent. His commitment toward recounting the history of the South and its injustices confirms the long-standing political involvement of southern Italian, and Italian musicians more generally, through post-1970s folk. It is possible to conclude that the folk music culture of the South, at least during the 1970s revival, "marks the outer limit of the hegemonic culture, whose ideological tricks it reveals, contesting at times only with its own presence, the universality, which is only superficial, of the official culture's concepts of the world and of life" (Lombardi-Satriani 1974, 104). In studying the current production of southern Italian folk songs, therefore, one of the questions that comes to mind is whether and to what extent the political and social commitment evident in much folk music from Campania in the 1970s, and in particular Bennato's attempt to narrate an alternative history of the South, can be identified in the current production of southern Italian folk music. As shown in the previous chapter, this question is already at play on the festival scene, as it is transforming into a big touristic venue, spurring many debates in recent years. The following sections will attempt to answer this question in relation to music production, distribution, and marketing. As for Bennato's own career, it is clear that "already in the late 1970s and early 1980s . . . Bennato had become aware that musical traditions of the South could become a vehicle of counterhegemonic resistance to the world's Northwest, for which . . . the South is synonymous with a backward society where misery, repression, and superstition dominate" (Bouchard and Ferme 2013, 111).

The 1990s Tarantella Music Revival: From Folk to World Music

The second wave of tarantella revival has contributed to shifting the production and distribution of southern Italian folk music onto a global scene and rearranging it for an urban and cosmopolitan audience. Table 2 shows only some of the main artists and groups involved in this process during the core years of this second tarantella revival—in the 1990s–2000s—as well as the way that their music is being marketed and labeled. As shown in table 2, the dynamics of globalization affect the work of both pizzica musicians from Salento and of Neapolitan musicians who work with both tammurriata and other tarantella forms.

Table 2. The post-1990s Tarantella music revival: From folk to world music

Artist/group	Album title	Date	Record	Genre
NCCP	*Medina*	1992	CGD (Global)	Folk
E Zézi	*Auciello ro mio: Posa e sorde* (My bird: Set down the money)	1994	Tide Records	Folk/world music
	Released in the United States as *Pummarola black* (Black tomato)	1995	Lyrichord	
E Zézi	*Zezi Vivi* (Live Zézi)	1996	Il Manifesto (Italy)	Folk
Officina Zoè	*Terra* (Land)	1997	Zoè/CNT (Italy)	Folk
Canzoniere Grecanico Salentino	*Ballati tutti quanti, ballati forte* (Dance you all, dance loud)	1998	Felmay (Italy)	Folk
NCCP	*Pesce d' 'O mare* (Fish of the sea)	1998	EMI (Global)	Folk
Bennato/Taranta Power	*Taranta Power*	1999	Rai Trade (Italy)	Folk
Spaccanapoli	*Aneme perze—Lost Souls*	2000	Real World Records (Peter Gabriel)	World music
Araknè	*Danzimania*	2001	Araknè	Tarantella
Bennato/Taranta Power	*Che il Mediterraneo sia* (Let the Mediterranean be)	2002	Rai Trade (Italy)	Folk
	Released internationally	2005	DiscMedi (Spain)	Folk/world music
Enzo Avitabile & Bottari	*Sacro Sud* (Sacred South)	2006	Folk Club Etnosuoni (Italy)	Folk
Araknè	*Legend of the Italian Tarantella*	2007	Arc (Global)	World music
Bennato/Taranta Power	*Sponda Sud* (Southern shore)	2007	Taranta Power/ Radio Fandango/Lucky Planets (Italy); Edel (Germany)	Folk/country/ world music
Enzo Avitabile & Bottari	*Black Tarantella*	2012	CNI—Compagnia Nuove Indie (Italy)	Folk

The table also illustrates how the passage from local to regional, national, and global music scenes has happened for many protagonists of the tarantella revival in the 1990s and 2000s. This shift is evident from several elements in the table. The same album is often released both nationally and internationally. In addition, several artists or albums are increasingly promoted by national and international labels, and some even by major labels such as EMI. Finally, the world music label is increasingly present. However, the chart also illustrates an important counterexample—the music experience of Neapolitan saxophonist and singer-songwriter Enzo Avitabile, whose 2012 album, *Black Tarantella*, was released by the Italian indie record company CNI (Compagnia Nuove Indie), the same company that has promoted some of the major countercultural groups since the 1990s, such as Almamegretta and Sud Sound System. Avitabile's 2006 album, *Sacro Sud* (Sacred South), was released by another Italian recording company specializing in Italian folk music, Folk Club EthnoSuoni. At the same time, both albums are usually included in the world music category; in fact, the albums helped consolidate Avitabile's role within the current world music scene, as suggested by the nomination for the Audience Award in the 2005 BBC Awards for World Music. Avitabile's eclectic music style, featuring jazz and southern Italian folk music rhythms and languages, as well as his collaboration with the folk drum group I Bottari, has also recently become the focus of Jonathan Demme's documentary *Enzo Avitabile: Music Life* (2012), which further suggests the artist's increased international visibility, even as his music production remains anchored to the Italian nonmainstream music context.

In the table, it can also be noted how albums' titles often reflect the artists' conscious attempt to publicize and participate in the current tarantella revival (*Danzimania*; *Ballati tutti quanti, ballati forte*; *Taranta Power*), a choice likely to bring these artists a much larger audience and fame as part of the larger Mediterranean music region (see, for example, the word *Medina*, very common within the Mediterranean). The increasing value of tarantella music internationally is evident in all these artists' official multilingual websites, designed for an international audience. This audience shift, in turn, affects some of the artists' musical orientation. Though NCCP's name, for example, remains a crucial reference point for the revitalization of southern Italian musical forms, their repertoire has largely changed in the 1990s. A quick look at their post-1990s album titles shows a major interest in Mediterranean music and world music aesthetics, while an interest in the folk aspects of this music, as well as in its rural context, remains. The album *Medina*, released in 1992, was an important step in this direction: Medina is not only the name of a well-known Arabic holy city, but also the name of several cities in Spain and one of the older gates in the city of Naples. This name therefore promises a closer attention toward the composite of Mediterranean sounds. The album also brought the group for the first time to the Festival di Sanremo, a national competition for Italian mainstream pop music. Here, the song "Pe' dispietto" (in Neapolitan, Out of spite) won the critics' prize, the most prestigious prize of the festival usually awarded to those songs that move beyond the realm of pop music thanks to their technical quality and style. At the same time, their participation in the Festival di Sanremo signals NCCP's closer involvement with mainstream Italian pop music. NCCP's more recent albums, from 1992 onward, have also contributed to increasing the group's popularity abroad, as suggested by their 2011 album, *Live in Munich.* These elements invite us to reflect on the complex relationship between folk and world music and discuss in particular the ways that world music aesthetics can paradoxically create a distance between local artists and their local audiences. As I will illustrate throughout this chapter, this type of dynamics appears very often within the panorama of contemporary tarantella.

An exemplary case in point is E Zézi's recent music production, in particular the song "Vesuvio," released first on the 1994 album *Auciello ro mio: Posa e sorde* (My bird: Set down the money) and then on the 1995 *Pummarola black* (Black tomato) album. This song represents an important shift in the career of E Zézi, while also raising questions regarding the ethics of marketing local folk music internationally. An example of *tammurriata,* the song depicts the ancestral fear of death through the overpowering figure of Mount Vesuvius, which dominates the city of Naples both physically and figuratively. Here E Zézi moves away from its main themes to describe the immense power of Vesuvius over the local population and its deep effects on the minds of its people, who constantly feel the presence of the mountain and its dangers:

Si' monte si, ma monte	You are a mountain, yes you are, but a mountain
e 'na iastemma	and a damnation
si' 'a morte si . . .	You are death, yes you are . . .
Muntagna fatta 'e lava	Mountain made of lava
e ciente vie	and a hundred roads
tu tiene 'mmano a te	you keep in your hands
'sta vita mia . . .	this life of mine
Quanno fa notte	When night falls
e 'o cielo se fa scuro	and the sky darkens
sulo 'o ricordo 'e te	just the thought of you
ce fa paura . . .	scares us . . .

Vesuvius is here personified as a gigantic living being whose decisions affect many people. The use of the invocatory *you* in the beginning attributes both human and divine aspects to the mountain, in whose hands lies everyone's destiny. Present in most rural cultures and especially in indigenous cultures, this personification of the natural forces is also part of the rural culture of tammurriata, which is characterized by a strong connection to the land. Furthermore, the mythical aspects of Vesuvius are not only reminders of the strong religious dimension present within tammurriata, but also symptoms of its peculiar sense of religiosity. The mountain, a synecdoche for the land as a whole, is here being prayed to in the same way as the Madonna. This attitude is in fact typical of a society in which the most common form of religiosity is popular religion.

Featured in the fourth season of the American show *The Sopranos* (in the fall of 2002), the song inaugurated the international fame of E Zézi. At the same time, this moment also spurred a long hiatus for the group, who was recruited by Peter Gabriel's Real World label. The group members ultimately did not agree over the terms imposed by the recording label. These conditions included the label's right to buy all the group's copyrights and also the exclusion of some pieces that sounded too political, traditional, and place specific (Cestellini and Pizza 2004). The result was the separation of some group members, who agreed to leave E Zézi for an international career in the global music market. These members included Marcello Colasurdo, whose artistic interests and popularity had already led him to create his own career path a few years earlier. The newly formed group Spaccanapoli released the album *Anime perze—Lost Souls* (2000), which rerecorded several of E Zézi's songs for an international audience.[5] This "global" version of E Zézi's music ultimately spurred an important debate within the group itself and the Italian folk music scene at large. The basic terms of the debate were authenticity and tradition, on the one hand, and international distribution via the world music label, on the other. E Zézi felt that the global distribution of their music through Spaccanapoli risked creating an irreparable break with their long-standing rejection of "cultural commodification and the selling of stereotypes" (51). According to scholars Cestellini and Pizza, for example, both the rearrangement of existing E Zézi's songs and the composition of new songs by Spaccanapoli illustrate a "reduction of political 'contamination' to the advantage of an objectification of the 'popular' or folk"; in other words, E Zézi's passionate and demystifying political satire is replaced by "a new exotic recipe" (53).

While Spaccanapoli's album was granted full entrance into the global world music market and spurred interest for southern Italian folk music in the United

States, the historical contingent of E Zézi has preferred to remain consistent with their 1970s agenda, attached to the values of the workers' movement and of Italy's extreme left wing. E Zézi's target audience and distribution, therefore, have never left the alternative space of anti-mainstream Italian music and of subaltern consciousness. Today, their songs remain known mostly by folk music connoisseurs and left-wing intellectuals and by those acquainted with the tarantella revival, while their unique political-artistic project has never received the national and international attention granted to NCCP. An article appearing in the February 5, 2000, edition of the left-leaning Italian newspaper *Repubblica* celebrated this continued social commitment by calling E Zézi "the other music of Naples" (Marchesano 2000). But the group's main interest still lies in the workers' conditions in the South, as shown by their involvement in the recent debate over the restructuring of Pomigliano D'Arco's Fiat. I had the opportunity to watch their July 2, 2010, performance at Carroponte, an old industrial building located in Sesto San Giovanni (on the outskirts of Milan) and now restored by Milan's municipal government into a space for art and music exhibitions. Throughout the performance, E Zézi repeatedly made explicit references to and commented on the current situation in Pomigliano and also reiterated their position in defense of the workers' rights.

This example illustrates an important aspect of the post-1990s tarantella phenomenon: that at least at the level of music production, the resurgence of tarantella allows for an often direct response to the larger Italian sociopolitical situation. It can be noted in the work of several southern artists who share with E Zézi a commitment to the social and cultural conditions of the South. Neapolitan artist Daniele Sepe, whose musical interests range from ethnic sounds to jazz, chamber music, and workers' songs, deserves special mention here both for his interpretation of southern folk songs and for his role as a "social agitator." Debuting with E Zézi in the 1970s, Sepe is particularly known within the 1990s tarantella revival context for his two albums *Vite perdite* (1993) and *Viaggi fuori dai paraggi* (1996), but also for his politically engaged music.

In particular, the award-winning 1998 album *Lavorare Stanca,* which discusses the nepotism of the Italian workplace through an eclectic music style, helped confirm Sepe's role together with Italian rap groups in the larger subcultural scene. Sepe represents one of the many faces of the current folk music revival, especially one of the most politically engaged ones. Most of his albums are distributed by alternative labels, such *Il Manifesto,* the historical paper of the Italian extreme left wing. Following a tradition initiated with the 1970s folk music revival, and in particular with the countercultural model represented by E Zézi, Bennato and Sepe have carried on this commitment into today's music scene.

At the same time, the debate within E Zézi's group over marketing choices illustrates how the risk of political and social disengagement is always lurking when it comes to global marketing of local music. This renewed interest in southern culture has in fact been celebrated by several scholars, musicians, and cultural brokers as a way to give a new dignity to the South, but it has also been criticized by others for being just a momentary craze, which does not deepen the visitors' interest and knowledge of this culture. Just as the current tarantella festival scene attracts the criticism of local performers and scholars, the current production of tarantella and distribution of tarantella music is equally spurring debate. The main concern here is that by disengaging this music from its sociopolitical and cultural scenario, one ends up transforming it into yet another example of "consumer-friendly multiculturalism" (Feld 2000, 168).

Eugenio Bennato's Taranta Power Movement

Bennato's Taranta Power movement, a crucial step toward the post-1990s global circulation of southern Italian folk music, offers a particularly complex example of the kind of dynamics discussed above. Announced in 1998, the movement's explicit goal was in fact to promote the tarantella phenomenon throughout the Italian peninsula and internationally. It pursues this objective by producing its own albums as well as promoting music by other southern Italian folk musicians, by organizing festivals and other events featuring tarantella music (in Europe, the United States, Canada, and South America), and by organizing schools, seminars, and workshops to teach this music tradition both nationally and internationally—for example, in Australia and Tunisia. As for its name, Taranta Power, the idea was to "provide a vivid contrast with the unfortunately inferior image that the 'Tarantella' has assumed in the collective imagination worldwide, perpetuated by bland folk groups and shallow musical expression, a very long way away from the hard reality of the Taranta ritual."[6] The need to uncover a more realistic and just image of tarantella and of its peculiar history is therefore a large component of Taranta Power's agenda. In addition, as Bennato explains in a 2008 interview, "I thought then the entire movement of ethnic music, which did not have a name, could be understood as 'taranta.' Before no one had thought of tying together the ethnic music of the South to one rhythm and dance. In Spain, this is what 'Flamenco' subsumes, as it is not only a dance, but a very strong identity-formation. The term 'Power' wished to convey its modernity. . . . Today 'Taranta Power' is our way of being southerners with an undeniable identity" (quoted in Bouchard and Ferme 2013, 112). This epistemological passage from tarantella to taranta is important to note, since it helps convey the full potential of Bennato's Taranta Power in terms of cultural production, as the movement has largely contributed to create a new cultural product, the "taranta" phenomenon, which can be seen advertised everywhere in Italy on music and dance concert, class, and workshop flyers. By semantically shifting from *tarantella* to *taranta*, Bennato is also making an important step toward ways of conceptualizing the Italian South within the contemporary globalized scenario. In fact, in Bennato's view, reconnecting to the power of tarantella springs, on the one hand, from a need to think locally, in musical as well as in many other cultural spheres, is a way to "reclaim a musical standard in which we recognize our roots, outside any xenophile or massifying fashion."[7] On the other hand, thinking locally for Bennato does not mean remaining fixed in one's own little village or region; rather, it is an alternative to the globalization of music, one that draws "parallels with other neighboring cultures, and . . . position[s] Italian popular music at the center of the Mediterranean region" (Bouchard and Ferme 2013, 112). In this sense, the huge success of the group—regionally, nationally, and internationally—has contributed to opening up the Italian folk music revival to both Mediterranean and global perspectives (ibid.).

On the *Taranta Power* album, Bennato makes extensive use of tarantella rhythms and lyrics from several regions, as well as of southern languages, and intertwines them with other musical and linguistic traditions from the Mediterranean. Moreover, Bennato's 1999 international tour largely contributed to making Taranta Power a world music phenomenon. For instance, Bennato's song "Taranta Power" was included in the world music collection *Womad 2001*. The opening of the song "Taranta Power" shows the importance of this moment for southern Italian folk music:

Nineteen ninety-eight
Taranta Power is up to date
Mille neuf cent quatre vingt dix-neuf   Nineteen Ninety Nine
Taranta Power est sortie de l'oeuf   Taranta Power is born
La tarentule en l'an deux mille   The tarantula in the year two
                                            thousand
de la campagne est venue en ville   from the country came to the city
Two thousand-o-one
Tarantella Power all the world around

The fact that this song starts off in English and French well represents the group's intentional opening toward an international music scene. By doing so, its power can remain "up to date." The next section recounts the taranta's myth and history by reminding the audience that "Taranta is deep South," as well as by adding lyrics in the Apulian language, the language of the spider dance, in the last line:

La taranta è il profondo sud	Taranta is deep south
è quella musica che tu	is that music that you
all'improvviso sentirai	will suddenly hear
è il ballo che non finisce mai	it is the dance that never ends
è il passo che dovrai imitare	it is the step you will need to imitate
per liberarti del male d'amore	to free yourself from love pain
così ballando meridionale	thus dancing the southern way
comme 'na taranta ca te pizzica	like a tarantula that bites your
lu core . . .	heart . . .

The celebratory tone of these lyrics is particularly important to note, since it reflects a larger ideological move from tarantella as a form of musical therapy to tarantella as a form of celebration, as promoted by several local scholars and cultural brokers since the 1990s. In fact, the scene represented here carries no direct connection with the ancient ritual of tarantism; rather, it illustrates a moment of initiation for the younger generations, as they learn to take their first steps of the spider dance and as they fill the taranta ritual with new desires and meanings. The musical structure of this song, as well as of several other songs contained on this album, also indicates this moment of revival: the basic rhythm of pizzica is accompanied by contemporary sounds, ranging from pop to rock to various ethnic sounds; the vocals, instead, feature both Bennato's solo singing, either in standard Italian or in southern languages, and choral singing in the Apulian language or other European languages. Bennato's words in this song have thus become the manifesto not only of the current tarantella phenomenon, but also for a "transnational Mediterranean music" (ibid.).

Bennato's more recent albums, *Che il Mediterraneo sia* (Let the Mediterranean be [2002]) and especially the following *Sponda Sud* (Southern Shore [2009]), have further developed this celebratory image of tarantella, and at the same time they have also contributed to popularizing the tarantella rhythms both within the larger Mediterranean and within the world music scene. Taranta Power's 2002–4 tour throughout the Mediterranean helped consolidate this project and also spurred Bennato's collaboration with other world music artists from the Mediterranean.[8] Yet as Bennato's musical composition embraces this new phase, his style seems to lack the spark that characterized his earlier works. His recent albums have in fact received criticism for their repetitiveness and lack of originality. Here is a sample review of the album *Che il Mediterraneo sia:*

The album is rich in melodies and motifs able to catch the attention of even those listeners who are not into ethnic music; as a result, this last work [of Bennato] is a product for less selective consumption, almost "consumer," one could add. But if this can be read as a positive note, it is also important to consider that all this has a big "cost": the album almost completely lacks that research spirit that characterized [Bennato's] masterpieces, so much so that [Bennato's] philological commitment . . . sounds considerably weakened. That commitment helped him popularize musical cultures otherwise destined to a slow and inexorable death. (Rettura 2003)

This transition in Bennato's music is already visible in the *Taranta Power* album, where Bennato's lyrics seem to lose the historical specificity and social message they contained in his previous albums—a message that was strictly connected to the situation of the Italian South—in favor of a celebration of the more generalizing notion of "taranta," a term associated with the current tarantella craze in Italy. While it is tempting to see this shift as simply the result of an artistic impasse, in examining global performances of local music, it is also important to look at "which meanings are repressed and which are taken up as metonyms of cultural identity" (Kapchan 2007, 150); it is thus possible to argue that, as it moves from "tarantella" to "taranta," Bennato's global performance of southern Italian folk music also ends up de-emphasizing his previous interest in a historical analysis of tarantella and its sociopolitical context, while at the same time "taking up" a celebratory perspective on tarantella.

Yet these examples also illustrate that extending one's audience to the international music scene does not necessarily mean completely disengaging from one's commitment to make socially involved music, whether it is about the conditions of the Italian South or those of African and other poor populations in the world. Even in Italy, Bennato's music is still very much listened to as socially committed music—see, for example, his recent concerts supporting Amnesty International and other humanitarian organizations as well as showing his continued support of Italian working-class struggles and values. The song "Grande Sud" (Great South) was also featured within the program Fabbriche in Concerto (Factories in concert), sponsored by the province of Savona, in the Italian Northeast, on September 10, 2010. At the same time, the more superficial tone of his "Mediterranean" albums raises a few questions: how can Bennato's music respect the specific history of tarantella, linked to a rather difficult social system and to dancing as a form of cure, while at the same time celebrating the taranta's "power" as a form of multicultural entertainment within the current world music scene?

This risk of commercialization in Bennato's recent albums is particularly striking since Bennato appears to be very much aware of the dynamics of massification lurking behind the tarantella phenomenon. The song "Alla festa della taranta" (At the taranta feast), which follows the pizzica rhythm, is an insider's reflection on the revival that throws some doubt on the current festival dynamics. This "staged taranta," Bennato suggests, can become a way to kill the taranta spirit rather than to keep it alive:

Quanta gente mieza via	How many people in the streets
e il maestro sul piedistallo . . .	And the master on the stage . . .
però attuorno nisciuno abballa	but look around nobody dances
E l'orchestra che sta sunanno	and the orchestra that is playing
è n'orchestra che nun va a tiempo	it's an orchestra that does not follow
the tempo	
alla festa della taranta	at the taranta feast
la taranta nun se sente	the taranta can't be heard
E sott'all'albero d'ulive	And under the olive tree
la taranta è ancora viva . . .	the taranta is still alive . . .
e te pizzica e te morsica lu core	and tricks and bites your heart . . .

These words ultimately seem to suggest that the nationwide celebration of tarantella since the 1990s has nothing to do with the history and the ritual of tarantella and directly contributes to overlooking them; while criticizing this superficial attitude, however, Bennato's own music, at least in the *Taranta Power* album, ends up contributing to popularizing an overly positive and thus more superficial perspective on tarantella.

Celebrating the Postcolonial South

It is important to contextualize Bennato's rewriting of southern Italian history within the larger postcolonial movement that in the 1990s invested southern music concomitantly with the pizzica revival (Chambers 2008; Anselmi 2002; Lombardi-Diop and Romeo 2012). While previous studies have looked at the South in relation to its difficult role within Italian national culture, recent scholarship has instead reframed the modern and contemporary history of the South as that of an internal colony whose relation with the national government is problematic even today (Schneider 1998; Gribaudi 1997; Gramsci 1995).

For Neapolitan musicians like Bennato, this has also meant to engage with the stereotypical image of Naples—historically the major city of the Italian South—an image conveyed by popular culture and still largely utilized by the tourism industry. The politically engaged Neapolitan hip-hop groups emerging in the 1990s, such as 99 Posse and Almamegretta, not only explicitly engaged with this representation of Naples and the South more generally, but also openly sought to dismantle it. Emerging in dialogue with other international sounds, this hip-hop music tradition is characterized by an explicit political content and an extensive use of local languages. Its lyrics often narrate the difficult position of southern Italy within its postcolonial and global configuration and reflect on its troubled history, while also making many references to local and folk culture. Its musical style often includes elements of folklore such as the traditional chanting style of tarantella and traditional instruments like the drums. It is true that the relation between this music and the post-1990s folk music revival has often been exaggerated and that Italian hip-hop groups usually tend to dissociate from the folk music revival (Plastino 1996); nevertheless, most scholars seem to agree that the Italian hip-hop phenomenon both preceded and encouraged the development of the current folk music revival (Gala 2002; Nacci 2001). For example, the song "Napoli" by 99 Posse ironically reiterates the stereotypes associated with this city through the use of rap sounds and political satire:

Napolì	Napolì
criature vuttate 'mmiez' 'a na vi'	children thrown in the streets . . .
Napolì	
crisciute cu 'e pippate 'e cucai' . . .	boys grown up on cocaine . . .
Napolì	
affiliate rint' 'a cocche fami'	belonging to some [Mafia] family
Napolì	
'o guverno ce ra sulo 'a polizi' . . .	the government gives us only the police . . .
Napolì . . .	
ma 'mmiez' 'a via continuano a murì	but in the streets they keep dying
Napolì	
ma tenimmo 'o sole 'a pizza e 'o mandulino	but we have sun pizza and mandolin
tarantelle canzone sole e mandulino	tarantella songs sun and mandolin
a Napoli se more a tarallucce e vino.	in Napoli you die happy.[9]

These last few lines seem to suggest that, as the city dies buried under its many problems, Neapolitan music, tarantella included, remains a consolation prize, while at the same time implicitly contributing to perpetuating the colonial image of a carefree and lazy people. It is interesting to contrast this image with the image of tarantella portrayed in Bennato's song "Popolo 'e tammurriata" (Tammurriata people), which appeared on Bennato's 2001 album, *Che il Mediterraneo sia*. The song borrows from the tammurriata rhythm and from the Neapolitan language and focuses on the tammurriata revival and its role in exposing a more realistic image of the city of Naples—well known worldwide for its exotic postcard visuals and melodious singing:

E mo parlammo 'e Napule	And let's talk about Naples
chella città addò so' nato	where I was born
c'a sape tutto 'o munno	all the world knows it
ma sape 'na cosa pe' n'ata	but mixes things up
Napule sole e mare	Naples sun and sea
e gente sempe felice	and always-happy people
ma chesta cartulina	but this postcard
'o riesto nun t' 'o dice	doesn't tell you the other side
'O riesto è 'na tammorra	The other side is a tammorra
ca vene da luntano	that comes from far[10]

The group Almamegretta has extensively drawn on the Southern Question debate to bring forth their protest against the political, cultural, and linguistic status quo. Almamegretta discusses the role of the South within contemporary Mediterranean culture on their 1993 album, *Animamigrante* (Migrant soul). The song "Sudd" ("South" in Neapolitan) recounts in dark tones the history of the South since Italian unification—a history of exploitation of southern lands and its people:

Who was deported for a few pennies a month?
Sicilian and Calabrian boys
hunger misery corruption disease
this is the price that my land has had to pay
to be this little luxury of civilization.

This process of exploitation continues today:

cars buildings heroin in large quantities
mafia 'ndrangheta sacra corona unita[11]
that's all they have left us.

At the same time, by mixing the dub music genre, Italian and Neapolitan, and Middle Eastern melodies, the song is also affirming the hybridism of southern Italian culture, which shares many elements with other parts of the Mediterranean and whose conditions can be viewed as part of a larger postcolonial context (Chambers 2008).

In a similar rhetorical move, the song "Figli di Annibale" (Hannibal's Children), from the same album, highlights African influence on Italian culture by recovering the history of Carthaginian general Hannibal and his invasion of the Italian peninsula in the second century BC. As the singer comments, "That's why many Italians have dark skin." As William Anselmi points out, in this song Almamegretta "stresses the *métissage* that has been constitutive of Italian history": "In a comparison of Hannibal's troops with the American army of occupation certain Italian 'racial' factors such as dark skin and dark hair are highlighted" (2002, 42). In other words, by embracing Africanness as a positive identity marker for southern Italians, Almamegretta is able to reverse the colonial binary linking North and South, center and margin, citizen and immigrant. Fighting discrimination, both toward southern Italian and international immigrants from the Mediterranean areas, is in fact a major theme in Almamegretta's music.

Partly thanks to increased global circulation, understanding the conditions of the South both in the 1990s and in the early 2000s also meant, and still means today, coming to terms with the extensive migratory flux from North Africa and the larger Mediterranean area and with the increasing plurality of languages and cultures that are in contact with each other within the already hybrid cultural area of the South. Indeed, globalization has "created a much more fertile ground for supplementary forms of belonging like Mediterranean-ness, which counteract narrow versions of identity linked to nation, religion, and class" (Fogu and Re 2010, 1). The popularity of this post-1990s Mediterranean discourse clearly emerges from Sud Sound System's 2003 hit "Le radici ca tieni," which in the Apulian language means "The roots you have."[12] The song opens with an invitation to celebrate the cultural hybridity and pluralism that have always characterized the Mediterranean. It is not by chance then that it is written in a particular variety of the Apulian language typical of the Grecia Salentina, an area where Greek cultural roots are still alive and their language now belongs to world heritage:

> We are from Salento, citizens of the world
> related to Messapians, with the Greeks and the Bizantines
> united in this style today with Jamaicans
> tell me now where you come from.

In addition, by mixing reggae and tarantella, this *tarantamuffin* group is looking for "correspondences with other exploited, subjugated cultures expressed through one's own local reality" (Anselmi 2002, 40).[13] Thus, the song reminds us not only that opening up to the Mediterranean is another way to discuss the role of the Italian South, but also that the only way to think both locally and globally is by retrieving, and sharing, one's own local cultural roots:

If you never forget your roots
you will also respect those of the foreign countries.
If you never forget where you come from
you will give more value to your culture.

Since these different places in the Mediterranean have in common a history of subalternity, as testified by the continued voyages of illegal migrants and refugees from North Africa to Italian shores, these common roots ultimately help these musicians reclaim the history of the Italian South as an internal colony and its current conditions as an integral part of the postcolonial Mediterranean (Chambers 2008).

Reimagining the South in Bennato's Taranta Power Movement

Bennato's early-2000s albums do not limit themselves to celebrate the tarantella craze; they also offer a new direction for southern Italian folk music by participating in the larger scene of "Mediterranean world music" (Plastino 2002, 282). The mix of southern Italian, Mediterranean, and North African rhythms and languages emerging from his "Mediterranean" albums assign new values and meanings to the southern Italian folk tradition. In this sense, Bennato's music moves beyond the consumerist model often associated with world music to participate in a larger Italian "process of self-identification with Mediterranean-ness" (Fogu and Re 2010, 1).

Bennato's "Mediterranean" albums, *Che il Mediterraneo sia* and *Sponda Sud,* explicitly participate in this discourse of Mediterraneanness by embracing the multiplicity of languages and cultures stemming from Italy's Mediterranean roots. Taking up world music aesthetics, particularly the emphasis on cultural pluralism, these albums call for a deeper understanding and respect for all the cultures of the Mediterranean, who meet by the sea, where the South-North migration begins. For example, both albums provide a booklet with English and French song translations to address English- and French-speaking audiences from the Mediterranean, while the sounds become more explicitly African and Middle Eastern. Peace in the Mediterranean is ultimately possible only if we treasure our common roots and are ready to share ideas and cultures with each other, as suggested in the song "Che il Mediterraneo sia":

We are equals
leaning over the shores of the same sea
and no one is a pirate
no one is a migrant
we are all sailors.

This is not only a reference to the increasingly discriminatory attitude toward immigrants from the Mediterranean, largely spurred by the Italian Lega Nord party since its inception in the early 1990s, but also a reminder that, being all sailors, our identities as people of the Mediterranean are in fact traveling identities. Indeed, here "immediate," or rooted, identities are "being referenced in an extraterritorial space where inherited traditions are breached to become the site of ongoing translations" (Chambers 2008, 47). In this sense, the song indicates that Bennato's agenda is both to celebrate this new Mediterranean perspective and to inaugurate Italian philosopher Franco Cassano's Meridian or Southern Thought, which seeks to bring the South back to the center of modernization by recovering its Mediterranean roots. In other words, the idea of a common Mediterranean identity for the South of Italy is now being recovered as an alternative identity to the one emerging from national discourse.

Che il Mediterraneo sia	Let the Mediterranean be
quella nave che va da sola	that boat that goes alone
tutta musica e tutta vele	all music and all sails
su quell'onda dove si vola	on that wave where you fly
tra la scienza e la leggenda	between science and legend
del flamenco e della taranta	of flamenco and taranta
e fra l'algebra e la magia	and between algebra and magic
nella scia di quei marinai	following those sailors
e quell'onda che non smette mai	and that wave that never ends
che il Mediterraneo sia . . .	let the Mediterranean be . . .

Like several other songs featured on the *Che il Mediterraneo sia* album, this song offers many references to the sea culture of the Mediterranean: waves, boats, and sailors as well as navigating and sailing. This imagery helps construct the larger metaphor of the Mediterranean Sea both as a point of convergence among the many different cultures navigating through it and as a source of power, a sort of positive energy sprung from these cultural encounters.

More important, by appealing to both algebra and magic, to both science and legend, the song suggests that tradition (or folklore) and modernization can complement rather than invalidate each other within the Meridian thought, as a counterpoise to Italian nationalist discourse, which has traditionally considered the South, and its folk culture, as too backward to be modernized. Another tool of resistance is reflected in the song's comparison between flamenco and taranta; in fact, "just like *flamenco* was a cultural movement of resistance that brought together Gypsy, Jewish, and Arab minorities in Spain, so the *taranta* belongs to a tradition that assimilated and consolidated early Dionysian rites with the sounds and dances of the southern peninsula, which owe a debt to Arab culture" (Bouchard and Ferme 2013, 112). The Meridian thought therefore "give[s] back to the South its ancient dignity as a subject of thought, thus interrupting a long history of subjugation to other subjects of thought" (Cassano 1996, 5); it represents an alternative not only to the long-standing marginalization of the South within the Italian context, but also to globalization discourse, which often ends up perpetuating old hierarchies of power, such as modern versus traditional as well as center versus periphery. In other words, the "southern shores" that Bennato refers to especially in his 2006 album "signify not only the Italian South but also all the (southern) shores that share with the Mediterranean the status of the other of globalization" (Bouchard and Ferme 2013, 114).

The celebration of the Italian South is further announced in the song "Grande Sud" (Great South). The song—which inaugurated an international tour including the Fiesta Festival in Toronto as well as several concerts in Africa—goes back to the Southern Question by representing tarantella as "third-class music" that empowers southern Italian migrants moving to the North:

C'è una musica in quel treno	There is a music in that train
che si muove e va lontano	that moves towards distant lands
musica di terza classe	third-class music
in partenza per Milano	leaving for Milan
c'è una musica che batte	there is a music that beats
come batte forte il cuore	beats as strong as the heart
di chi parte contadino	of those who leave as peasants
ed arriverà terrone . . .	and arrive as *terroni*[14] . . .

The reference to internal migration in this song helps the artist complete a full circle by creating a logical connection with the early phase of his career, when the migrants were still mostly southerners moving to the northern Italian industrial triangle of Milan, Genoa, and Turin. In fact, since the current economic conditions are spurring a new generation to look for jobs in the North and especially Milan, South-North migration remains an important topic for southern Italian music in the 2000s and 2010s. It is indeed also possible to note clear similarities between this song and two songs written by Bennato in the early 1980s, "Te saluto Milano" (Goodbye Milan) and "Vento del Sud" (Southern wind), which deal with South-North migration in Italy as part of the larger Southern Question. The first song, in particular, is inspired by Bennato's failed attempt to find a music sponsor in the big northern city and his consequent decision to go back to the South. As Bennato (2010) recalls, the song thus represents a continuum with "Brigante se more," which focuses on the history of the South.

The main difference between these two songs and the ones contained in his Mediterranean albums is that, in the latter, Bennato compares the southern Italian experience to that of international migrants from northern Africa, thus making a clear connection among different Souths, while also reminding us that the Southern Question has never been solved.

The song "Ritmo di contrabbando" (Bootleg rhythm) further shows continuity between Bennato's first albums and his Taranta Power project by explicitly linking the current tarantella phenomenon to the Southern Question and by highlighting the countercultural aspects of this type of music. The title further reminds us that southern Italian music is subaltern music, since the South of Italy is a subaltern place, or, in Bennato's own words, an "Italia minore" (lesser Italy). A look at the first few lines will give a sense of the musician's intention:

Quando sona la taranta	When the taranta plays
è il mio sud che dal suo ghetto	it's my South that from its ghetto
sta sfidando tutto il mondo	is challenging the whole world
col suo ritmo maledetto . . .	with its cursed rhythm . . .
Quando sona la tammorra	When the tammorra plays
è il mio sud che sta partendo	it's my South that is heading out
come parte Don Chisciotte	like Don Quixote
contro i mulini a vento . . .	tilting against the wind mills . . .

Even though it speaks of the subaltern, the song is written in both standard Italian and Neapolitan language. This choice shows how tarantella has now come to reach the national music scene and to attract audiences from all over the peninsula; at the same time, this choice also reflects the album's contribution to the increasingly mainstream consumption of tarantella.

Yet the following stanza seeks, once again, an emotional and artistic connection with the other Souths of the world—"It's my heart that is migrating to all the Souths in the world"—while also bringing linguistic samples from Swahili, an African and in its European setting a subaltern language, thus suggesting that a purely commercial interpretation of this phenomenon is reductive. Countercultural aspects of tarantella during both 1990s and 2000s are then emphasized in the next stanza, where Bennato celebrates tarantella for its challenging both mainstream forms of communication and big music-production companies. The inclusion of this second element is ironic to say the least, since Bennato's albums are now distributed by major labels and also considering that the lyrics of this song are once again in standard Italian.

Quando sona la battente	When the *battente* plays
è il mio Sud che sta suonando	it's my South that it's playing

contro l'indice d'ascolto	against the audience ratings
contro il telecomando	against the TV remote . . .
e quel suono che si sente	and that sound you hear
è il mio Sud che va lontano	it's my South that goes far
clandestino e dissidente	clandestine and dissident
fino al sound di Manu Chao . . .	to meet the sound of Manu Chao . . .

The final reference to Manu Chao, a world music artist who sings about migration and third-world poverty and is well known within Italian left-wing circles, suggests Bennato's full participation in the world music scene.

To further complicate Bennato's position on this album, as his work moves from southern Italy to the Mediterranean, the geographical and historical specificity of his previous songs tends to be replaced by a more generalized representation and celebration of the global South; in this sense, the South and the Mediterranean cease to represent purely spatial concepts and become examples of what Italian scholar Francesca Saffioti calls "geosimboli": "spatially determined images exemplifying the revaluing of those historical and cultural characteristics that can transform a marginalized space into a qualitatively emerging space" (2010, 2). In other words, the Italian South turns into a global southern perspective from which to look at modernity, globalization, and their agents. In this latter sense, Bennato's position reflects a common view within much contemporary scholarship on the post-1990s tarantella revival, particularly from the Salento area. These scholars consider the liberating potential of tarantella, the main folk music genre in the South, as crucial to the construction of antihegemonic identities that are shared by a large population throughout the Mediterranean and contrast the homogenizing effect of both globalization and nationalist discourse (Lapassade 2001). In the case of the Salento, the need to understand, and celebrate, southern Italian identity is also due to the growing role of this area as the center for Mediterranean migration since the 1990s and therefore the need to understand the changing identity of the area. The importance of tarantella consists therefore in its affirmation of a local identity that exists within a larger Mediterranean culture. However, while the image of the South celebrated here certainly challenges previous stereotypes offered by the nationalist discourse, tourism promotion, and popular music discourse, it also assigns an absolute value to the South. Viewed in this light, I believe that this new representation of the South risks perpetuating the long-standing image of the South as a mythical figure, thus creating distance, once again, from the reality of the South and of its problems.

Even the Southern Thought model offered by Cassano has been criticized for its essentializing the South, as well as the Mediterranean, and thus perpetuating the same ideological mechanisms involved in the creation of the Southern Question: "Mediterraneo, as well as South and North, are material, intellectual and sentimental products that can be felt as pre-existing and natural only through the enforcement of ideological structures" (Pizza 2002, 53). However, in his preface to the 2005 edition of *Il pensiero meridiano,* Cassano is committed to moving beyond this essentializing notion of the Mediterranean and toward a more transnational dialogue, in which "the Mediterranean becomes a metaphor for the 'global South(s)' and for an idea of *sud-alternità* ('South-alternity')" (Bouchard and Ferme 2013, 90). This model has been further developed by other scholars engaged with the Southern Question. Saffioti, for example, points out the need to avoid "attribu[ting] to the Mediterranean... a saving role," since "the South is not an immutable substance, a generic element, or a form of geographic determinism. Becoming Mediterranean is possible if we accept the experience of mediation with the Other, without being able to exclude violence" (2010, 1–2). Saffioti's words remind us that the Mediterranean encounters are not always simple and peaceful and that celebrating Mediterraneanness does not necessarily help us understand it. The increased influx of refugees to the Sicilian island of Lampedusa, for example, has spurred much debate within Italian government circles and public opinion, and it has often created friction between refugees and the local population, as is often discussed in the local and national media and as is brilliantly described by Italian filmmaker Emanuele Crialese's feature film *Terraferma* (2012).

Still, Bennato's social message in these albums remains an important one, albeit at times a generalizing one, insofar as it contributes to rowing against the flattening of the linguistic and cultural richness of the Mediterranean that is potentially at risk within globalization, as suggested by the song "Ogni uno" (Each one):

> No global that music and that African sand . . .
> No global that tammurriata . . .
> No global this song that belongs to the brigand
> and therefore
> even though it tours the world
> will still be no global.[15]

Full Circle: Bennato Sings Ninco Nanco

Bennato's 2011 album, *Questione meridionale* (Southern question), seems to have inaugurated yet a new phase in the artist's career, as it moves away from a celebration of Mediterranean identity and toward a reassessment of Italian national history through the story of the brigandism movement and its link to the Southern Question. In fact, the album rewrites the history of brigandism as a form of resistance to the nineteenth-century colonization of the South on the part of the Savoia government. To add to this music endeavor, Bennato comments extensively on the genesis and significance of this album in his 2013 book, *Ninco Nanco deve morire* (Ninco Nanco must die), titled after one of the main songs in the album. The book is divided into two parts; in the first, Bennato discusses the brigandism phenomenon in relation to the Southern Question and also analyzes several songs that appeared on the 2011 album; in the second part, Bennato traces back his entire career according to this southern perspective and also discusses the history of his tarantella music production since the 1970s and throughout the Taranta Power movement. Studied together, the album and the book thus offer an overview of Bennato's use of folk music to represent the Italian South.

Written by Bennato and D'Angiò, the ballad entitled "Ninco Nanco deve morire" focuses on the figure of the brigand Ninco Nanco, who was killed by northern troops during the occupation of the South in the name of the Risorgimento. Against the silence imposed by colonialism on the history of brigandism, in the song Ninco Nanco's story emerges loud and clear. The theme of silence pervades the whole song, as clearly shown by the catchy refrain:

E Ninco Nanco deve morire
perchè si campa putesse parlare
e si parlasse putesse dire
qualcosa di meridionale

And Ninco Nanco has to die
because if he lives he could talk,
and if he talked he could say
something Southern.

In typical Bennato style, the song contains metatextual references to tarantella, in this case tammurriata:

It is the idea that makes the war, a declared war
to see who wins
between the gun and the tammurriata.

The verse echoes another famous line in Bennato's "Brigante se more" song, in which the brigand's war is made with both guns and "tambur" (drums). Bennato makes further reference to tammurriata by reclaiming the importance of folk music against the allegations of superstition, which aim at demonstrating the ignorance and inferiority of the southern populations within colonial discourse:

And tammurriata is superstition
and this story has to end
and here we make Italy or we die
and Ninco Nanco has to die.

The term *storia* (in Italian both "history" and "story") is significant since it represents the opposition between the official history of Risorgimento and the often reiterated idea of the necessity of "making Italy" and the fact that southern culture is consequently relegated to an unreliable "story" made up by ignorant folks.

The song "Mille" (Thousand), appearing on the same album, rewrites the story of General Garibaldi's troops, also known as "i Mille" (the Thousand) and their "liberation" of the southern regions; the song follows a typical ballad-like structure in its repetition of the phrase "One thousand" at the beginning of each stanza. While the first part of the song recounts Garibaldi's expedition according to its propaganda, particularly the notions of freedom and equality to be attained through Risorgimento or resurgence,[16] the second part shows the other face of Risorgimento—the falsity of its promises, the violence perpetrated on those who tried to stop Garibaldi's troops, and the silence to which they have been relegated. The effect of this misinformation on the Italian nation is still clear in the following stanza:

> What a beautiful tale they told us . . .
> what a beautiful tale that one has to memorize
> because it is written in all school books.

But the power of the past to disrupt national discourse is equally strong once one starts to uncover it:

> One thousand lies that go farther and farther
> and the truth that advances slowly
> among the words of canceled songs,
> this is a war of brigands and tammurriata.

Once again, the tammurriata rhythm directly contributes to disrupting this false history and bringing back silenced stories. The song's ending repeats the first two lines of the first stanza, which speaks of victory, heroism, and national pride ("One thousand carnations taken from the gardens / one thousand crowns of diamonds and rubies"), but replaces the last two lines ("One thousand flags under the Sicilian sun / this is a war of justice and so on") with two more lines that go in the opposite direction and thus highlight the less heroic aspects of Risorgimento: "One thousand rifles to strike and go away / this is damned war and so on."

The song entitled "Questione meridionale" announces in a much more explicit way the themes discussed above; written on the occasion of the 150th anniversary of the Italian unification, the song starts each verse in every stanza with "Noi" (We), as opposed to "them" (northerners), which seems to suggest a renewed sense of historical awareness on the part of southern Italians today, a deeper understanding of who we were and who we are today:

> We with the "brothers" came down from the North
> Who "liberated" us to form a "Nation."
> We under the same flag,
> from the Alps to the sea.
> But if we become a Question?
> The Question is "Southern."[17]

These verses brilliantly describe the sense of betrayal felt by several southern scholars, who believe that the "Southern Question" has consistently been used as a way for the national government to blame the South for its own problems, when in fact this question emerged as part of the colonization discourse (Gramsci 1995; Schneider 1998; Orizzonti Meridiani 2014). The song ends with a powerful statement: if brigands' music, which was silenced for more than a century, "goes on," it is because "we are brigands." It is possible to trace many similarities between this reclaiming of southern identity as brigands and the reclaiming of "Africanness" and "Mediterraneanness" as forms of empowerment that often emerge from the 1990s Mediterranean discourse discussed above. They are both ways to counteract the official history of the South as written by nonsoutherners.

Finally, on this album, Bennato shares his view in agreement with recent Italian and Italian American scholarship that makes a strong connection between the history of southern colonization and the history of southern migration (Gabaccia 2000; Verdicchio 1997). In the song "Si va" (We go), composed by Bennato, the artist relates the emigration of southern Italians to the United States—a process that is directly connected to Italian unification and its consequent impoverishment of the South (Bennato 2013, 61). As a result, "Napoli which was the capital . . . / now is only a departure point." The urgency of migration, as connected to colonization, is explicitly expressed in the song in the following lines: "One goes far from the paese [country/village] / one goes to America not to die." But the song does not limit itself to lament the end of the cultural, economic, and artistic grandeur that was the city of Naples before unification; on the contrary, it broadens the listeners' view to a transnational perspective via American migration. On a textual level, this change of perspective is confirmed by the song's refrain, written in English,

> Oh let's go let's go to America.
> People says this land is mine!

But if you come you're welcome
in America paisà.[18]

Sung by both Bennato and his band's chorus, the refrain takes on a fast tarantella rhythm that contrasts the ballad-like rhythm of the stanzas; by combining
the tarantella rhythm with the English language, Bennato is here participating
in yet a different form of cultural hybridism, a type of hybridism that looks at
migration over the Atlantic rather than the Mediterranean. As Bennato himself
comments,

One goes on that boat
that as soon as it passes Gibraltar
transforms a tarantella rhythm
in the new swing that it will find on its way.

As it goes back to renarrating the history of the Italian South, Bennato's
latest album indicates the artist's return to a more place-specific expression of
the local. In fact, while its extensive use of standard Italian makes the album
"nationally consumable," the choice of a ballad-like song structure, frequent
references to the tammurriata folk-song tradition from the Campania region,
and the use of phrases in Neapolitan bring this album closer to Musicanova's
albums from the 1970s rather than to Bennato's Mediterranean albums from the
1990s. And even if on a textual level the album contains many references to the
South as part of a larger postcolonial entity, the focus on a specific moment of
southern history helps anchor this music endeavor to a specific time and place,
thus moving beyond the essentializing representation of the South emerging
from much tarantella music production from the late 1990s and early 2000s. At
the same time, the violent history of southern brigandism also frees this project
from any overly positive celebration of the South and of the Mediterranean. This
new approach to southern history is indeed part of a larger historical movement that seeks to readdress southern history and is reclaiming brigandism as
an important historical phenomenon that can help us better understand Italian
national history—a movement that sees Italian journalist Pino Aprile, with his
well-known book *Terroni* (2013), as one of its main proponents; it is not surprising then to read Aprile's foreword to Bennato's book on Ninco Nanco.[19] Yet as it
moves away from an explicit representation of a Mediterranean identity emerging from his previous albums, Bennato's discussion of migration, as reflected
by the song "Si va" analyzed above, remains transnational besides being local;
in other words, Bennato's expression of the local seems to ultimately come
from a clear understanding of the global forces that still shape Neapolitan and
southern cultures today.

Conclusion

As shown through my analysis of Bennato's work, particularly its representation of the Italian South, post-1990s tarantella music has the potential to become a constructive response to the harsh conditions of southern Italy and a constructive alternative to the exotic image of southern Italy still emerging in national and transoceanic discourse today. In the actual practice of revival music, however, and especially as it is classified as world music, tarantella risks losing the countercultural role it played in the first wave of its folk revival, during the 1970s, and being perceived as simply another item of mass culture. The celebration of a Mediterranean identity at play within the post-1990s revival has often been at risk of essentializing the South and, once again, attributing a mythical value to it, one reminiscent of the mythical tropes popularized by the Neapolitan song tradition. Nevertheless, Bennato's commitment to narrating the troubled sociopolitical condition of the South is still present in his most recent music production, as is his willingness to represent both southern Italy and the Mediterranean as hybrid postcolonial entities. This complexity ultimately suggests Bennato's development of a new cultural product, which is the result of the interaction and mediation between the local and the global (Motherway 2013); it also makes Bennato's work with tarantella a unique and enduring one.

CHAPTER 4

Tarantella for U.S., Italian American, and Cosmopolitan Markets

Alessandra Belloni's Performance from New York City to Honolulu

When the University of Hawai'i's French and Italian Division first hosted Alessandra Belloni's tarantella music and dance workshop on April 26, 2006, I did not know what a "tarantella workshop" might look like. While the image of tarantella that most people in the United States are familiar with is the refined sixteenth-century Neapolitan tarantella, my participation in the local festivals had taught me to appreciate tarantella as a complex family of folk dances, to be learned within the space and time of the festival rather than in a workshop. Which version would Belloni's workshop feature and how? I also wondered how Hawai'i's audiences might respond to a tarantella event, considering not only its general lack of familiarity with Italian culture but also the scarce knowledge of Italian folklore among students and aficionados of Italian culture in the United States (Del Giudice 2009b).

As a matter of fact, the tarantella performance presented by Belloni, and especially her dance choreographies, offered a rather different version of tarantella than the ones I had watched at the festivals at home; neither was this a typical example of ethnic music and dancing featuring typical tarantella costumes—the type that you would expect to see at displays of Italian American culture (Rauche 1990). Judging from the audience's enthusiasm, her representation of tarantella was also a very successful one, given its ability to resonate with the University of Hawai'i's diverse and international audience. As Belloni herself asserts in her publications and interviews, her performance offers a unique version of tarantella that not only reinterprets these music and dance traditions from a woman's perspective (Belloni 2007),[1] but also projects them onto world music and New Age scenarios by focusing on the cross-cultural, universal, and spiritual aspects of these traditions. For the goal of this study, it is important to ask what allows the tarantella folk genre to relocate from the southern Italian festivals to both world music and New Age scenes as well as what Belloni's role is in this process of relocation.

While this chapter's main focus is Belloni's own use of the tarantella rhythms in her performance, through Belloni's example I hope to find answers to the questions above as entry points into the dynamics of recontextualization of tarantella in the United States from the 1970s until today. Employing Belloni's tarantella performance as a starting point, then, I explore what new aesthetics and sociocultural values have become associated with tarantella, a folk tradition representative of the local culture of southern Italy, as it was marketed as "ethnic" music first and more recently as a "world" music product to consume on a global scale. While these dynamics are already at play within the Italian festival context (see chapter 2), Belloni's own adaptation of tarantella but confirms the presence of these dynamics in the United States and highlights a New Age perspective that is only starting to emerge in Italy, within Milan's cosmopolitan context, thus helping create a unique cultural product. My analysis of Belloni's work, as well as of what I call the "identity narrative" emerging from her work, suggests that Belloni's own adaptation of tarantella for a U.S. audience is a rather complex cultural product. On the one hand, it confirms a collective image of Italy as an exotic place in the eyes of American and international audiences (Schneider 1998; Gribaudi 1997); on the other hand, it replaces the religious and patriarchal legacies of tarantella with a gendered and New Age type of performance, thus allowing both Italian and Italian American women to reconnect to ancient women's healing practices in the Mediterranean and to reclaim gendered aspects of their ethnic heritage.[2]

A "Mediterranean Volcano"

Singer, actress, dancer, and percussionist Alessandra Belloni first moved to New York City in 1971, at the age of seventeen, to find a venue where she could express herself in music (Del Giudice 2009a).[3] In her book *Rhythm Is the Cure: Southern Italian Tambourine,* Belloni recounts how she "had been living in New York for several years, studying theatre and music, and on one of [her] trips back to Italy [she] met a group of women who invited [her] to be part of a women's concert. There [she] learned some amazing women's work chants from Naples,

Puglia, Calabria, and Sicily. The music was haunting and powerful, and [she] wanted to learn more as [she] found that it touched [her] heart deeply" (2007, 9). After debuting on New York City's theatrical scene, in 1976 Belloni met Italian American guitarist-composer John La Barbera in Greenwich Village in New York, and they discovered a shared passion for southern Italian folk music (ibid.); La Barbera had just returned from Italy and was as familiar as Belloni with the 1960s and 1970s Italian folk music revival (La Barbera 2009; Del Giudice 2009a). During his stay in Italy in 1973 on a music scholarship, La Barbera had come to associate with the Italian student movement, which strongly encouraged the recovery of Italian traditional music as a way to move beyond the increasing industrialization and Americanization of Italian pop music. A group of southern Italian students living in Florence had then introduced La Barbera to southern Italian folk music in 1975. Called Pupi e Fresedde, the group was inspired by the socially progressive and American-based 1960s Bread and Puppet Theatre, but its originality consisted in its loans from Italian Renaissance puppet theater and Commedia dell'Arte. As an official theater company, the group soon came to participate in the Italian folk-revival movement (La Barbera 2009). "We were committed to bringing the lost Italian traditions of music and theatre from Southern Italy back to the United States," La Barbera states. "I also hoped," he continues, that "[this music] might inspire other Italian Americans in search for their own roots, just as I had mine years before" (112). Through La Barbera, Belloni also met Sicilian tambourine player Alfio Antico and was "bewitched by [his] wild power on the drum." Belloni marks this moment as a crucial one in the development of her career, since "this [drumming] power convinced [her] that [she] could learn how to play that way, too, if [she] really wanted to" (2007, 9).

In 1979 Belloni and La Barbera founded I Giullari di Piazza (Jesters of the Square), a performing troupe devoted to "recreat[ing] the type of street dance theatre done in the piazzas of Italy and present[ing] it to audiences in New York City." Thus, the group's main goal was to reclaim the "ancient musical folklore of Southern Italy" (La Barbera 2009, 112). Together with La Barbera and the troupe I Giullari di Piazza, since the late 1970s Belloni has helped popularize southern Italian folk music in the New York City area (where she resides), throughout the United States, and internationally, in both academic and cultural circles. I Giullari di Piazza has toured and performed nationally in important cultural venues, such as Carnegie Hall, the Lincoln Center for the Performing Arts, the Metropolitan Museum, and the Smithsonian Institution, while also touring in California, Florida, and Canada. Its members have also been invited to perform in academic settings, such as the Caramoor Center for Music and the Arts, where they also teach Commedia dell'Arte. As of 2015, I Giullari di Piazza is artist-in-residence at the Cathedral of St. John the Divine in New York City. Its repertoire includes concerts and folk operas, a mix of music, dance, and theater narrated in both English and Italian. These operas include *Stabat Mater: Donna de Paradiso,* based on the thirteenth-century Italian lamentation in honor of the Madonna, and *La Cantata dei Pastori* (The shepherds' cantata), an adaptation of a seventeenth-century Neapolitan Christmas play told in music and dance by masked characters and puppets and still performed in the Naples area today. Of special relevance to this study is *The Voyage of the Black Madonna,* a folk opera that follows the encounter between the Roman poet Virgil and seven Black Madonnas, who help him save the world from self-destruction. The opera therefore "draws on pagan and Christian traditions to convey a New Age message" (Merkling 1993, 3). Conceived and written mostly by Belloni, this work reflects her strong devotion for the Black Madonna, a cult very common throughout southern Italy, in Europe and the Mediterranean, as well as in South America. In Belloni's understanding, however, the "Black Virgin is a Christian phenomenon as well as a preservation of the ancient goddesses who represent the healing power of nature" (quoted in Brooks 1996, 29). As I will explore in detail later in this chapter, this understanding has ultimately shifted the framework for Belloni's work beyond the music tradition of southern Italy and toward New Age spirituality.

At the same time, the opera features several performances of southern Italian folk music and dance; these are traditional versions, but the opera also contains original songs written by Belloni and put to music by La Barbera. The folk opera *1492–1992: Earth, Sun and Moon,* was conceived by I Giullari as an adaptation of the *Voyage* from a multicultural perspective. Commissioned by the Lincoln Center on the occasion of the five hundredth anniversary of Columbus's trip to the Americas, this opera features a traditional trickster figure within Neapolitan culture, Pulcinella, and his American Indian counterpart, Coyote, who get together to save the planet. Featuring a mix of both southern Italian and American Indian songs, dances, and musical instruments, the show seeks to offer an alternative version of Columbus's story, one that highlights the similarities between the two cultures, mainly a similar history of domination under Spanish rule. While this comparison seems to overlook the gravity of the American Indian genocide, which is incomparable to the Italian situation, this work as a whole reflects an explicit political commitment of I Giullari, especially in the early stage of its career. This commitment seems to be replaced by a New Age framework in Belloni's one-woman show, as well as in favor of a social commitment to helping women across different cultures, as confirmed by her more recent show *Drums of Illuminations* as well as by her female ensemble, Daughters of Cybele. Finally, I Giullari's most recent show, *The Dance of the Ancient Spider*, goes back to the southern Italian tradition by focusing on the tarantula myth and its music rituals, while also reframing them within a pre-Christian and shamanistic context. *The Rhythm Is the Cure* workshop analyzed later in this chapter has developed largely out of this show.

In recent years, Belloni has not only developed her own one-woman show, *Rhythm Is the Cure,* but also worked on several cross-cultural productions featuring Thunderbird American Indian Dancers as well as African and Latin American artists. A talented singer and dancer, Belloni has released two albums: *Tarantata: Dance of the Ancient Spider* (2000), which won the Best World Percussion CD nomination by *Drum* magazine, and *Tarantelle & Canti d'Amore* (2003). Belloni is also an exceptional percussionist. Employing the southern Italian tambourine style, she rearranges it to create original pieces or combines it with African and Brazilian percussion rhythms. This professional and personal experience has ultimately allowed Belloni to emerge on the international music scene as an exceptionally gifted and eclectic artist and a spiritual woman. For example, Belloni has taught workshops at Mount Sinai Hospital in New York City as well as in both Italy and Brazil, employing dance and percussion for healing purposes; since 2011 she has also been leading a drum circle at United Hebrew Nursing Home. Belloni's work with dance therapy and shamanic rituals is featured in the video *The Tarantella Trance: Towards the Origins of a South European Shamanism* within the *Living Shamanism* TV series.[4] Belloni's various honors, reported on her website, include the New York State Council on the Arts Award, the Italian American Woman of the Year 1996 Award, the Carnahan Jackson Humanities Fund in Women Studies Award, and, most recently, the Association of Italian American Educators' Award in Performing Arts (2016).

Belloni's Tarantella as World Music

Belloni's successful marketing of tarantella as world music stems from her ability to appeal to the cross-cultural elements of this folk tradition. Both in her shows and in her workshops, Belloni highlights what she calls the "universal" aspects of tarantella, such as the importance of the drum rhythm, common to several Mediterranean cultures and elsewhere in the world; the cult of the Black Madonna, which Belloni has studied in several places in the Mediterranean and in South America (Birnbaum 1993); and a shared closeness to the earth among Mediterranean peoples and several indigenous populations around the world. This focus on cross-cultural performance is evident in the Honolulu workshops in which I participated—for example, in Belloni's search for common elements between Mediterranean and Hawaiian culture, such as her comparison of the Mediterranean Black Madonna to the Native Hawaiian goddess Pele.

Similar to other world music projects, Belloni's performance also highlights the "traditional, authentic, and primal" aspects of southern Italian music (Taylor 2007, 180). In fact, the artist explicitly appeals to both organic and exotic aspects of southern Italian culture; she also underlines the traditional quality of her performance and her own authenticity as an Italy-born artist who is very familiar with the world of tarantella. Both ethnomusicology and folklore scholars have noted how this appeal to authenticity and tradition, along with exoticism, raises questions over the artist's own ethical positioning toward the culture that they are representing (Born and Hesmondhalgh 2000, 26). How does Belloni's tarantella project respond to these questions?

In my experience as a workshop participant, I have noted that both *authenticity* and *tradition* are used by Belloni as key terms to describe tarantella. Personal anecdotes illustrating her experience at southern Italian festivals and her acquaintance with the local performers help define Belloni as a genuine representative of this expressive culture and to establish her authority on the matter, thus shifting her role from the artist to the cultural broker and to the "Italian." Moreover, while Belloni's public shows extensively feature her own original work as a percussionist and a singer, her workshop, at least in the University of Hawai'i case, included several songs and rhythms that are part of the southern Italian tradition and are commonly performed at the festivals in Italy. The very act of performing live, embedded in both stage performances and dance workshops, adds yet another layer of authenticity to these performances, since live performances perform authenticity even more than the actual music (Silverman 2012, 246). This attention to tradition in the workshops does not reflect Belloni's perspective on tarantella as a folk genre; on the contrary, Belloni has explicitly expressed preference for those cultural expressions that show an effort to continually transform and adapt to changing tastes and times (Del Giudice 2009a). A case in point is the artist's experimentation with the tarantella rhythm and dancing through her *Tarantella—Spider Dance* show, which features what Belloni calls the "techno Tarantella Ecstasy."

Because it does not concur with Belloni's art philosophy, this focus on tradition in the workshops seems therefore designed solely as a marketing strategy to establish credibility for the artist as an authentic performer of southern Italian culture. Marketing her own performance as authentic ultimately allows Belloni to reduce the distance between the tarantella sounds that she is recovering, adapting, and rearranging and their original context (Feld 1994). In other words, it enables the artist to advertise her own version of tarantella as authentic at the same time that it transforms tarantella into a product that is suitable for an international audience. This representational choice is perfectly understandable as a marketing tool; however, on a representational level, it also ends up participating in a process of self-stereotyping (Silverman 2012, 257–58), as is the case with other phenomena of folk revival that are now being globally exported and exhibited. In fact, Belloni's contribution to recontextualizing tarantella as world music comes largely from the exoticized image of southern Italian culture emerging from her performance.

This focus on authenticity is important to note especially since the actual choreographies employed in Belloni's workshop are the result of a complex process of rearrangement and are only loosely based on their Italian versions. This is particularly evident for the choreography that Belloni has put together for her tammurriata performance. More than a single set of dance movements, the tammurriata includes a range of choreographies, even when the rhythm and melodies are the same. The tammurriata is in fact danced differently in different towns and villages, each style taking the name of the place from which it originates (see the introduction and chapter 2). This variety in turn reflects the extremely local quality of this dance and the place-specific knowledge it carries with it. The tammurriata featured in Belloni's workshops, on the contrary, combines a whole range of steps that belong to different styles, and to different areas, into a single choreography. Furthermore, the artist's tammurriata choreography features some steps that, to my knowledge, are absent or at least uncommon in the Italian festival context. These steps, which show close bodily interaction between the two dance partners, have been arranged to appear toward the end of the choreography to assign a particularly sensual tone to the dance finale. By inserting these steps, Belloni is able to emphasize the erotic quality of this dance and therefore to confirm the common representation of Italy as an exotic land of passion. My students' loud reactions during this portion of the dance testify to the marketing success of this choice. An article appearing in the University of Hawai'i student paper *Ka Leo,* soon after the 2007 workshop, was entitled "Pagan-Catholic Dance Takes a Spin," thus confirming that these sexualized representation of tarantella had a strong impact on the workshop participants (Sherreitt 2007).

It is important to note that there are obvious logistic reasons for this rearrangement and that Belloni often acknowledges her own personal interpretation during her workshop by stating that these are her own choreographies. Regardless of Belloni's interpretation, her tarantella performance ends up engaging in "self-stereotyping" as a way to lure foreign audiences. In this sense,

Figure 22. Final steps to Belloni's tammurriata choreography during the 2013 workshop at UHM; the author (*left*) is shown dancing with Belloni (*right*). In this choreography, both dancers gradually lower their bodies to the floor; at that point, one dancer gradually bends his or her body backward and toward the ground, while his or her partner gradually leans on him or her. The sexual innuendo of these movements is usually reiterated by Belloni, who speaks about the symbolic quality of these movements in their resembling a lovemaking act. Photo courtesy of Lenny Kaholo.

this example confirms dynamics of exoticization affecting folk dancing within the larger Mediterranean, such as Spanish tango (Savigliano 1995).

The artist's appeal to the sensual exoticism of southern Italy was particularly evident in the workshop held on the UH Mānoa campus on February 13, 2010, in concomitance with Valentine's Day. Focusing her attention mostly on tammurriata, Belloni made sure to underline the erotic quality of the dance and invited the workshop participants to picture the dance in this way. In response to my questionnaire on their experience in Belloni's 2010 workshop, several participants confirmed the success of this marketing strategy. In response to my question, "What did you learn about southern Italian folk music in this workshop?" A graduate student from England stated: "That sexuality and its expression is a large part of the dance." Another graduate student from Japan stated, "I think if I had just seen Belloni alone somewhere and didn't have the input that her dance was indeed 'Southern Italian' I would have just thrown it into one of the many 'exotic-ethnic-feminine' styles of dance like the Brazilian samba, Turkish belly dance, etc."

Figure 23. Belloni's outfit at her February 2013 workshop at the UHM campus. The photo also shows the image of the Black Madonna in the back, which constitutes an important element of her workshop and show settings. Photo courtesy of Lenny Kaholo.

Belloni's use of costumes in both her shows and her workshops actively contributes to the representation of southern Italy as an exotic and eroticized place by forging an artist's image that I would call an "imagined Mediterranean gypsy." While, on the one hand, this gypsy style emulates that of current festivalgoers throughout Italy, on the other hand, it also increases its picturesque qualities. In fact, to the gypsy outfit Belloni adds the colors of the spider-dance myth: white, symbolizing virginal purity, and red, symbolizing the menstrual blood, passion, love, and ritual death.

In the workshops, Belloni explains that this choice of colors is crucial to her art philosophy, because it pays homage to and attempts to re-create the tarantella dance ritual; for example, tarantism studies report that the *tarantati* would often dress in white (De Martino 2005; De Giorgi 1999). Unfortunately, in the eyes of an international audience, especially one that is not familiar with Italian culture, these props may end up reinforcing the image of an exotic southern Italian culture—an image too often associated with the colonial stereotyping of the South (see the introduction), while at the same time affirming the authenticity of Belloni's performance (Silverman 2012, 250). This effect is even more striking since Belloni explicitly reiterated her awareness of the ideological implications embedded in the world music market in our interview. The exotic quality of this image is further emphasized by the Hawaiian hibiscus that appears in Belloni's dark hair. Coming from Waikīkī's ABC Stores, the artificial flower suggests not only the pervasive globalization of culture, but also an unusual intercultural fusion between two famously exotic places in the eyes of both American and international audiences—Hawai'i and Italy.

Finally, the exoticizing effect of Belloni's representation of Italy is echoed by her summer workshop. Set in a luxurious seventeenth-century Tuscan villa in the Chianti wine region, the workshop promises to fully deliver a lusty experience of Italy—the one most often portrayed in films and TV shows about Italy, such as the comedy *Under the Tuscan Sun*—where Tuscany as a synecdoche equals Italy and where everybody is rich and happy and owns a gorgeous balcony from which to observe the lush countryside while sipping good wine. This metonymic image of Italy—which excludes the South and so many other less known places to American tourists—portrays a "staged" version of Italy (MacCannell 1999) that ultimately ends up silencing the reality behind the myth, which has to do with the difficult living situation for people in Italy, especially in the South, today. At the same time, this limited representation of Italian folk culture is largely counterbalanced by Belloni's recent project based in southern Italy, her annual Black Madonna tour in the Campania region, which allows her to create a direct line of communication between her mostly international students and well-known southern Italian musicians and tradition bearers, such as Raffaele Inserra, as well as to promote different locations and aspects of Italian culture.

Representing tarantella for a world music audience, as in Belloni's case, thus remains a complex endeavor that is constantly at risk of confirming the exotic image of southern Italy (the land of wine, passion, and erotic dance practices) and of Italian culture more in general for U.S. audiences, while at the same time presenting a version of tarantella that foreign audiences will perceive as authentic.

Belloni's Tarantella as a Woman-Centered New Age Practice

Belloni's largest contribution to the global resignification of tarantella consists of her appeal to tarantella as a woman-centered music and dance ritual, which operates as a progressive adaptation of tarantella. While the marketing of Belloni's shows as New Age can be read as a strategy for consuming southern Italian culture as a global commodity, her performance as a whole plays an important role in challenging the southern Italian patriarchal tradition and reclaiming women's shamanic roles within the Mediterranean context.

It is important to note that Belloni does not consider herself or her work New Age and also denies her participation in the New Age culture, especially in its more commercial aspects; as she reiterated both in her interview with Del Giudice and in our own interview, she also criticizes New Age theorists for their overly positive reinterpretation of ancient women's rituals, such as female drumming rituals in tarantism, since they fail to understand the difficult social and cultural conditions in which those women lived (Del Giudice 2009a, 223–25). Nonetheless, as Belloni herself admitted during our interview,[5] her performance does retain many elements that are common to New Age culture—thus the success of her performance within New Age circles.

The successful marketing of Belloni's tarantella performance as New Age comes not only from her focus on the ritualistic and pre-Christian aspects of tarantella, but also from the artist's description of tarantella as a "primeval" and "organic" form of performance that is closer to nature (Taylor 2007, 178). In her adaptation of tarantella for American and international audiences, Belloni revitalizes what she believes to be the pre-Christian aspects of southern Italian folk music, particularly women's ancient roles as drummers, thus embracing the "magic-ritualistic origins" of tarantella (Belloni 2007, 11). She also appeals to what she calls the people's "knowledge of the . . . Earth" (9). The importance of tarantella as an example of organic culture is confirmed in her workshops; I asked the 2010 workshop participants, "Can you recall any particular concept or fact related to the history of the tarantella?" Several of them were able to remember that it originated in agricultural areas and was closely tied to the land. But by using the term *earth* with a capital *E,* Belloni takes a further step: she transforms southern Italian land into a sacred space sharing similarities with several indigenous cultures worldwide. This semantic shift ultimately indicates a cultural shift from a local knowledge of the peasant world to its nostalgic reclamation, as is often the case with neo-paganism in the United States (Magliocco 2004). This New Age framework seems particularly fit for Belloni's weeklong retreat in Hawaiʻi, which she started in 2013 at Kahumana Organic Farm and Café, a place used for spiritual and therapeutic retreats as well as yoga and meditation classes.

Belloni's privileging, especially in her workshops, of the *pizzica tarantata* subgenre that is closer to the tarantism ritual—as well as her outfit, which pays homage to the tarantella myth—similarly allows the artist to enact what Biagi calls a "staged healing ritual" (2004, 279–315) that goes beyond the music and dance performance. However, as she constructs her own image as a female drum performer, a teacher, and a spiritual woman, Belloni is also fulfilling important cultural and social roles. To start with, she is able to share common ground with Italian feminist scholarship. Several scholars have looked at the tarantella rituals and values, as well as at the Black Madonna cult, as still an important moment of empowerment for Italian women today (Birnbaum 1993; Magrini 1994, 2003). By introducing a gendered perspective on tarantella in the United States, Belloni actively participates in the process of resignification of tarantella that is already occurring within the Italian context. Thus, her woman-centered tarantella performance represents an important site of reflection on the patriarchal legacy of southern Italian culture. Furthermore, by capitalizing on the healing power of tarantella, Belloni is also reaching women of different ages, languages, and cultures, both in Italy and internationally. Belloni's professed social commitment to creating a universal bond among women and helping women's liberation worldwide from what she calls the "spider's web" of repression (Del Giudice 2009a, 219–20) also speaks to her use of southern Italian rhythms to forge a cross-cultural, universally feminine perspective. Belloni's signature line of southern Italian tambourine featuring the image of a Black Madonna equally contributes to create a woman-centered shamanistic atmosphere around her performance.

Belloni's employment of tarantella rhythms as music therapy focusing especially on women is evident in her workshops. As one female participant in the 2010 Honolulu workshop put it: "I love dancing and I think there's something common underlying all dances across cultures that women, especially, are more capable of tapping into. . . . I think it's great to be able to share that 'universal' experience and the 'particular' style of femininity of dancing, not to mention the bond I share with other women who are equally passionate about expressing themselves through the medium of dance!"

The UH Mānoa workshops represented a shortened version of Belloni's *Rhythm Is the Cure* workshop; having participated in the full-length version in February 2007 and 2010, I can, however, testify to the similarities between the two events. Although the UH Mānoa workshops did not feature extensive breathing and relaxation exercises, they surely did involve an overall therapeutic effect through extended group dancing and the final breathing and meditation exercise, as suggested by the later remarks of many participants. In response to my question, "Can you describe your experience as a workshop participant?" one participant in the 2010 workshop wrote, "Very fun, energetic, positive, joyful, memorable. I shared so many laughs with my four friends and also connected with a few total strangers. I moved all my body, emptied my mind, danced with the beat, listed to Alessandra's words, and did not care about anybody or any-

Figure 24. Breathing and meditation exercise at the end of Belloni's 2013 workshop at UHM. Photo courtesy of Lenny Kaholo.

thing." In this sense, the therapeutic effect of the workshop on the local audience seems to confirm the audience response in New York City and elsewhere (Biagi 2004) as well as the testimonials contained in the *Living Shamanism* video. Having participated in her workshops during difficult times, like other fellow participants I can also testify to Belloni's genuine effort to create a therapeutic environment and especially a context in which to help other women.

In this sense, Belloni's tarantella performance as a whole becomes a complex project that illustrates how dancing southern Italian tarantella can become an important moment of self-discovery and "self-fashioning" (Bock and Borland 2011, 13) for both Italian and American women, who can often find "a release from restrictive notions of the female body derived from contemporary American popular culture" (3) and Western culture more generally. As suggested by Bock and Borland, from a scholarly perspective it is often tempting to dismiss world music performances as simply moments of cultural appropriation; at the same time, from the perspective of the (female) participant who experiences these performances through her own body, the social value of Belloni's performances is an important one to take into account.

Finally, it is important to note that this social role also occurs thanks to Belloni's own bodily enactment of southern Italian folk music and dances in

her workshops (Grace 2005). Both her shows and her workshops constantly
negotiate between her artistic reinterpretation of southern Italian folk music
and dances, her personal belief in the healing power of the tarantella rhythms,
and her experience of the southern Italian folk music festivals. Her enactment
of the tarantella's healing power is therefore strictly connected to her artistic
persona, in particular her role as a spiritual woman with a direct experience of
the tarantella music rituals, as Belloni herself points out both in her book and
in her interviews. Because it creates an intimate space for the artist and her
audience to connect on a personal level, this close intersection between Belloni's performance and her performed identity is crucial, I believe, in forging a
world music performance that also works as a "discourse of identity" (Kapchan
2007, 180). This "discourse of identity" in turn reflects the artist's position as a
representative of Italian culture abroad and as an artist operating both within
and beyond New York City's Italian American scene.

Belloni's Representation of (Southern) Italianness

Belloni's commitment to reaching women of different ages, languages, and
cultures ultimately places her work beyond both Italian and Italian American
cultural contexts and toward a transcultural understanding among women all
over the world. At the same time, her work does have a direct impact on the ways
that Italian culture is portrayed in the United States, as it furthers American
audiences' understanding of southern Italian culture and Italian culture more
generally. In fact, a challenge for Belloni or for any artist working with Italian
folk culture in a transnational context is that the term *Italian* usually evokes a
highly polished, upper-class image resonating with Dante's and with opera
masterpieces but certainly not with the rural, unschooled tarantella folk music
and dances from the South (Del Giudice 2009b). Yet Belloni's work goes beyond cultural brokering, since it also reimagines the Italian South according to
world music, New Age, and gendered perspectives. In addition, this work reflects the artist's position at the intersection of different linguistic and cultural
spheres—Italy, her place of origin; Italian American groups in New York City,
with whom she is in a "love-hate relationship" (Del Giudice 2009a, 228); and
the larger white American culture, especially through the world music scene,
as confirmed by the type of audience who gravitates toward Belloni's shows
and workshops. Belloni's performance therefore embodies the complexity of
defining one's work (and oneself) as "Italian" within the Italian diaspora context in the United States.

In both her concerts and her workshops, Belloni introduces the audience to the historical and cultural significance of the southern Italian folk music tradition by providing key cultural concepts and historical information. Her effort to familiarize the audience with southern Italian traditions places her in the role of a cultural broker who is committed to translating the tarantella cultural world into a different linguistic and cultural context, thus explicitly operating at the level of cultural production. But while introducing the tarantella rhythms to a different linguistic and cultural context, Belloni also reinterprets these rhythms to respond to the needs of her international audiences. In performance student Laura Biagi's words, Belloni has "re-created the ritual of tarantismo to make it suitable to the social context of contemporary New York City. Belloni takes the ritual of tarantismo overseas and adds to its practice the worship of other saint figures that were not present in the ritual as it was practiced in Salento (particularly the cult of the Black Madonna in her many forms, from Southern Italian Madonna de' Poveri to Brasilian Yemanja)" (2004, 276–77). While contributing to marketing her work as both world music and New Age, these elements also suggest similarities between Belloni's own project and the Italian American "folklore reclamation" movement, with its "focus on forms, elements, and even words formerly marginalized, silenced, and discredited by the dominant culture" (Magliocco 2011, 198). In this sense, they also reflect the impact of Belloni's work on the Italian American scene.

The workshop format employed by Belloni is an important example of her adaptation of the Italian festival scene—where participants learn to play the tambourine, sing, and dance from expert practitioners—into the American cultural environment, where professionalism and specialization are key concerns. Through the workshop format, Belloni is able to communicate different aspects of southern Italian culture to U.S. and international audiences, at the same time (and in the same way) that Italian practitioners are now importing the workshop format into the Italian context as a way to popularize, to educate, but often also to commercialize southern Italian folk music (Gala 2002; Pizza 2004). This is to say that adaptation here works both ways: not only are Americans embracing southern Italian folk music and dance traditions, but festivalgoers in Italy, with fewer ties to the original festival context, are now adapting cultural models that are foreign to the southern Italian context in order to make sure that southern expressive culture can live today in a new globalized form. In this sense, Belloni's performance plays an important role within the larger context of the tarantella revival—both the 1970s revival and the "neotarantism" phenomenon started in the 1990s. In addition, Belloni introduces her audience to several regional varieties and choreographies of tarantella, thus actively expanding her U.S. audiences' image of tarantella beyond previous representations of this folk tradition. By bringing to the fore issues of cultural change related to the Italian context, and by exporting them to various linguistically and culturally differ- ent scenarios, since the 1970s Belloni has performed an important task: that of popularizing the Italian revival not only for Italians living abroad but also for Italian American and larger U.S. music settings.

The originality of Belloni's performance lies in her ability to translate the current tarantella revival in Italy, such as the gypsy-style festival costumes, into an essential component of ancient southern Italian traditions. By doing so, she is able to call attention to her style as "authentically" Italian. This focus on the authenticity of her work in turn allows her to contrast her own version of south- ern Italian folk dances to the allegedly distorted version popular among Italian Americans. From this viewpoint, Belloni's promotion of her work as "Italian" provides an implicit commentary on, and criticism of, other representations of Italian culture in the United States.

By separating the artist from the diasporic Italian American cultural context, Belloni's "identity narrative" also ends up de-emphasizing the artist's own his- tory as an Italian immigrant to the United States. A midway stage between her country of origin and her acceptance as a U.S. citizen, Belloni's immigrant his- tory, which in turn echoes the longer history of Italian migration to the United States, rarely appears throughout her tarantella workshops or shows. In addi- tion, given her effort to market her own performance as authentic, any reference to Italian American history and culture—such as the continued importance of tarantella for Italian American groups in New York City and elsewhere—would undermine not only her knowledge of Italian culture but also the uniqueness of her performance in the eyes of her U.S. and international audiences. At the same time, even as she often acknowledges her indebtedness to several south- ern Italian artists who have introduced her to southern Italian tambourine and dances (Belloni 2007; Del Giudice 2009a), Belloni does not choose the Italian music scene over the U.S. one, nor does she define herself as part of the Italian folk music revival. As Biagi also observes, "The artist does not seem to locate her work as part of neo-tarantism. The way she markets her ritual interpretation is as an 'original practice' which nevertheless she modifies to suit the needs of contemporary women in New York City, the United States, and other countries around the world" (2004, 261–62). Belloni's focus on the uniqueness of her own tarantella performance ultimately distances her work both from other Italian American artists who also work with the southern Italian rhythms and from Italy-based artists who operate within the current neotarantism context.

Tarantella as an Italian American Tradition

Even as Belloni presents and markets her work as an "original practice" (ibid.) featuring what she considers the authentic Italian tarantella tradition, her work is of great significance within the larger context of post–World War II Italian migration to the United States vis-à-vis Italian American culture. Her forty-year commitment to reclaiming the tarantella tradition in all its complexity and to popularizing it in New York City and elsewhere in the United States resonates with the work of several Italian American artists, especially southern Italians who in some cases were first introduced to tarantella directly by Belloni. Biagi also underlines the important role played by Belloni's Italian American audiences. After interviewing several Italian American women who have participated in Belloni's tarantella workshops and classes in New York City in the 1990s—including Mary Ciuffitelli and Michela Musolino, whose stories I report below—Biagi concludes that "Belloni helped restore a link to Italian traditions that most of [these women's] families had left behind when they emigrated" (287). More important, Biagi notes that "exposure to Southern Italian traditions (through Belloni's work) gave some of these women a key to re-interpret their past and their present" (290). The bigger lesson for these women therefore consisted in learning about their mothers' and grandmothers' stories and about their often difficult roles within the southern Italian patriarchal system, which system had in turn led to the rise of the tarantism myth and to its musical traditions.

Belloni seems to have more or less directly inspired a generation of Italian American women and artists to recover the southern Italian folk heritage through both her shows and her dance workshops. Vocalist Michela Musolino, who first joined Belloni's southern Italian tambourine and dance class at the Cathedral of St. John the Divine in New York City in 1997, studied and worked with Belloni for three years. A singer, percussionist, and dancer, Musolino has performed in both Italy and the United States and has also collaborated with several Italian artists, including world-famous Sicilian percussionist Alfio Antico, who is also featured in her 2003 debut album, *Songs of Trinacria*. In the United States, she has performed with Italian American dancer and choreographer Natalie Marrone, whose work also makes use of the rhythms and cultural world of tarantella.[6] Of Sicilian origin, Musolino specializes in Sicilian folk songs, but she also performs and teaches Sicilian tarantella, which she considers an important type of "group celebration."[7] Her more recent interest in southern Italian folk music relates to the troubled history of the Italian South, in particular the history of brigandism as a resistance movement to the nineteenth-century colonization of the South (Aprile 2011). While her work departs from Belloni's approach to tarantella, especially Belloni's focus on tarantella as a healing practice, it is thanks to Belloni and I Giullari that Musolino was first attracted to tarantella's complex history as well as to its musical and choreographic aspects. "It was the beginning of a journey," she states. Musolino shares with Belloni an equally strong devotion for the Black Madonna; in the 1990s, she reports, several Italian Americans with whom she is in contact started to become interested in the Black Madonna as well as in tarantella rituals. After doing some research on the matter, Musolino realized that the Black Madonna cult was an essential component of her own family heritage and her identity as an Italian American; therefore, this became an important moment of both ethnic and personal self-realization.

Mary Ciuffitelli, who joined Belloni's classes at St. John the Divine in 1996, is a pivotal figure in this context, since she was able to connect with several Italian American artists to promote tarantella rhythms in New York City, including Michela Musolino and Natalie Marrone, while also promoting the work of southern Italian group Aramirè—Compagnia di Musica Salentina as well as their tours, appearances, and workshops in New York, New Jersey, Pennsylvania, and Florida.[8] Ciuffitelli recalls that when she first saw Belloni's performances in the 1980s, she was simply "blown away," since Belloni first introduced her to rhythms and choreographies that were not part of the tarantella repertoire typical of Italian American celebrations. According to Ciuffitelli, therefore, Belloni's biggest merit lies in her ability to "open this dance" to Italian American communities. Over the years, the impact of Belloni's work, and especially her dance workshops, was very strong on Ciuffitelli and on several other Italian American women, who would gather together with Belloni on a regular basis to dance as well as to talk about their own heritage and their own roles as women, particularly Italian American women. "We really bonded," Ciuffitelli states. By "going into ritual time," these group members—called *le tarantate* (or "women bitten by the spider's bite") as homage to the tarantism rituals—were able to use the tarantella rhythms as a way to heal from everyday life problems and thus to support each other on both spiritual and emotional levels. Belloni's workshops therefore became moments of cultural therapy for several Italian American women in New York City.

The important role played by Belloni not just in New York City but within the larger Italian American folk music scene is also confirmed by artists who do not have a direct connection with Belloni. Natalie Marrone, a (southern) Italian American from Hoboken, New Jersey, is the artistic director of The Dance Cure company, an all-female modern dance company established in 1998 and based in North Carolina. As the name suggests, the company takes its inspiration from the tarantism dance rituals and "fuses the athleticism of contemporary dance with folk dances, myths and rituals of [Marrone's] Southern Italian background." Marrone first came in contact with southern Italian folk dance while in New York City in the 1990s, where she also met Michela Musolino and Mary Ciuffitelli. Since then Marrone's work has been to choreograph, perform, and teach southern Italian folk dances. Although she has never worked with Belloni, Marrone confirms that Belloni's albums, particularly *Tarantata: Dance of the Ancient Spider* (2000), was very inspirational because it was able to reach so many people and laid the groundwork for any artist who wanted to work with the tarantella rhythms in New York City and elsewhere in the United States.[9] Like Belloni, Marrone focuses on women's role in southern Italian folk dances, and she is committed to "performing and teaching an accessible yet diverse body of dances that explores the many rites of passage woven through the fabric of human experience" (ibid.).

Given the importance of Belloni's legacy for much of New York City's and the Italian American folk music scene, as suggested by the life stories reported above, Belloni's attitude toward Italian American culture becomes even more striking. In an interview with folklorist Luisa Del Giudice, Belloni explains her conflicted relationship with Italian American audiences, whose perceived political conservatism—especially in the 1970s—seemed to reflect, in I Giullari's eyes, an equally conservative understanding of southern Italian music (Del Giudice 2009a, 228–30). Originated in Italy, where the folk music revival was fueled by the student movement and Italian left-wing ideology (Santoro 2009), Belloni and I Giullari's folk music project suited the political climate of post–Vietnam War United States, especially its celebration of U.S. diversity (Gabaccia 2002, 221). This appreciation for multiculturalism seems to have both spurred Belloni's interest in world music—and its idea that "we are all one" (Del Giudice 2009a, 240)—and further distanced her from Italian American audiences and what she perceived as their "blatant racism" (230). According to La Barbera, the negative reception of this type of work on the part of Italian American groups confirmed how unfamiliar Italian Americans were with Italian folk music. This reaction was evident to him since he first started touring on the East Coast with his Italian folk group Pupi e Fresedde in 1977. The audience's immediate reaction simply was, "That's not Italian music" (2009, 110).

As a matter of fact, La Barbera's and I Giullari's were not the first encounters of Italian Americans with Italian folk music and culture, but rather the introduction of performing styles as well as music and dance varieties that went beyond the typical ethnic folk-performance style. This difference ultimately illustrates two different cultural and ideological backgrounds: the folk movement–inspired urban intellectual effort of Belloni and I Giullari and the southern Italian peasant culture of the immigrant families (Gabaccia 2000). Furthermore, as Luisa Del Giudice points out in relation to Italian folk music among Italian Canadians, the "young Italian folk revivalists were just entering, as new areas for fieldwork, the very lands that these immigrants had left behind. An impulse to hide one's humble origins rather than publicize them was also likely" (Del Giudice 1994, 83). Therefore, while I Giullari sought to reconnect Italian Americans to the tarantella folk culture that was being revitalized in Italy at the time and to do away with the stereotyped version of tarantella that local musicians played at Italian American weddings (La Barbera 2009), these group's rather different social and cultural backgrounds led to a different reaction to the pseudoritualistic music that Belloni and I Giullari were proposing.

In my interview with Belloni, she acknowledges that the Italian American cultural scene is profoundly changed since she was first introduced to it in the 1970s, partly because "we educated them," she states. However, she also confirms her distance from the Italian American scene as well as from what she perceives as a "disconnect" of Italian Americans from their cultural heritage, in particular the tarantella rituals and rhythms. At the same time, Belloni confirms her commitment to educating and helping Italian American women to liberate themselves from their spider's web—in other words, from what she perceives as the deeply patriarchal environment of Italian American families still today.

Belloni's view of Italian American tarantella as a stereotyped and reductive version of tarantella echoes the comments of several Italian American women I interviewed. Both Ciuffitelli and Musolino confirm that their knowledge of tarantella as they grew up in the Italian American context was limited to Neapolitan tarantella, so they had no knowledge of other tarantella subgenres such as pizzica or tammurriata before they danced with Belloni. Like Belloni, they are committed to bridging this gap with the southern Italian tarantella tradition, but they also believe that there are continuities among the tarantella they grew up with, the one promoted by Belloni, and the one promoted by the current tarantella revival in Italy. As Musolino states, growing up Italian American also meant learning about the spider bite and its rituals, though in a more superficial way that was more suitable to an audience of children. Therefore, for Musolino, reclaiming tarantella as part of her own Italian American background means understanding a history of women's repression and thus learning about the cultural and social significance of tarantism rituals for both southern Italian and southern Italian American women. At the 38th Annual Conference of the American Italian Historical Association held in Los Angeles in 2005 and organized by the Italian Oral History Institute's director, Luisa del Giudice, Ciuffitelli spoke of her interest in the rhythms and history of tarantella, a "familiar voice I had never heard," thus suggesting a willingness to reclaim an important component of her Italian American background that had been silenced for generations. Furthermore, as Marrone points out, for Italian Americans like her, it is important but also difficult to "bridge the gaps" with the culture of the previous generations, whose goal was to assimilate into the white U.S. culture. By recovering the ritual energy of tarantella, Marrone continues, we can heal Italian communities in the United States from the shame of being Italian immigrants, especially for those with southern Italian ancestry. In turn, this will also help contemporary Italian Americans to reconcile with the culture of their ancestors. As a contemporary Italian American artist, Marrone's goal is both understanding and negotiating the Italian American voices she grew up with, and she does this by combining contemporary folk-fusion performances with the folk dance–festival circuit, thus negotiating between different generations and audiences. These acts of negotiation in turn enable Italian American artists like Musolino and Marrone to look beyond discourses of authenticity in relation to Italian culture and to embrace their performing arts as a way to go back to their own roots without losing the sense that folklore traditions, and cultures more generally, are constantly evolving (Bendix 1997). As an Italian American, Marrone states, "I get to create the kind of dance that makes sense to me in this time and place."

Tarantella in New York City and Beyond, 1970s–2010s

While Belloni's approach to tarantella is unique to her own artistic and personal temperament, the tensions that inform her discursive frameworks, performance practices, and ethnic identification reflect larger dynamics that have to do with the process of circulating tarantella in the United States since at least the 1970s—particularly the tensions between different notions of tarantella, and of Italian (folk) culture more generally, as well as different understandings of what it means to be "Italian" within Italian American and larger U.S. contexts.

The interviews reported above clearly illustrate how, forty years after I Giullari's first tour in the United States, and partly thanks to their and Belloni's own work with southern Italian rhythms, both the ritual power of tarantella and its complex history have come to be appreciated and cherished within cultural and artistic circles in New York City and elsewhere in the continental United States. However, it is important to understand that both La Barbera's and Belloni's importation of tarantella music from Italy to New York City in the late

1970s did not happen in a cultural vacuum; La Barbera's curiosity about Italian folk music, for example, had started at an early age, thanks to his Italian family and neighbors. In addition, when I Giullari debuted on New York City's folk music scene, there were already several other folk groups involved in Italian folk music, such as the one founded in 1976 by southern Italian Tony Morsella, who had migrated from the small town of Duronia in the Molise region in 1962; Morsella's experience with his folk music and dance group—including their tours throughout the United States, Canada, and Italy—ultimately led him to create the TV show *Mondo Italiano,* an educational program that has lasted more than thirty years and focuses on Italian culture and is geared toward Italian American communities.[10] Indeed, Italian immigrants "have continued many cultural practices long transformed in Italy . . . making Italian American communities a focus of particular interest to folklorists" (Del Giudice 2009b, 4). This is largely thanks to the fact that from the late nineteenth century until the period immediately following World War II, Italian immigrants to the Americas were mostly peasants and laborers from the poorest areas of Italy, especially the rural South. With little or no education, and a strong use of the language, they were "firmly rooted in regional *oral* cultures" (ibid.). Even a quick search in the Library of Congress online archives confirms the presence of a variety of tarantella recordings from several southern Italian regions, collected on the East Coast between the 1910s and 1970s. At the same time, Neapolitan tarantella remains the main type of tarantella featured in these music collections, and it is accompanied by other well-known examples of *canzone napoletana* such as "Funiculì Funiculà," which have little to do with the folk culture of tarantella. Of course, an important reason for the inclusion of *canzone napoletana* in these collections is the popularity of the genre across both sides of the Atlantic and its long-standing association with the Italian song per se (together, of course, with, and often performed as opera), given not only the presence of Neapolitan musicians in New York and elsewhere at the turn of the century and their export of Neapolitan songs (Frasca 2014), but also the popularity of the Neapolitan song genre throughout Italy. More important, the Neapolitan song genre, through its themes of passion and sentimentality, migration, and nostalgia, "easily entered the immigrant repertoire wherever Italians went" (Del Giudice 1994, 81).

In departing from this type of representation, I Giullari's and Belloni's own fascination with tarantella was part of the larger folk-revival movement that was investing both the United States and Italy at the time. Indeed, rediscovering Italian folk music at the time went often hand in hand with a renewed interest in the ethnic cultures of America. The collection of recordings from central Pennsylvania titled *Oh Mother It Hurts Me So,* edited by Ray Allen and published in

1980, presents a variety of folk music samples from different ethnic groups and includes one mouth-organ tarantella performance by fiddler Marty D'Addario, of Italian and Irish descents.

A major resource for I Giullari and any U.S.-based musician inspired by Italian folk music at the time was the 1957 *Folk Music of Southern Italy* (Columbia) and the 1958 *Music and Song of Italy* (Tradition Records), both featuring Alan Lomax's and Diego Carpitella's recordings from 1954 and 1955, as well as the multivolume LP collection *Italian Folk Music* (1972), authored by Lomax and Carla Bianco and featuring Lomax's recordings. The Campania volume, for example, contains on-site recordings of both tarantella and pizzica. "The recordings made [in Italy] by Alan Lomax and Diego Carpitella," La Barbera states, "inspired others to continue where the earlier ethnomusicologists had left off. This new enthusiasm motivated the younger generation to research its own roots and present this music to wider audiences in what has come to be called a folk revival" (2009, 104). In addition, both the 1965 collection *Italian Folksongs: Collected in Italian-Speaking Communities in New York City and Chicago,* assembled by Lomax and Bianco, and the 1979 collections *Calabria bella dove t'hai lasciate* and *In mezz' una strada trovai una pianta di rosa,* both recorded and curated by anthropologist Anna Lomax Chairetakis, testify to a renewed interest in tracking down this complex folk genre in the United States, as also confirmed by Bianco's 1974 book, *The Two Rosetos,* which studied several folk expressions among Italian groups in northeastern Pennsylvania and focused particularly on the oral culture of families coming from a rural background.[11] They also suggest the continued presence of a variety of tarantella subgenres beyond Neapolitan tarantella among Italian American groups at the time on the East Coast and Chicago as well as in Canada.

Chairetakis's two-volume collection (1979), in particular, includes several recordings of tarantella from several regions, including Campania, performed by immigrants living in New York, New Jersey, and Rhode Island.[12] The importance of this publication in the United States at that time is confirmed by the collection editor:

> In America today the music of the Italian working people is ignored or belittled by many rising members of the Italian community itself—not so much because of its associations with poverty, but because of the insidious and pervasive form of class prejudice which the Italian peasant and worker, especially of the South, have for centuries experienced, and still encounter. However, a new and enlightened appraisal will reveal that Italian folk music can hold its own with the best European and American music of its genre. It is certainly the most genuine musical expression of the Italians who immigrated to these shores.

The role of Calabrian immigrant musician Giuseppe De Franco, one of the leading artists in the Calabria volume, is significant in this context (Wood 2011). Moving to the United States in 1968, in his mid-thirties, to settle in Nutley, New Jersey, De Franco first started playing Calabrian folk music at friends' parties and local bars and later decided to start a music career. His 1975 participation in the Smithsonian Folklife Festival, together with several other members of his southern Italian Acrese community as well as several groups from Italy, represented a turning point for De Franco and his wife, Raffaela, who participated in the 1981 New York City concert series of Italian folk music and the 1983–85 Italian Music Tours produced by Chairetakis and the Center for Traditional Music and Dance. In 1990 they won a National Heritage fellowship and also helped form the group Calabria Bella (Beautiful Calabria). Having learned to play *chitarra battente, organetto* (button accordion), and *tamburello* during his youth in southern Italy, De Franco brought with him to the United States an extensive knowledge of a variety of tarantella, *villanella,* and several other folk-song genres. De Franco's example clearly illustrates not only a continued dialogue between Italian groups living on both sides of the Atlantic, but also that Americans at the time had direct access to the rich composite of southern Italian folk music, including tarantella.

Besides the recording projects discussed above, the Italian Folk Art Project—initiated in 1977 at the Nationalities Service Center of Philadelphia thanks to the help of Elba Farabegoli Gurzau—reflects an active interest in studying and disseminating knowledge of Italian folk culture within the larger U.S. multicultural context. Gurzau's 1964 book, *Folk Dances, Costumes, and Customs of Italy,* was meant to provide educational material on Italian folk culture—from music scores to choreographic suggestions and costume description—particularly to Italian American communities, "which . . . have a rich opportunity of encouraging, in the larger American community, an interest in things Italian and at the same time stimulating better understanding among people" (3). As the book's preface suggests, since the term *tarantella* was already well known at the time in the United States, the author decided to offer "some of the interesting legends that surround its origin as well as some of the differences in character that are evident in the various regions in which it is popular" (1–2). This statement makes clear that although *tarantella* was a popular term, not much was known about this complex music and dance genre besides the Neapolitan tarantella subgenre. Not surprisingly, then, the costumes described for tarantella performances in the book are those typical of Neapolitan tarantella.

In 1979 the project consolidated as a nonprofit educational institution called the Italian Folk Art Federation of America (IFAFA), a major magnet for both education and research on Italian folk arts as well as for information regarding U.S.-based performing groups. As of 1984, the Italian Folk Arts Federation of America counted among its members at least twenty-four folk groups, of which fourteen were based on the East Coast, but there were also groups from Ohio, Michigan, Minnesota, Iowa, and Illinois, while two were based in Canada ("Musica Popolare" 1985). This list shows how all of the groups provided dance entertainment, while some of their names explicitly mention "folk dancing" or "heritage dancing," which further confirms the resilience of Italian folk dancing among immigrant groups in the United States at the time—and given the large numbers of southern Italians among immigrant groups in the United States, it is safe to assume that tarantella was extensively featured in many of these groups. The "heritage dancing" label also suggests that these forms of Italian folk culture were exhibited within a U.S. multicultural framework, as does the fact that all the groups in the list also featured traditional costumes. In other words, this new interest in Italian folk culture can be explained within the larger multicultural ideology movement in the United States, a movement that choreographer Anthony Shay describes as a continuation of Eurocentric imperialism, whereby benevolent Anglo-Americans act as champions of diversity, while at the same time dictating the way that these ethnic cultures get represented. According to Shay, the Anglo-American control of these ethnic cultural forms ranges from adapting dances to a reductive slot time performance to using stereotyped dances and costumes.

One of the groups listed is the Italian Folklore Group of Washington, D.C., founded in 1976 by Celest Di PietroPaolo. IFGW comprised about fifteen Italian-born and fifteen American-born singers and dancers. Di PietroPaolo was also one of the founders of the Italian Folk Art Federation of America and served as chairman of the folk dance section for many years. He has performed traditional music at all of the major festivals in the Washington, D.C. area, including those sponsored by the Smithsonian Institution, the Folklore Society of Washington, and the Italian Embassy. Since 1975 Di PietroPaolo has also led the performing group Italian Village Music and Dance together with his wife, Marie di Cocco, who has also been teaching Italian traditional dances. It is important to note that on their website they explicitly differentiate their own work from previous Italian folk ensembles, since their goal from the start has been to share with American audiences the variety and richness of Italian traditional dances in the hopes of educating them to the "true folk heritage for italian-americans [*sic*]—the music of the immigrants." They thus remind their American audience that "for many years the commonly held belief in this country has been that the body of Italian folk music contains little more than 'the' tarantella, Santa Lucia, and a few other choreographed dances and songs in proper italian [*sic*] (i.e., not traditionally in language)." This comment further testifies to the existence of different and conflicting images of Italian folk music, and of tarantella, in the United States even today.

Indeed, the need for a deeper understanding of Italian folk culture, including tarantella, was circulating among both musicians and scholars of Italian folklore in the early 1980s beyond I Giullari. In October 1984, Musica Popolare, the Ethnic Folk Arts Center's Italian music tour, visited several communities in the Northeast; the tour featured several musicians from Italy, particularly Sicily and Campania, and Calabrian musicians living in the United States. Their participation attests to the presence of tarantella musicians on the East Coast at the time and also to their direct contact with musicians in Italy. As project director Anna L. Chairetakis put it in her introductory speech, "Many Italian Americans of the 2nd and 3rd generations, descendants of the first big immigration, have come to identify Neapolitan urban music, which emerged in its present form in the late 19th century, as the core of their traditional music, and sometimes as the badge of their ethnic identity. The same is true of the gay, sophisticated Neapolitan tarantella. . . . As appealing, familiar, and powerful as these expressions are, the Southern Italian folk music tradition encompasses much more" ("Musica Popolare" 1985). Chairetakis's words confirm not only the widespread popularity of the classic Neapolitan tarantella among contemporary Italian American communities, but also her project's goal of moving beyond this reductive version of tarantella and toward the larger and more complex tarantella genre. Nevertheless, contemporary Italian American performances of tarantella, especially heritage events and parades, often continue to perform a stylized and reductive version of tarantella, as confirmed by the performance videos of folk groups currently featured on the IFAFA website.[13]

The existence of such competing images of tarantella still circulating in the United States today confirms the dual role of Italian folk culture within Italian immigrant groups. While Italian Americans have shown a great deal of interest in preserving an Italian cultural heritage, including its musical aspects, Italian oral cultural heritage is at the same time ignored, and even rejected, not only by many Italian Americans but often also by Italian educational programs and other cultural organizations. In other words, while a "vast, capillary musical underground still thrives in myriad spontaneous effusions that echo local, even familial tradition . . . [t]his patrimony has been largely overlooked from within the Italian community and from the scholarly community without" (Del Giudice 1994, 75). Italian American artist Natalie Marrone confirms that, as a peasant tradition, tarantella represented an element of Italian culture that many immigrants, including her relatives, were committed to distancing themselves from (Marrone 2013). This attitude is not limited to Italian groups in the United States; as Luisa Del Giudice also points out in her autobiographical study of folk songs among Italian groups in Toronto, "I suppose my family was a little dismayed to discover I wanted to study their songs. Had they not been ridiculed for those very songs by my generation just a decade before?" (Del Giudice 1994, 75). In fact, Del Giudice explains, "The post-fascism Italian immigrants bore with them what might at times seem like a double inferiority complex—of Italian versus North American culture, and more covertly, of local and rural vis-à-vis Italian national culture" (77).

These words suggest that the only way for tarantella to survive within this immigrant context was by becoming codified into a stereotyped choreography with *costumi antichi* (antique costumes) (Marrone 2013) and other elements resembling what the larger white American culture expects ethnic cultures to display. This reference to *costumi antichi* is corroborated by Anthony Rauche, who, writing in 1990, underlines the continued importance of tarantella for Italian Americans as a symbol of ethnic belonging, as this music and dance tradition helps "bridg[e] the gaps between their 'American' and 'Italian' identities"; nevertheless, he also observes, based on his own observation of Festa Italiana in Hartford, Connecticut, that these performances have moved from a spontaneous performance among the audience to a stage performance by a dance troupe who also performs other types of ethnic music. He thus believes that it is important to look at this change because it shows a "staged, stylized version of tarantella" (1990, 194).

Several elements indicate that by the late 1990s, a new wave of tarantella music was circulating in the United States following the Italian pizzica revival, one that also encouraged the performance of tarantella within a world music framework, while also promoting other genres of southern Italian folk music and dances (Del Giudice 2016). In 1999 Rounder Records released a newly edited version of Lomax's collection of Italian folk songs, titled *Italian Treasury: Folk Music and Song of Italy*, which testifies to the recently growing interest in Italian folk music both in Italy and in the United States. In addition, Del Giudice's seminal work at the Italian Oral History Institute in Los Angeles—especially her organization of two conferences, Essential Salento in October 1998 and Performing Ecstacies: Music, Dance, and Ritual in the Mediterranean in 2000—have certainly sparked a new interest in tarantella in the United States, especially on the East Coast (Del Giudice 2005b, xv). Beside scholarly presentations, the Performing Ecstasies conference featured several cultural exhibits, as well as music and dance performances. Among the artists invited to perform were

Luigi Chiriatti with his group Aramirè, Musicantica, and Belloni and I Giullari di Piazza, who performed the *Tarantata: Dance of the Ancient Spiders* show. The conference also continued the successful collaboration between Del Giudice and Aramirè that had started with the Essential Salento conference: for several years, they worked together in writing and translating field recordings from Chiriatti's archive.[14]

The strong impact of the conference on Italian American groups is confirmed by Mary Ciuffitelli's experience. While Belloni's workshops and classes represented a first step toward rediscovering tarantella music and dance traditions, Ciuffitelli's experience at the Performing Ecstacies conference was illuminating because it showed her both the musical and choreographic variety of the tarantella genre and its various artistic interpretations and performing styles. In other words, this event illustrated the many possibilities of this folk music tradition: "It was an eye opener," Ciuffitelli recalls. In fact, it was this conference that first put Ciuffitelli in contact with the group Aramirè and spurred her to promote their music in New York City, which, in turn, helped spread this music to other places in the United States. This became a "life-changing moment" in Ciuffitelli's life, as she felt she was not only "bridging the gap" with these cultural traditions from Italy, but also getting in touch with modern Italy—a place that, as an Italian American, she did not know. The video *Pizzica with a NY Accent,* directed by Ciuffitelli and released in 2007, contains a sampling of events produced or created by Ciuffitelli in New York City in the period 2000–2005, including a workshop on music traditions from Salento by Roberto Raheli of Aramirè. The video clearly illustrates that by the mid-2000s, the complex history and various music traditions of tarantella were becoming more and more popular in the Italian American cultural circles in New York City. By giving the video a "NY accent," Ciuffitelli underlines the importance of recovering tarantella rhythms and rituals as part of the Italian American diasporic culture.

This increased interest in Italian folk culture on the part of Italian American groups, particularly in New York City, is further confirmed by the steady growth of the Black Madonna del Tindari gatherings, which have been taking place on September 8 at Phoenix Bar on Manhattan's East Thirteenth Street and are organized by Italian American folklorist Joseph Sciorra (2004). Since 2004 the gathering happens in the same spot where a private chapel in honor of the Black Madonna del Tindari was located until 1987, and since 2005 it has featured tarantella music and dancing, particularly Apulian pizzica. An article appearing in the *New York Times* on September 5, 2004, reported the event as being organized by "an informal group of scholars and artists who see Black Madonnas as symbols of feminine strength, racial harmony and spiritual power"

(Duffy 2004); in fact, a common trend to the celebration seems to be a "linkage between pagan earth goddesses and the Virgin Mary" (Sciorra 2008b). The title of Duffy's article, "Showering a Madonna with Affection, Not Devotion," also suggests that the Black Madonna figure has assumed new meanings for current generations of Italian Americans. As Sciorra also comments, "A new generation of Italian Americans has adopted and transformed the Madonna Nera image into an icon of *italianità* by linking it to a reconfigured, ecumenical spiritually, a politically progressive position, and a multicultural perspective, as an ongoing reimagining of what it means to be 'Italian' in the 21st century" (2008a).

The increasing popularity of southern Italian folk music culture in New York City is additionally confirmed by the work of artists who operate both within and outside Italian American cultural circles, such as Italian Argentinean dancer and choreographer Anabella Lenzu. Lenzu's work departs from other tarantella performances, as it is essentially aimed at a theater audience; her "dance dramas" offer a unique mix of theater and modern dance performances, while also borrowing from both southern Italian and Argentinean folk music and cultures, in particular tarantella and tango.[15] A first-generation Italian Argentinean immigrant to the United States, Lenzu is particularly interested in the immigrant experience in New York City and the United States and is committed to exploring it through theater and dance.[16] Lenzu was also the founder and artistic director of the Ciao Italy Performing Arts Festival in Williamsburg, Brooklyn, from 2006 to 2010; in Lenzu's words, the festival features "traditionally-based and Italian-inspired work by contemporary performers and scholars," to "create a bridge between the historic Italian community in Williamsburg and the more recent community of artists who are living and/or working in the neighborhood." Among Lenzu's repertory, the show *Entroterra* (2004) especially reflected the artist's interest in southern Italian folk performance; based on her two-year work and dance experience in the Caserta province of the Campania region, the show paid homage to several southern Italian folk dance genres, including pizica and tammurriata, as well as the global tammurriata rhythm of Neapolitan artist Enzo Avitabile. Through this experience, Lenzu was able to uncover her "Italian roots as a daughter of Italian immigrants who arrived in Argentina in 1952" and to "rediscover [herself] as a person and reconsider [her] function as a choreographer" (ibid.).

It is important to note that this new wave of interest in tarantella is characterized both by a more direct access to folk music groups from Italy and by the labeling of this music as "world music." The group Aramirè, for example, has widely performed in Europe and the United States since the early 2000s, largely contributing to the current craze for the Salentine pizzica. After being invited to the Performing Ecstacies conference in 2000, Aramirè performed at the World Music Institute in New York City, as well as in Philadelphia and New Jersey in September 2002, and then again in New York City at Carnegie Hall in January 2007. Roberto Raheli, lead vocalist and violinist, also conducted workshops on Salentine music and drumming in New York City. Edizioni Aramirè, the group's publishing arm, further contributed to circulating Salentine music in the United States through the release of Aramirè's recordings, which feature booklets of commentary and lyrics in Italian, the Apulian language, and English. More recently, the Apulian group Canzoniere Greganico Salentino, one of the leading voices of the post-1990s pizzica revival in Italy, has been touring in the United States since 2011 as well as in Europe and elsewhere internationally; they also performed in New York City again on February 1, 2013. Finally, the Los Angeles–based group Musicantica arrived in the United States in the 1980s, and their work has been included in major publications on the southern Italian folk music revival in the United States; their experience in the United States can be read within the larger Italian "brain drain" phenomenon, and in this sense it reflects a continuity between the experience of immigrant folk musicians from the nineteenth and early twentieth centuries and that of Italians who have recently migrated (Del Giudice 2016).

The 2008 World Festival of Sacred Music hosted by the Getty Museum, co-sponsored by the Italian Cultural Institute in Los Angeles, featured Neapolitan saxophonist and vocalist Enzo Avitabile, one of the leading voices in the current Neapolitan music scene, including folk music. Avitabile's recent collaboration with I Bottari, a percussion-based group devoted to the tammurriata rhythms of the Campania region, gave rise to the internationally successful Sacro Sud Project, "an imaginary journey from Nazareth to Napoli, exploring the spiritual vitality of the many 'souths' of the world and featuring songs from a variety of epochs" (J. Paul Getty Trust 2011). This participation, together with Jonathan Demme's recent documentary *Enzo Avitabile: Music Life* (2012), reflects Avitabile's increasing visibility in the United States. As these examples suggest, the key to success in the United States for these artists largely lies in their ability to adapt and "translate" their work for a world music audience, similar to Belloni's tarantella performance and its successful adaptation of these southern Italian rhythms into a product suitable for an international world music market.

Partly because it was spurred by the current revival in Italy and also built on more homegrown revivals, most interest in southern Italian folk music in New York City and elsewhere in the United States has focused on Apulian pizzica and on the music rituals connected to the tarantism phenomenon. Stimulated by the many Apulian pizzica–related events now occurring both in Italy and in the United States, as well as by the intensive cinematic production in the Apulia region, in July 2009 the Calandra Institute organized the first Puglia Film Festival in New York City, partly geared toward the large Apulian population living in the city's metropolitan area (Melchionda 2009). This climate of general enthusiasm over things southern Italian, however, has also slowly brought to the attention of New York City audiences the tammurriata music tradition from Campania. In particular, the work of Neapolitan tammurriata performer Marcello Colasurdo reached the U.S. musical scene in September 2007, when the project *A Global Dionysus in Napoli: The (Un)Real Story of Marcello Colasurdo* was presented at Manhattan's La Mama Experimental Theatre. Based on Colasurdo's life, the original version of the project, entitled *A Global Dionysus in Napoli* (and produced by OPS, a Naples-based cultural association), is an "interdisciplinary cultural project blending music, theatre, art, and video, that takes place on an imaginary television show dedicated to contemporary incarnations of Dionysius" (Calandra Italian American Institute 2007). In concomitance with the La Mama show, Colasurdo himself participated in the symposium Folk Music and Modernity in Southern Italy, organized by the Calandra Institute on September 17, 2007, and featuring the authors of U.S. theatrical adaptation, as well as Marco Messina, founder of the Neapolitan hip-hop group 99 Posse, who had participated in creating the original project.

This brief overview of the dynamics of tarantella performance in the United States since the 1960s ultimately confirms what Anthony Shay describes as the general framework for the historical development of immigrant dances in North America. In particular, Belloni's debut years can be read within what Shay calls the second phase, in which national and state-run folk ensembles started to provide a polished and stereotypical representation of ethnic dances, and from there Belloni's search for an alternative way of representing Italian tarantella beyond the Italian American framework. The third phase, since the 1990s, has seen an increased emergence of ethnic choreographers who are committed to moving beyond these stereotypical folk representations, while also contributing to attracting to the United States music and dance groups directly from Italy.

Viewed in this light, the strong revival of tarantella in Italian American and larger U.S. contexts since the late 1990s—thanks not only to the work of several Italian American artists but also to the recent presence of southern Italian groups in the United States—helps enrich and diversify the representation of southern Italian folk music and culture offered by Belloni and I Giullari since the 1970s. This multiplicity of voices confirms the complexity, and many possibilities, of representing Italian culture within transnational and diasporic contexts. It also suggests a central role played by tarantella within the current representation of Italian music in the United States; for tarantella scholar Luisa Del Giudice (2016), tarantella, and pizzica in particular, may even go so far as replacing the Neapolitan song genre as the "next pan-Italian heritage" within the U.S. diasporic culture.

Conclusion

Belloni's unique reinterpretation of southern Italian folk music and dances for an international audience is particularly significant for this study, as it illustrates the artist's established role as a cultural broker; in fact, Belloni actively participates in the process of resignification of tarantella that is already occurring within the Italian context. Her successful marketing of tarantella as a world music and New Age product raises important questions about the representation of Italian culture for an international audience; at the same time, her woman-centered tarantella performance represents an important site of reflection on the patriarchal legacy of southern Italian culture.

Furthermore, the tensions in Belloni's narrative as described in the previous sections—between what she presents as part of the southern Italian tradition and what she excludes from her representation—make her work a complex moment of cultural brokerage. As an effect of this complex narrative, Belloni's work ends up de-emphasizing the artist's involvement within Italian American groups in New York City, an important component of her audiences since the 1970s. Yet the profound influence of Belloni's work on many Italian American women and artists since the 1970s has actually helped them embrace their diasporic Italian American culture on a deeper level; this is remarkable, especially given Belloni's focus on her own performing art as an original practice reflecting tarantella traditions from Italy and unconnected to the Italian American context.

Final Thoughts

The performances of Eugenio Bennato and Alessandra Belloni play with different representations of the Italian South in a constant negotiation between artistic impulse, sociopolitical concerns, audience motivations, and commercial opportunities. Furthermore, the complexity of Belloni's project derives from her own artistic persona and from her own performance as a southern Italian woman and artist. Insofar as her tarantella performances and workshops affect the representation of southern Italy among U.S. and cosmopolitan audiences, Belloni's positionality and ethics play an important role as a recorder of southern Italian folk music for an international audience—as it does my own, I might add, since I too study the revival and translate it, both linguistically and culturally, for a U.S. academic audience. In representing the musical and cultural world of tarantella for national and global audiences, the performer, the folklorist, the popularizer, the cultural critic, and the intellectual are not only structurally affected by their positionalities in relation to the topic of study, but should carefully reflect on them and their agency. In fact, in the study of folk cultures, a major risk is that of romanticizing or exoticizing the folk, and as I have illustrated throughout this study, neither the folklorist, the performer, nor the intellectual can easily stay away from such an inevitably romanticizing attitude.

Problems of representation have consistently been central to both folklore studies and cultural studies scholarships, two major scholarly frameworks for this study, given the attention paid in both fields to the cultural expressions of socially marginalized groups. This focus on the marginal reached Italian scholarship in the earlier part of the twentieth century through the work of Antonio Gramsci, whose main concern was over what he saw as a "split between the people and the intellectuals" (1985, 168). This reflection ultimately led him to a new conception of the intellectual, which was based on the assumption that "the intellectual function cannot be separated from productive work in general" (275). But reflecting on the role of the intellectual also led Gramsci to consider the role of folklore within both cultural and political spheres. According to Gramsci, the intellectual's role was in fact crucial in helping people "regain importance" (168), and this placing of the people (also to be understood as groups or communities) at the center of the intellectual endeavor meant giving new importance to the marginal, the repressed, the local. Gramsci's attention to folklore, conceived as the culture of the lower classes, therefore developed out of his Marxist political orientation, while at the same time inaugurating the study of folklore within Italian Marxist scholarship.

This concern about giving voice to the culture of marginalized groups still remains central to folklore studies today. Yet the history of this discipline offers many examples of folklore scholarship that declared to give voice to the people, but in actual practice often constructed these voices according to the folklorist's own perspectives and biases. A case in point is the brothers Grimm's nineteenth-century folklore scholarship. As documented by German scholar Heinz Rölleke in the 1970s and further analyzed by Richard Bauman and Charles Briggs, the Grimms were constantly concerned with authenticity when they transcribed oral texts and transformed them into collections of folktales; however, they did make many stylistic changes and revisions. It was exactly these stylistic additions, such as the introduction of direct discourse, that helped to make the texts "authentic" in the eyes of the collectors and their readers, when in reality no actual peasant had been interviewed by the Grimms, but only middle-class families who often knew the story from previous publications (Bauman and Briggs 2003, 212–14). This practice ultimately reveals the Grimms' central concern with building an idealized image of what "the folk" said or what they felt.

This paradox, inherent in the early formulation of folklore studies in nineteenth-century Europe, is confirmed by Gramsci's view of folklore. While capitalizing on the crucial role of the marginal classes within Italian society and advocating a renewed interest in these classes' "conception of the world," he also reminds us that "this conception of the world is not elaborated and systematic because, by definition, the people . . . cannot possess conceptions which are elaborated, systematic and politically organized and centralized in their albeit contradictory development" (1985, 189). This contradiction is explained in Gramsci's view by the need to understand the people's conception of the world *in order to* help them move beyond it, to educate them, and in this way to contribute to the construction of a national consciousness, while maintaining a cosmopolitan dialogue with other nations. In doing so, he also constructs a rather negative and limited conception of the folk, which deeply influenced several generations of Italian folklorists. My brief examination of De Martino's 1961 study of tarantism in the first chapter asserted both De Martino's indebtedness to Gramsci's thought and his belief that the "backward" southern folk culture was a sign of the lack of social and cultural development in the region.

Both 1970s and 1990s tarantella scholarship, which is deeply influenced by Italian Marxism and by Gramsci's thought, certainly moved beyond Gramsci's conception of folklore only to embrace an overly positive image of the South and of tarantella. This leads us to ask how their understanding of southern Italian folklore takes into consideration questions of agency and appropriation. De Simone's 1979 study of Campanian folk songs, which first made available the folk culture of this region to a national and middle-class audience, was informed by a much more positive notion of the folk than De Martino's. Yet local performers and old-timers were and are very aware of the distance separating them from De Simone's intellectual position, as he interpreted the peasant world of tammurriata for the Italian urban middle class. As I illustrated throughout my analysis of the post-1990s festival scene, a nostalgic return to the land and to the peasant culture of the South is embedded in the extensive participation in the current festivals of young urbanites often unfamiliar with the peasant world of tammurriata, in the same way as it was in the 1970s revival. These elements raise important questions regarding not only the role of folklore within Italy's social formation but also the roles of both the intellectual and local communities and interest groups within the current sociopolitical structure of Italy. A look at Italian folklore scholarship thus confirms that the representation of southern folk and their cultural expressions has constantly gone hand in hand with its romanticization. Even as contemporary scholars of tarantella recount the history of the Italian South as a postcolonial location, they confirm such an attitude in their embracing an often mythicized Mediterranean identity.

Both European and U.S. scholars have now consciously moved away from such a romanticizing notion of the folk, not only by deconstructing the notions of the "folk" and the "popular" these disciplines constructed and relied upon, but also by exposing the ideological filter through which we perceive these concepts. As a result, folklorists have come to replace the word *folk* with either *small groups, communities,* or *networks,* while also focusing on communicative, linguistic, and performative aspects of folklore as "expressive culture." For cultural theorist Stuart Hall, instead, "there is no whole, authentic, autonomous 'popular culture' which lies outside the field of force of the relations of cultural power and domination" (1981, 232). His observation reminds us that we should not attribute a truth-value to the popular and also that, once again, different representations of the popular have historically been produced within different ideological frameworks, and thus none of them has a truly "authentic" value.

Furthermore, one of the main problems with the representation of the popular or folk is that it is always "staged," and thus it becomes important to "deconstruct the scientific and political operations that staged the popular" (Canclini 1995, 146). We can conclude that, although local and marginal knowledges are now given renewed attention within globalization, they are actually staged versions of those knowledges. The romanticization of the folk that often comes with the revival is therefore only another face of staging the folk. This staging of the folk and its dynamics need to be taken fully into account in order to uncover and understand their ideological mechanisms, that is, who is staging the folk, for whom, and to what end. However, I do not believe that the act of staging is always negative per se. I argue that these practices become problematic when they create a mystification of local culture that either paves the way for or confirms common stereotypes about that given culture.

Nowhere is this more evident than in the world music scene. A much-discussed aspect of world music concerns the claims of authenticity that usually come with the world music package and that help advertise this music's special value within the contemporary globalized market as a more "truthful" and "organic" musical expression. Among the discursive strategies of world music is in fact "the use of language that emphasizes the diversity of the music, its freshness," and "new sounds, musics and musicians unpolluted by the market system of the late capitalist west" (Taylor 1997, 19). In addition, "Consumers at the traditional metropoles look toward the former margins for anything real, rather than the produced" (22). At the same time, "the authentic" work[s] in retail terms as a redescription of the exotic," and "in the context of the denunciation of Western pop artifice and decadence . . . the authentic itself becomes the exotic (and vice versa)" (Frith 2000, 320). In other words, by exhibiting and marketing previously marginalized sounds as authentic, the world music label also inevitably reinforces stereotypical images of exoticism associated with those sounds. In the case of southern Italian folk music, it ends up reinforcing the image of the South as the Italian Other. Of course, this is not to say that local traditions should not be globally displayed. Rather, it reminds us to ask who gets to narrate the folk and the South. I will now return to Eugenio Bennato's performance of the song "Grande Sud" at the Festival di Sanremo on February 2008, which represents an important example of the national and global display of tarantella as supported by a local musician.

As illustrated in the third chapter, Bennato's increasing popularity within both national and global music scenes can be looked at as a point of departure from the local and a move toward the "ethnic" marketed by the world music label. I have also illustrated, however, how the powerful rhetoric embedded in his songs about the South still makes his music politically crucial to narrating the South today. When Neapolitan folk musician Eugenio Bennato, perhaps the biggest name of the current tarantella revival, participated in the Festival di San-remo, a national venue for Italian pop songs since the 1950s, his participation was widely noted by the media. Bennato had in fact finally managed to bring the *taranta* to the Festival di Sanremo. Watching tarantella music and dances performed on the Sanremo stage was definitely a first, and it also meant that the popularity of the tarantella revival had now reached the larger mainstream stage of Italian music. A live show with millions of viewers, the Sanremo Festival continues to be one of the most watched and discussed shows on Italian TV. Thus, for musicians and singers, performing at Sanremo means that their music acquires nationwide resonance; it means that their songs are going to be part of the larger imaginary of Italian song. In terms of performance, this carries great responsibility but also professional opportunities for the local musician to become nationally visible. While confined by TV and national fes-tival protocols, Bennato's staged and televised performance thus also enabled the representation as presence or visibility within the cultural industry of both southern Italian and Mediterranean musicians.

What makes this stage appearance especially important to this study is Ben-nato's choice to perform the song "Grande Sud," written and sung by a southern musician and explicitly narrating the South for a national audience. Thus, the performance of this song on the Sanremo stage becomes an important site to visualize the tarantella revival and analyze what happens to tarantella when it is performed for national consumption. Two different videos of this performance circulate on YouTube—one by Bennato and his chorus and another one mainly performed by him and his life and music partner, Pietra Montecorvino. In the first version, Bennato plays his acoustic guitar and sings, accompanied by clas-sic guitar, beating guitar, bass, and tambourine; a chorus of voices from Mo-roccan, Mozambique, Madagascar, and southern Italy sings in their respective languages—the Italian voices both in Italian and in southern languages—while one of the Italian singers also dances pizzica onstage. The second performance instead features Bennato and Montecorvino singing together at center stage, but soon joined by another musician singing in Arabic and performing rap. Bennato's choices in both performances, featured on different nights of the festival, reveal not only the many connections between narrating the South and narrating the Mediterranean, but also that, at the center stage of an Italian music festival, southern Italians and other peoples from the Mediterranean *can* in fact perform together. This means that they both get represented on national and world music scenes and that the southern and the Mediterranean are in dialogue with one another in performance, and at least in that one show this dialogue was not flattened into the mystified world music idea of "we are all one." In this sense, the "connections between the Mediterranean and the global South(s) are not meant to elide the differences and asymmetries. . . . Rather, they establish a transnational dialogue among peripheral zones that, despite their differences, share many commonalities" (Bouchard and Ferme 2013, 91). By sharing the stage with other Mediterranean voices who tell their own story, while southern Italians narrate theirs, and by showing respect for linguistic and cultural differences, Bennato's use of the world music stage makes a very powerful and critical statement.

Even as we stage tarantella (or "the popular," "the folk," "the local") through global performances, therefore, we must still exercise agency in narrating its history and in striving to convey its linguistic and cultural specificity. The result will always be a translated and transformed version of the local tarantella, but it can also become a valuable new sociocultural project with an important social impact, especially given the troubled conditions of Mediterranean immigrants living in Italy today. As Bock and Borland also remind us, "By examining these embodied practices, we hope to begin a conversation about how people engage with the cultural practices of others in ways that extend beyond processes of (mis)representation and mastery." At the same time, they also warn that "such an approach should not ignore the potential damage to others these practices might entail. It should, however, complicate our understanding of how and why people interpret and draw upon cultural differences in their own expressive behaviors" (2011, 6).

Another point to reflect on in this discussion is that, even when these romanticized ideas of the folk, the popular, and the local are deconstructed in scholarship, as I illustrated in the case of the tammurriata revival, local performers and audiences themselves often still cling to notions of the folk, place, and tradition as something fixed in time. While for performers and cultural brokers the claim to authenticity works both as a marketing strategy and as a political move aimed at garnering funds from local and national authorities, for many southern locals who have grown up with the traditional tammurriata festivals, this tends to be the only way to celebrate tammurriata. How should the folklorist and intellectual deal with such a complex network of experiences, interests, and values?

An important scholarly answer lies in the need to recognize that folk groups are, in fact, an "invention" as much as communities and nations are (Noyes 1995, 449). *Community* and *group* are in fact two much-debated terms within folklore studies scholarship, following Dan Ben-Amos's 1967 definition of folklore as "artistic communication in small groups" (quoted in Bronner 2002, 30). In folklore studies, this approach not only guaranteed the specificity of the folklorist's analysis, but also opened up his or her reflection to the exploration of the contested definitions of folklore, and of tradition, both within the same group and in relation to other groups. As Dorothy Noyes shows through her analysis of the Italian Market Festival in downtown Philadelphia, folk groups are often extremely heterogeneous units, where different members have different ideas about what the group is about, what connects group members together, and who belongs or doesn't belong to it. Proposing the alternative framework of "networks," Noyes concludes that although we (folklorists) may, in theory, believe in the integrity of groups, "working ethnographically, we are aware of the fragility of the group concept put to the test" (1995, 449). Roger Abrahams similarly complains that folklorists are not doing enough to address the increasing level of hybridity and multivocality of contemporary society; according to Abrahams, the very notion of community needs to be redefined according to this new perspective: "As long as we imagine folklore to reside primarily in small groups, especially those organically connected to the land in small and self-enclosed communities, we will continue to romanticize the folklore enterprise" (1993, 22). Foregrounding this fragility of a constructed "whole" and mapping the overlapping networks in which people are implicated thus become significant parts of the ethnographic project.

Another way in which this problem of representation has been dealt with in the scholarly sphere is by moving toward more autoethnographic types of research, that is, toward an either personal or situated perspective that allows for a deeper understanding of the topic studied. However, as shown in the last chapter, being Italian or having spent many years in the South does not solve the problem of representation in Belloni's case, nor does my participation in her workshop and familiarity with tarantella dancing. Even as I employ an autoethnographic approach, I am not able to *fully* discern, and make sense of, my double roles as an outsider-scholar and a local woman migrated to the United States. As a local, I cannot but cling to the genuine quality of the local festivals. How can I speak about my South without clinging to a sense of its authenticity?

Yet as I write about southern cultural traditions for foreign and global audiences, I am aware and hopeful of not only the social implications but also the social impact of my work. As I suggest in the introduction, several factors motivated me to conduct this study. First was the need to provide U.S. academic and cultural audiences with a local perspective on tarantella, one that takes into consideration the place-specific knowledge and community values embedded in this folk dance tradition. By illustrating this perspective, I hoped to provide a deeper, more historically and culturally layered, understanding of tarantella than the one displayed by world music, while at the same time reminding myself and my southern Italian readers that our local perspectives, far from being the only valuable and authentic ones, are in fact multiple, dynamic, and as ideologically driven as national, diasporic, and global perspectives. Furthermore, as a southern Italian writing for a U.S. audience, I am committed to challenging the idealized image of Italian culture constantly reiterated by U.S. popular culture generally, and by centuries of Italian music in particular, and to highlight the historical, cultural, and linguistic complexity of Italy. While I am aware of how other scholars and I too have limitations as both linguistic and cultural brokers, our social, cultural or aesthetic, and political investment is an inherent part of our work, and it most certainly plays an important role in the struggle that any affirmation or translation of cultural tradition necessarily entails.

As cultural brokers work at the conjuncture of local specificity and global reception, we should especially reflect upon and treasure Gramsci's lesson about the important task of the intellectual in the larger cultural and political spheres. This task, I suggest in relation to the current tammurriata festival scene in Italy, is ultimately one entailing responsibility toward both the local communities we are translating from and the international and global audiences we are writing for. If we accept the definition of "tradition" as the "transfer of responsibility for a valued practice or performance" (Noyes 2009, 234), then as we broker cultural traditions we need to constantly "assum[e] our responsibility to our own past and our own hoped-for future" and remind ourselves that, even as it is "unavoidably constrained by its own dispersed and often stigmatized tradition, our accumulated disciplinary knowledge offers some insight into the nature of hand-to-hand transfers" (249). To put it, once again, in the words of local performer and student Peppe Dionisio, "attention, passion, and respect" are something that, as engaged scholars, we cannot afford to forget.

Here I have tried to fulfill this responsibility by addressing the multivocality of the tarantella traditions, by providing examples of different dynamics and problematics involved in translating tarantella for a global audience, and by addressing the risks of flattening these diverse representations of southern Italian folk music, and of the South more generally, into one reductive image, that of the "global tarantella."

Notes

Introduction

1. The Italian "brain drain" movement refers to the exodus of Italian intellectuals, artists, and especially academic scholars since the 1990s; a 2004 study calculated that between 1990 and 1998, among Italian emigrants the number of people with degrees quadrupled (*Economist,* June 6, 2011). For more details, see Foadi 2006.

2. Raffaele Inserra grew up and lives today in the small town of Gragnano, in the province of Naples, where I also grew up and lived until 2004. We also happen to share a surname, since Inserra is a very common name in the area; while we are not immediately related, having common relatives and family friends certainly helped secure his collaboration and support during my interview with him as well as my fieldwork research in the area.

3. While the Italian "brain drain" is currently contributing to an increasing number of Italian scholars and researchers moving to the University of Hawai'i, since I moved to Hawai'i in 2004 I have encountered only a few people from southern Italy; in addition, southern Italian folk music and dances remain a niche cultural trend even among southern Italians, even as the larger population is more and more exposed to them within the current revival phenomenon.

4. In standard Italian, "tarantella napol*e*tana" is a more common spelling (emphasis added).

5. Its common attribution to Neapolitan painter and writer Salvator Rosa (Paliotti 1992; Cossentino 2013) already testifies to tarantella's gradual move away from folk music and toward a more refined music and dance form.

6. Several scholars of the post-1990s tarantella revival have further developed De Martino's study and in some cases moved beyond De Martino's to illustrate the centrality of the trance element within the tarantism phenomenon (Lapassade 2001; De Giorgi 1999) and the similarities between tarantism and other cults of possession around the world, as well as between southern Italian and other examples of Mediterranean tarantella and tarantism (De Giorgi 1999). See, in particular, the Italian volume *Trance, guarigione, mito: Antropologia e storia del tarantismo* (2000), curated by Gino Di Mitri.

7. All translations from Italian, as well as from the Neapolitan language common to the city of Naples and the Campania region, are mine unless otherwise noted. Neapolitan was recently established as an official Italian language by UNESCO (1995–2010), but also a "vulnerable" one since it is gradually weakening due to the pressure of standard Italian both in school and in the media. This is one of the reasons why many contemporary writers do not follow a common orthography; for example, the phrase *ballo sul tamburo* (or dance on the drum) can be written in Neapolitan as "balle 'ncopp' 'o tambur," where *tambur* is the same as *tammurre* or *tambure*, à la variants of the standard Italian *tamburo* (drum).

8. De Martino argues that this interpretation created an "irreconcilable conflict between the popular ideology of the *taranta* and the new science," which then led to the "progressive folkloric isolation [of tarantism] and its gradual reduction to a 'relic' and 'fragment'" (2005, 235).

9. In 2004 the group changed its name to Spakka-Neapolis 55.

10. As Bennato puts it, "When on a ternary base the chant suddenly explodes, in an unexpected binary pattern, it creates a swing effect, and therefore a sense of disruption, as if the *tarantato*, past or present, was caught between a reassuring basic rhythm and an unpredictable chant pattern" (2001, 91).

11. The Neapolitan equivalent of Italian *tamburo* (drum). Tammurriata is also called "tammorriata" in standard Italian by nonlocal performers and practitioners.

12. As the dance component has acquired a complex structure with many geographical variants, so has the singing component been used for different purposes, namely, as a narrative subtext to the dance choreography, as an invitation to dance, as a dialogue between the protagonists (singers), and as a representation of everyday or extraordinary events through the use of pantomime. A complex and interdisciplinary art form by definition, *canto a ballo* has been used to express the collective identity of a group or a community and represents one of the most successful forms of social interaction. According to Gala (1993), the presence of a textual component allows for a verbal exchange among the participants and for the singers to "show off" their vocal abilities; at the same time, the dance allows for physical expressions of love, physical strength, and competition among group members, while also educating the participants to the accepted norms of social behavior and body posture.

13. Schneider explains, "Italy was certainly affected by Orientalism. For, although the imperial powers of the north did not envision the Italian peninsula as a land they had to colonize—its inhabitants were European Christians, after all—it was nevertheless their goal that Italian resources and products circulate freely in international

markets, that Italian markets be open to English and French manufacturers, and that Italian elites share and support the world civilization system that these powers believed it was their prerogative to create. As such they critically scrutinized the divergent polities of the peninsula on the eve of their unification in 1860, much to the disadvantage of the Neapolitan Kingdom of the Two Sicilies that governed the Southern region and Sicily" (1998, 5).

14. This position also ends up perpetuating a commonly held assumption at the time, both in European and in U.S. scholarship, that folklore is by definition something belonging to the past and about to vanish (Bendix 1997).

15. On July 7, 2015, the Italian newspaper *IlSole24ore* reported data collected by the Registry of Italians Resident Abroad (AIRE); according to this data, in 2014 the number of Italian nationals migrated abroad was more than one hundred thousand, the largest number since 2004 (Nava). The article also warns that the actual number of Italians requesting a visa in foreign countries is often much larger than the number registered by AIRE. According to another 2015 report, the *Dossier Statistico Immigrazione,* in 2014 the number of Italians migrating abroad has grown faster than the number of foreign immigrants to the country for the first time since 1994 (Programma Integra).

16. In an article that appeared on April 13, 2015, the Italian newspaper *La Stampa* reports a large gap in terms of 2014 unemployment rates between southern and northern regions, with the South carrying an unemployment rate of more than 20 percent—similar to Spain and Greece—against much lower rates in the North, including the city of Bolzano with 4.4 percent, even lower than Germany (Baroni 2015).

17. The increasing interest in the Southern Question on the part of both Italian and Italian American scholars can in turn be understood within a larger critical movement toward a reassessment of postcolonialism in Italy, which draws on the history of southern Italy as both an internal colony and a migration host for populations coming from its former colonies and from elsewhere in Europe, North Africa, and the Mediterranean (Verdicchio 1997; Chambers 2008; Lombardi-Diop and Romeo 2012). Neapolitan musician Eugenio Bennato's recent work with the tarantella rhythms, for example, explicitly moves in this direction.

18. In the words of Neapolitan singer Teresa De Sio, Salentine music, much more so than the more melodic and refined Neapolitan music, contains "a very dark aspect, linked to a violent gesture that cannot be made without beating your hand on the skin of the drum. It is a music . . . that follows a psychedelic rhythm and repetitiveness. . . . [I]t is something that takes you into trance" (Romanazzi 2006, 11).

Chapter 1. A Brief History of the Tarantella Revival

1. Leydi remains one of the major scholars of Italian ethnomusicology; his volume *Il folk revival italiano* (1972) represents a reference point for any study of Italian folk music still today.

2. *Saracen* is a generic term for "Muslim" widely common in Europe since the Middle Ages; in Naples, in particular, Saracens, or *sarracini,* often appear as a theme in the *canzone napoletana* genre.

3. The name "Zézi," masculine plural form of "zeza," comes from old street-theater figures, who went around villages to represent "The Song of Zeza," a comedy centered on the Neapolitan trickster figure of Pulcinella and his wife, Zeza. See their website, http://www.zezi.it/sito/.

4. "Flobert" is the name of the fireworks factory where the explosion occurred.

5. In an interview, singer Marcello Colasurdo, for many years a leading figure in the group, comments on this aspect: "Alfasud has been a mess. . . . [Alfasud] has changed the life of the country, but it has also brought cultural backwardness. . . . Some workers used to say: 'It's true that in the fields I had to work more hours, [but] I worked when I wanted, and I could breathe fresh air, and if I wanted to lie down I could do it. Even working for fourteen or fifteen hours a day, the rhythms were not the same as here [in Alfasud]" (quoted in Vacca 1999, 109).

6. The continued interest in *pizzica* and its relation to tarantism is evident not only in the Italian context but also in the international one, as suggested by several European and North American publications. See, for example, Daboo 2010, Lundgren 2008, Lüdtke 2009, and Blackstone 2009.

7. The history of the festival and its protagonists since its start in 1998 is narrated by musical critic and essayist Pierfrancesco Pacoda in his 2012 study, *Tarantapatia: Le lunghe notti della taranta.* The book focuses on the role of the many *maestri concertatori*, or artistic directors, who have alternated on the festival stage and contributed with their artistic choices to transforming the notion of *taranta* into a global and cosmopolitan phenomenon.

8. Gargano is the name of a geographical area in the province of Foggia, in the Apulia region, that is located by the Adriatic Sea.

9. Both terms *pizzicato* and *tarantolato* refer to the person metaphorically bitten by the tarantula, who then develops the spider-bite syndrome.

10. Torsello also notes that the changing fortune of De Martino's 1961 famous study of tarantella's music and dance therapy in the past fifty years is directly related to the changing attitudes toward folk culture in Italy. Not very popular at the time of its publication, the book remained unnoticed until the 1970s, precisely because it was about the Southern Question and the marginality and poverty of the South (2006b, 29). At the time of its publication, in fact many complained that focusing on tarantism, as well as on other aspects of folk culture, would be detrimental to the promotion of modernization and tourism in the southern regions. The 1970s folk-revival movement, however, spurred a renewed attention to *cultura popolare* (folk culture); in this new scenario, De Martino's study of tarantism received new attention in academic circles, and in the 1980s several scholars, including French anthropologist George Lapassade, started taking ethnographic trips to Salento, following in De Martino's steps. By the early 1990s, De Martino's work was fully reappraised within Italian academia; this rediscovery coincided with the increasing curiosity of scholars and tourists toward the music and dance rituals of tarantella. Finally in 2005, De Martino's book was translated into English.

11. *Mezzogiorno* is another term for southern Italy.

12. In 2011 the book was translated into English as *Southern Thought, and Other Essays on the Mediterranean*, coedited and cotranslated by Norma Bouchard and Valerio Ferme.

Chapter 2. Exporting Southern Italian Festivals from South to North

1. Giuseppe (Peppe) Dionisio, discussion with the author, Scafati, Italy, June 11, 2009.

2. Raffaele Inserra, discussion with the author, Lettere (Naples), June 6, 2009.

3. While my initial fieldwork dates back to the 2007–10 period, I was able to conduct several interviews in the summer of 2014, when I also had the opportunity to return to some of the calendrical festivals and participate in several tammurriata events unrelated to the older festivals.

4. Groups formed by several musicians who visit different festivals and are often invited to perform on the stage. Each area or town has its own *paranza*, and it is a matter of pride both for the group and for the community it comes from (Lamanna 2004).

5. Rosa Maurelli, discussion with the author, Milan, June 10, 2014; Francesca Di Ieso and Armando Illario, discussion with the author, Milan, June 12, 16, 2014; Valeria Lista, e-mail to the author, August 28, 2014.

6. Antonio Matrone, conversation with the author, Lettere (Naples), July 26, 2014.

7. "E vvide 'sti guagliune? Chill'anno 'a sulo venì â festa cu' 'a butteglia 'e vino, pensano ca chéll' è 'a festa.... [C]histi so' fricchettoni.... [P]utessero ij all'agriturismo a fa' 'a stessa cosa."

8. The title of this section draws on Karen Lüdtke's book (2009), which provides an in-depth analysis of time and space dynamics at play within the pizzica revitalization phenomenon.

9. It is actually difficult to generalize even for this type of events; for example, the genesis of the Notte della Tammorra Festival, initiated by the Canto di Virgilio association and directed by Neapolitan musician Carlo Faiello, draws inspiration from an old feast that takes place in the Neapolitan town of Nola in concomitance with the Epiphany celebration (January 6) and signals an encounter and exchange between older and younger music and dance practitioners. The festival takes place in Naples around the summer solstice and applies the same format to an urban music festival, while also paying homage to the Catholic celebration of San Giovanni (Saint John) (Faiello 2005b).

10. Ugo Maiorano, discussion with the author, Pagani (Salerno), July 21, 2014.

11. Tiziana Torelli, e-mail to the author, July 22, 2014.

12. Pasquale Pierri, conversation with the author, Salerno, July 7, 2014.

13. Figures 13 and 14 show musicians and festival participants in the church of the Madonna dei Bagni on May 6, 2016 (photo by Luigi Coppola). Bringing music inside the church as homage to the Madonna is a long-standing practice in this festival, as I was able to observe on several occasions.

14. Andrea Iozzino, conversation with the author, Castellammare di Stabia (Naples), July 9, 2014.

15. Torelli, e-mail to the author.

16. Luigi Coppola, conversation with the author, Agerola (Naples), July 19, 2014.

17. This phrase, first used in the early 2000s following a police investigation, refers to a vast area around the provinces of Naples and Caserta in the Campania region, sadly famous for the presence of toxic waste, which is often burned, giving rise to unprecedented pollution problems. These illegal activities, often conducted in agricultural areas, are operated by the local Mafia, or *camorra,* and often with the complicity of northern companies, who also dump on these sites, as famously described by Neapolitan journalist Roberto Saviano in his best-selling book *Gomorrah* (2007). As a result, the "Land of Fires" has been defined as the biggest underground dump in Europe (Borrelli 2015).

18. Ferraiuolo also worked on a documentary film on the topic titled *The Tammorra Displaced* (2005).

19. "Forse è per questo che le donne suonano di solito solo strumenti che consentono un atteggiamento fisico più composto, quali il flauto, il violino, il pianoforte e, naturalmente, la voce. . . . Il discorso del ballo va in maniera simile: ci si aspetta che la donna balli, perché il corpo della donna che ondeggia in maniera sexy è un valore nel sistema estetico moderno."

20. Raffaella Coppola, Facebook message to the author, October 21, 2012.

21. See Raiola's documentary films *Tam-Tam Tammorra* (1999) and *Voci del popolo contadino* (2007).

22. Canto Antico Movimenti, http://www.cantoantico.it/. The website has recently changed, and this statement cannot be found anymore; the updated home page focuses on the notion of "South Beat," the group's most recent project, while at the same reiterating the importance of the southern roots: "The South is music, spirit, life. . . . South Beat is our way of narrating this, it is artistic research that combines cultural diversity, current cultural expressions and knowledge of the past, within an individualistic urban landscape, which more than ever needs to retrieve expressivity and choral breath."

23. Antonio Ricci and Armando Soldano, conversation with the author, Milan, June 12, 2014. See also my interviews with Rosa Maurelli, Ashti Abdo, and Filippo Renna.

24. Gino Perri, discussion with the author, Milan, July 4, 2014. Perri has helped manage Metromondo for more than fifteen years and has largely collaborated on many tarantella events in Milan.

25. The type of song called *fronna* or *fronne 'e limone* is a full-throated, improvised type of song that is not accompanied by any instruments and allows the singers to initiate a creative dialogue with some fixed patterns but also much room for improvisation (De Simone 1979).

26. Ashti Abdo and Filippo Renna, discussion with the author, Milan, June 17, 2014.

27. Arci, or Associazione Ricreativa e Culturale Italiana (Italian Recreational and Cultural Association), is an association that promotes various cultural activities and operates within a left-wing ideological framework.

28. It is important to note that as of 2015 there is an equivalent page for tammurriata aficionados in Campania as well.

29. Antonio Ricci and Armando Soldano, conversation with the author.

30. "Fare divulagazione di una cultura che in realtà è la fotografia di un pezzo d'Italia che non esiste nei libri, nella storia ufficiale, andare un pò a distruggere quell'immagine olografica, il cliché . . . [quella musica] è un'altra cosa, c'è una poetica, c'è una musica, c'è una storia, una funzione, un rito etc."

31. "Raccontare un sud possibile diverso che non è nostalgico, che non è un cliché, e che è anche una proposta musicale italiana alternative."

32. "Un mondo fatto in un certo modo, fatto di relazioni, passato attorno al tavolo la domenica."

33. "Gli fai una pizzica e si esaltano, non posso immaginare che quella è la punta di un iceberg di un mondo complesso pieno di contraddizioni, di cose anche orrende."

34. Gianpiero Caruso, conversation with the author, Milan, June 19, 2009.

35. "Ed è questo concetto che è alla base del south beat"; "la pulsazione sud e l'appartenenza che noi ci portiamo dentro ma che non guarda indietro con nostalgia, ma va, si mouove verso altre pulsazioni."

36. Its name derives from the local town of Pimonte.

Chapter 3. Images of the Italian South within and beyond World Music

1. "Putipù" refers to a folk music instrument common to southern Italy, particularly in Naples and surrounding areas; it is a type of friction drum featuring a closed cylindrical sound box with a bamboo cane attached at the center.

2. Nuie simme d' 'o Sud
   nuie simme curte e nire
   nuie simme buone pe' cantà
   e faticamme a faticà . . . venimme d' 'o Sud
   e camminamme a pere
   datece 'o tiemp d'arrivà
   pcché venimme d' 'o Sud
   'O sole
   'o mare
   'o ciel blu
   'o mandulin e 'o putipù
   'e pummarole p'o ragù
   'a pizza, 'a muzzarella
   'o core 'e mamma e 'a tarantella
   'e maccarune pe' magnà

'nu filo 'e voce pe' cantà
è overe o nun è overe?
Ma facitece 'o piacere
pcché nuie simme d' 'o Sud.

3. Sanfedismo was a popular anti-Republican movement, which activated peasants against the Parthenopaean Republic in 1799 and ultimately contributed to the restoration of the Bourbon Kingdom of Naples under Ferdinand I of the Two Sicilies. Its members were called Sanfedisti.

4. *Villanella* is a rural song genre originating in Naples and was very popular by the sixteenth century. It was a parodic reaction against the more refined madrigal; however, some of the most famous *villanelle* were composed by madrigal poets. *Villanella* represented, therefore, a sort of conversation between the music culture of the Spanish court and the folk culture of the lower classes (Gala 1992). For this reason as a genre, *villanelle* well suited NCCP's music project as part of the larger 1970s folk music revival; from there comes Bennato's familiarity with this form. NCCP conducted careful work of research and musical arrangement on sixteenth-century *villanella* and tarantella in Naples, while at the same time composing several new songs in the *villanella* and tarantella mode.

5. Their name refers to one of the main streets of Roman origins that divides the modern city of Naples in two parts. As of 2004, their name is Spakka-Neapolis 55.

6. Taranta Power, http://www.tarantapower.it/en/chi_siamo.aspx.

7. Ibid.

8. Ibid.

9. The ending in the Italian original contains the phrase *a tarallucce e vino* (literally "with biscuits and wine"), a phrase that is used in Neapolitan to denote a general idea of an argument that ends well, but also implies that there is no solution to the problem and the arguers simply decide to make up with a glass of wine. Therefore, to die "*a tarallucce e vino*" implies a typical Italian way of postponing problems by eating and drinking on it, which in this case is ironically attributed to one's death.

10. This commitment to denouncing the sociocultural conditions of the South can also be noted in the work of Neapolitan artist Daniele Sepe, whose music interests range from ethnic sounds to jazz, chamber music, and workers' songs; Sepe deserves special mention here both for his interpretation of southern folk songs and for his role as a "social agitator." Debuting with E Zézi in the 1970s, Sepe has become known, both in Italy and abroad, thanks to his folk music albums *Vite Perdite* (1994) and *Viaggi fuori dai paraggi* (1996). Released during the height of the post-1990s folk music revival, these albums recover tarantella rhythms from several regions through a skillful and unique musical style, while also adding South American and other world music rhythms. The award-winning 1998 album *Lavorare stanca* (Work is tiring), which discusses the nepotism of the Italian workplace through an eclectic musical style, helped confirm Sepe's role together with rap groups in the Italian subcultural scene. Renowned on the world music scene, Sepe represents one of

the many faces of the current folk music revival, especially one of the most politically engaged ones. Most of his albums are distributed by alternative labels, such as *Il Manifesto,* the historical newspaper of the Italian extreme left wing. Following a tradition initiated with the 1970s folk music revival, and in particular with the countercultural model represented by E Zézi, Bennato and Sepe have carried on this commitment in today's music scene.

11. 'Ndrangheta and *sacra corona unita* are terms used to describe organized crimes in the southern regions of Calabria and Sardinia, respectively.

12. Coming from the Apulia region, their music has been labeled *tarantamuffin* for its mix of Jamaican ragamuffin (reggae and rap together) and tarantella (Plastino 1996).

13. As William Anselmi puts it, "This particular form of hybridization conveys tradition and otherness in terms of their similarity as a means to re-appropriate one's anthropological culture embedded in a discourse of militancy against oppressive Power, whatever its globalized expression" (2002, 40).

14. *Terrone* (singular) is a common derogatory term to describe migrants from the South of Italy. The term derives from *terra* ("land" or "dirt") and refers to those who dig in the earth and therefore are dirty and unrefined.

15. Quoted in Bouchard and Ferme 2013, 114. Here is the original text:

No global quella musica e quella sabbia d'Africa . . .
No global quella tammuriata . . .
No global chistu canto c'appartene a nu brigante
e accussì pure si gira o munno
no global sarà.

16. Risorgimento was a political and social movement started in the early decades of the nineteenth century and culminating in the independence of Italy from foreign influence and a unified Kingdom of Italy.

17. Noi con i 'fratelli' scesi giù dal settentrione
che ci hanno 'liberato' per formare una 'Nazione'
Noi sotto lo stesso tricolore,
dalle Alpi fino al mare
Ma se diventiamo una questione?
La Questione è Meridionale.

18. *Paisà* is a southern term meaning "paesano," that is, from the village. It is very common among Italians migrated abroad, since for many of them the village dimension was more immediately comprehensible than the idea of a nationally unified Italy, especially since the idea of a unified Italy was mostly a recent one and, in the case of southerners, also one that they did not share.

19. In 2012 Bennato and Aprile worked together also on the music show *Profondo Sud* (Deep South), featuring Bennato's music as well as excerpts from Aprile's books and focusing on the history of the colonization of the Italian South and its legacy within the Italian sociocultural milieu.

Chapter 4. Tarantella for U.S., Italian American, and Cosmopolitan Markets

1. See also Belloni's website, http://www.alessandrabelloni.com/.

2. My analysis of this performance is based on my organization and observation of the workshop that Belloni held on the University of Hawai'i's Mānoa campus in 2006, 2007, 2008, 2010, and 2013; on my participation in Belloni's concert at Red Elephant, Honolulu, on April 29, 2006; on her website information and other publications; and on my interview of (February 2013) and informal conversations with Belloni as well as with several Italian American women and artists who also work with the tarantella genre and who in some cases have been in direct contact with Belloni—namely, Michela Musolino, Mary Ciuffitelli, Natalie Marrone, and Anabella Lenzu.

3. The phrase "Mediterranean Volcano," reported on Belloni's website as well as in Luisa Del Giudice's interview with Belloni (Del Giudice 2009a), has been often used to describe Belloni's personal and artistic energy and fits well with the image of passionate (southern) Italian culture that she conveys in her shows and workshops.

4. The video trailer can be found at http://vimeo.com/channels/livingshamanism/59786628.

5. Alessandra Belloni, discussion with the author, Honolulu, February 28, 2013.

6. Natalie Marrone and The Dance Cure, *The Dance Cure*, 2003.

7. Michela Musolino, discussion with the author, January 22, 2013.

8. Mary Ciuffitelli, discussion with the author, February 7, 2013.

9. Natalie Marrone, discussion with the author, February 1, 2013.

10. http://www.duronia.com/tonymorsella.htm.

11. Anna L. Chairetakis's work of research and recording continued into the 1980s, as testified by the 1986 anthology, with Domenico Carbone and Filippo Riggio, *Chesta e la Voci ca Canuscite: Southern Italian Mountain Music from Calabria, Campania, Basilicata, and Abruzzi.*

12. Chairetakis's work of research and recording with Calabrian groups in Brooklyn in 1975, particularly their performances of Calabrian *villanella* is discussed in detail in her article "Tears of Blood" (1993).

13. Italian Folk Art Federation of America, http://www.italianfolkartfederation.org.

14. The result was the publication of two albums: *Canto d'amore: Canti, suoni, voci nella Grecia salentina* (Love song: Songs, sounds, and voices from the Griko-speaking area of the Salento), translated by Luisa Del Giudice, with Edizioni Aramirè (Lecce, 2000), and *Bonasera a quista casa: Antonio Aloisi, Antonio Bandello "Gli Ucci": Pizziche, stornelli, canti salentini,* by Luigi Chiriatti, translated by Luisa Del Giudice, Edizioni Aramirè (Lecce, 1999) (Del Giudice 2005b, xv).

15. Anabella Lenzu, http://www.anabellalenzu.com/.

16. Anabella Lenzu, discussion with the author, New York, January 29, 2013.

Works Cited

Abrahams, Roger D. 1993. "Phantoms of Romantic Nationalism in Folkloristics." *Journal of American Folklore* 106, no. 419: 3–37.

"Alessandra Belloni and the Daughters of Cybele." 2013. *Percussive Notes* (September): 18–19.

Anselmi, William. 2002. "From Cantautori to Posse: Sociopolitical Discourse, Engagement and Antagonism in the Italian Music Scene from the Sixties to the Nineties." In *Music, Popular Culture, Identities,* edited by Richard Young, 17–45. Amsterdam: Editions Rodopi.

Apolito, Paolo. 2000. "Tarantismo, identità locale, postmodernità." In *Quarant'anni dopo De Martino: Atti del convegno internazionale di studi sul tarantismo,* edited by Gino L. Di Mitri, 1:137–46. Nardò, Italy: Besa.

Appadurai, Arjun. 1996. *Modernity at Large: Cultural Dimensions of Globalization.* Minneapolis: University of Minnesota Press.

Aprile, Pino. 2011. *Terroni: All That Has Been Done to Ensure That the Italians of the South Became "Southerners."* New York: Bordighera Press.

Aubert, Laurent. 2007. *The Music of the Other: New Challenges for Ethnomusicology in a Global Age.* Translated by Carla Ribiero. Burlington, Vt.: Ashgate.

Ausiello, Emilio, and Michele Maione. 2012. *Tammurrianti: Metodo pratico per tammorra e tamburello.* Vol. 1, *Approccio alle tecniche tradizionali.* Naples: Polosud.

Baroni, Paolo. 2015. "Disoccupati: L'Italia divisa tra inferno e paradiso." *La Stampa,* April 13.

Barwick, Linda. 2012. "'Oltre l'Australia, c'è la luna': Maggio Garfagnino and the Emigrant Experience." In *Italy in Australia's Musical Landscape,* edited by Linda Barwick and Marcello Sorce Keller, 179–200. Melbourne: Lyrebird Press.

Bauman, Richard, and Charles L. Briggs. 2003. *Voices of Modernity: Language Ideologies and the Politics of Inequality.* Cambridge: Cambridge University Press.

Belloni, Alessandra. 2007. *Rhythm Is the Cure: Southern Italian Tambourine.* Pacific, Mo.: Mel Bay.

Bendix, Regina. 1989. "Tourism and Cultural Displays: Inventing Traditions for Whom?" *Journal of American Folklore* 162: 131–46.

———. 1997. *In Search of Authenticity: The Formation of Folklore Studies.* Madison: University of Wisconsin Press.

Bennato, Eugenio. 2001. "Le leggi musicali della tarantella." In *Tarantismo e neotarantismo,* edited by Anna Nacci, 83–92. Nardò, Italy: Besa.

———. 2010. *Brigante se more: Viaggio nella musica del sud.* Rome: Coniglio Editore.

———. 2013. *Ninco Nanco deve morire: Viaggio nella storia e nella musica del Sud.* Soveria Mannelli, Italy: Rubbettino editore.

Bennato, Eugenio, and Carlo D'Angiò. 1987. *A sud di Mozart.* Naples: Pironti.

Bermani, Cesare. 1997. *Una storia cantata, 1962–1997: Trentacinque anni di attività del Nuovo Canzoniere Italiano.* Milan: Editoriale Jaca Book.

Bevilacqua, Salvatore. 2003. "Tarantismo e slancio della musica etnica nel Mezzogiorno d'Italia: Nessi sociali molteplici di una produzione culturale che rivisita la questione meridionale." In *L'eredità di Diego Carpitella: Etnomusicologia, antropologia e ricerca storica nel Salento e nell'area mediterranea,* edited by Maurizio Agamennone and Gino L. Di Mitri, 385–401. Nardò, Italy: Besa Editrice.

Biagi, Laura. 2004. "Spider Dreams: Ritual and Performance in Apulian Tarantismo and Tarantella." Ph.D. diss., New York University.

Bianco, Carla. 1974. *The Two Rosetos.* Bloomington: Indiana University Press.

Birnbaum, Lucia Chiavola. 1993. *Black Madonnas: Feminism, Religion, and Politics in Italy.* Boston: Northeastern University Press.

Blackstone, Robert Lee. 2009. "'The Spider Is Alive': Reassessing Becker's Theory of Artistic Conventions through Southern Italian Music." *Symbolic Interaction* 32, no. 3: 184–206.

Bock, Sheila, and Katherine Borland. 2011. "Exotic Identities: Dance, Difference, and Self-Fashioning." *Journal of Folklore Research* 48, no. 1: 1–36.

Boissevain, Jeremy. 1992. Introduction to *Revitalizing European Rituals,* edited by Jeremy Boissevain, 1–19. London and New York: Routledge.

———. 2008. "Some Notes on Tourism and the Revitalization of Calendrical Festivals." *Journal of Mediterranean Studies* 18, no. 1: 17–42.

Borio, Gianni. 2013. "Music as Plea for Political Action: The Presence of Musicians in Italian Protest Movements around 1968." *Music and Protest in 1968:* 29–45.

Borland, Katherine. 2009. "Embracing Difference: Salsa Fever in New Jersey." *Journal of American Folklore* 122, no. 486: 466–92.

Born, Georgina, and Dave Hesmondhalgh. 2000. "Introduction: On Difference, Representation and Appropriation in Music." In *Western Music and Its Others: Difference, Representation, and Appropriation in Music,* edited by Georgina Born and Dave Hesmondhalgh, 1–58. Berkeley: University of California Press.

Borrelli, Antonio. 2015. "A Caserta la più grande discarica sotterranea d'Europa." *Il Giornale,* June 16.

Bouchard, Norma, and Valerio Ferme, eds. and trans. 2011. *Southern Thought, and Other Essays on the Mediterranean.* Race and Ethnic Studies. New York: Fordham University Press.

———. 2013. *Italy and the Mediterranean: Words, Sounds, and Images of the Post–Cold War Era.* New York: Palgrave.

Briggs, Charles L. 1996. "The Politics of Discursive Authority in Research on the 'Invention of Tradition.'" *Cultural Anthropology* 11, no. 4: 435–69.

Briggs, Charles L., and Richard Bauman. 1992. "Genre, Intertextuality, and Social Power." *Journal of Linguistic Anthropology* 2, no. 2: 131–72.

Bronner, Simon J. 2002. *Folk Nation: Folklore in the Creation of American Tradition.* Lanham, Md.: Rowman & Littlefield.

Brooks, Iris. 1996. "Alessandra Belloni." *Percussion Source* 1, no. 2: 26–29.

Cachafeiro, Margarita Gómez-Reino. 2002. *Ethnicity and Nationalism in Italian Politics.* Burlington, Vt.: Ashgate.

Calandra Italian American Institute. 2007. "Folk Music and Modernity in Southern Italy." http://qcpages.qc.cuny.edu/calandra/folk-music-and-modernity-southern-italy.

Camuffo, Francesco. 2004. "I repertori della tradizione musicale campana." In *Tammurriate: Canti, musiche e devozioni in Campania,* edited by Antonello Lamanna, 142–49. Rome: Adnkronos.

Canclini, Nestor Garcia. 1995. *Hybrid Cultures: Strategies for Entering and Leaving Modernity.* Minneapolis: University of Minnesota Press.

Carnevale, Nancy C. 2009. *A New Language, a New World: Italian Immigrants in the United States, 1980–1945.* Urbana: University of Illinois Press.

Carpitella, Diego. 1974. "Ethnomusicology in Italy." In "Folklore Studies in Italy." Special issue, *Journal of the Folklore Institute* 11, nos. 1–2: 81–98.

Carrera, Alessandro. 2001. "Folk Music and Popular Song from the Nineteenth Century to the 1990s." In *The Cambridge Companion to Modern Italian Culture,* edited by Zygmunt G. Baranski and Rebecca J. West, 325–35. Cambridge: Cambridge University Press.

Cassano, Franco. 1996 [2005]. *Il pensiero meridiano.* Bari: Laterza.

Catalano, Roberto F. 1999. Review of *Italian Treasury: The Alan Lomax Collection* [Rounder Records, 1999]. *Music & Anthropology* 4.

Cestellini, Daniele, and Giovanni Pizza. 2004. "La 'tradizione' contesa: Riflessioni sulla scissione del Gruppo Musicale Operaio 'E Zézi.'" In *Tammurriate: Canti, musiche e devozioni in Campania,* edited by Antonello Lamanna, 46–88. Rome: Adnkronos.

Chairetakis, Anna L. 1993. "Tears of Blood: The Calabrian Villanella and Immigrant Epiphanies." In *Studies in Italian American Folklore,* edited by Luisa Del Giudice, 11–51. Logan: Utah State University Press.

Chairetakis, Anna L., Domenico Carbone, and Filippo Riggio. 1986. *Chesta e la Voci ca Canuscite: Southern Italian Mountain Music from Calabria, Campania, Basilicata, and Abruzzi.* Recorded in the Niagara Frontier Region. New York: Global Village Music 675.

Chambers, Iain. 2008. *Mediterranean Crossings: The Politics of an Interrupted Modernity.* Durham, N.C.: Duke University Press.

Cohen, Erik. 1988. "Authenticity and Commoditization in Tourism." *Annals of Tourism Research* 15, no. 3: 371–86.

Cohen, Ronald D., ed. 2003. *Alan Lomax: Selected Writings, 1934–1997.* London: Routledge.

Cossentino, Raffaele. 2013. *La canzone napoletana dalle origini ai nostri giorni: Storia e protagonisti.* Naples: Rogiosi Editore.

Cresswell, Tim. 2004. *Place: A Short Introduction.* Malden, Mass.: Blackwell.

Daboo, Jerri. 2010. *Ritual, Rapture and Remorse: A Study of Tarantism and Pizzica in Salento.* New York: Peter Lang.

De Giorgi, Pierpaolo. 1999. *Tarantismo e rinascita: I riti musicali e coreutici della pizzica-pizzica e della tarantella.* Lecce, Italy: Argo.

Del Giudice, Luisa. 1994. "Italian Traditional Song in Toronto: From Autobiography to Advocacy." *Journal of Canadian Studies* 29, no. 1: 74–89.

———. 2005a. "The Folk Music Revival and the Culture of Tarantismo in the Salento." In *Performing Ecstasies: Music, Dance, and Ritual in the Mediterranean,* edited by Luisa Del Giudice and Nancy van Deusen, 217–66. Ottawa: Institute of Mediaeval Music.

———. 2005b. Introduction and acknowledgments to *Performing Ecstasies: Music, Dance, and Ritual in the Mediterranean,* edited by Luisa Del Giudice and Nancy Van Deusen, xv–xviii. Ottawa: Institute for Mediaeval Music.

———. 2009a. "Alessandra Belloni: In Her Own Words." In *Oral History, Oral Culture, and Italian Americans,* edited by Luisa Del Giudice, 193–252. New York: Palgrave Macmillan.

———. 2009b. "Speaking Memory: Oral History, Oral Culture, and Italians in America." In *Oral History, Oral Culture, and Italian Americans,* edited by Luisa Del Giudice, 3–18. New York: Palgrave Macmillan.

———. 2016. "Folk Revival, Migrations, and Cultural Politics in the Italian Diaspora." Paper presented at Musicians in the Mediterranean: Narratives of Movement, a joint symposium of the International Council for Traditional Music and the International Musicological Society, Naples, June 24.

Del Giudice, Luisa, and Gerald Porter. 2001. Introduction to *Imagined States: Nationalism, Utopia, and Longing in Oral Cultures,* 1–7. Logan: Utah State University Press.

De Martino, Ernesto. 2005. *The Land of Remorse: A Study of Southern Italian Tarantism.* Translated by Dorothy Louise Zinn. London: Free Association Books.

De Simone, Roberto. 1974. *Chi è devoto: Feste popolari in Campania.* Naples: Edizioni Scientifiche Italiane.

———. 1979. *Canti e tradizioni popolari in Campania.* Rome: Lato Side.

———. 1982. *Il Segno di Virgilio.* Puteoli, Italy: Sezione Ed.

———. 2005. "Tammurriata: Così scompare la tradizione." *Il Mattino,* December 27.

Dickie, John. 1997. "Stereotypes of the Italian South, 1860–1900." In *The New History of the Italian South: The Mezzogiorno Revisited,* edited by Robert Lumley and Jonathan Morris, 114–47. Devon: University of Exeter Press.

———. 1999. *Darkest Italy: The Nation and Stereotypes of the Mezzogiorno, 1860–1900.* London: Macmillan.

Di Mitri, Gino L. 2000. *Trance, guarigione, mito: Antropologia e storia del tarantismo.* Lecce, Italy: Besa.

———, ed. 2003. Introduction to *Breve storia del tarantismo,* edited by Henry E. Sigerist, 7–18. Nardò, Italy: Besa.

Dionisio, Giuseppe, and Cinzia D'Aquino, eds. 2003. *Il volto della tradizione: Riti e tammurriate nella festa di Bagni.* Sarno, Italy: Labirinto.

Duffy, Peter. 2004. "Showering a Madonna with Affection, Not Devotion." *New York Times,* September 5. http://www.nytimes.com/2004/09/05/nyregion/thecity/showering -a-madonna-with-affection-not-devotion.html?_r=0.

Erlmann, Veit. 1996. "The Aesthetics of the Global Imagination: Reflections on World Music in the 1990s." *Public Culture* 8: 467–87.

Fabbri, Franco. 2001. "Nowhere Land: The Construction of a 'Mediterranean' Identity in Italian Popular Music." *Music & Anthropology: Journal of Musical Anthropology of the Mediterranean* 6.

———. 2015. "Five Easy Pieces, 1964–2006: 40 Years of Music and Politics in Italy from B(ella Ciao) to B(erlusconi)." *Forum Italicum* 49, no. 2: 638–49.

Faiello, Carlo. 2005a. "Per monti e Madonne." In *Il suono della tradizione: Un progetto di Carlo Faiello,* produced by Il Canto di Virgilio. Rome: Squilibri.

———. 2005b. *Il suono della tradizione.* Rome: Squilibri.

Falassi, Alessandro. 1987. *Time Out of Time: Essays on the Festival.* Albuquerque: University of New Mexico Press.

Feld, Steven. 1994. "From Schizofonia to Schismogenesis: On the Discourse and Practices of World Beat." In *Music Grooves,* edited by Charles Keil and Steven Feld, 257–89. Chicago: University of Chicago Press.

———. 2000. "A Sweet Lullaby for World Music." *Public Culture* 12, no. 1: 145–71.

Feld, Steven, and Keith Basso. 1996. *Senses of Place.* Santa Fe, N.M.: School of American Research Press.

Ferraiuolo, Augusto. 2004. "A Dance of the Earth." In *Performing Ecstasies: Music, Dance, and Ritual in the Mediterranean,* edited by Luisa Del Giudice and Nancy Van Deusen, 133–50. Ottawa: Institute for Medieval Music.

———. 2009. *Religious Festive Practices in Boston's North End: Ephemeral Identities in an Italian American Community.* New York: State University of New York Press.

———. 2015. "The Tammorra Displaced: Music and Body Politics from Churchyards to Glocal Arenas in the Neapolitan Area." *Cultural Analysis* 14.

Foadi, Morano. 2006. "Key Issues and Causes of the Italian Brain Drain." In *Innovation: The European Journal of Social Science Research* 19, no. 2: 209–23.

Fogu, Claudio, and Lucia Re. 2010. "Italy in the Mediterranean Today: A New Critical Topography." In "Italy in the Mediterranean," edited by Claudio Fogu and Lucia Re. Special issue, *California Italian Studies Journal* 1, no. 1.

Fournier, Laurent-Sébastien. 2008. "Festivals, Games, and Ludic Performances as a New Potential Intangible Cultural Heritage in the Mediterranean World." *Journal of Mediterranean Studies* 18, no. 1: 1–15.

Frasca, Simona. 2014. *Italian Birds of Passage: The Diaspora of Neapolitan Musicians in New York.* New York: Palgrave.

Frith, Simon. 2000. "The Discourse of World Music." In *Western Music and Its Others: Difference, Representation, and Appropriation in Music,* edited by Georgina Born and David Hesmondhalgh, 305–22. Berkeley: University of California Press.

Gabaccia, Donna. 2000. *Italy's Many Diasporas.* Seattle: University of Washington Press.

———. 2002. *Immigration and American Diversity: A Social and Cultural History.* Malden, Mass.: Blackwell.

Gala, Giuseppe M. 1992. "'Io non so se ballo bene': Canzoni a ballo e balli cantati nella tradizione popolare italiana." Special issue, *Choreola* 7–8, no. 2.

———. 1993. "Ballo sul tamburo della Campania." In "'Io non so se ballo bene': Canzoni a ballo e balli cantati nella tradizione popolare italiana." Special issue, *Choreola* 9, no. 3: 196–202.

———, ed. 1999a. "Feste e tamburi in Campania." Special issue, *Etnica* 14.

———. 1999b. *La tarantella dei pastori.* Florence: Ed. Taranta.

———. 2002. "'La pizzica ce l'ho nel sangue': Riflessioni a margine sul ballo tradizionale e sulla nuova pizzicomania del Salento." In *Il ritmo meridiano: La pizzica e le identità danzanti del Salento,* edited by Vincenzo Santoro and Sergio Torsello, 109–53. Lecce, Italy: Edizioni Aramirè.

Gammella, Pasquale. 2009. *Fabbriche e tammorre.* Phoebus: Casalnuovo.

Grace, Sherrill. 2005. "Performing the Auto/Biographical Pact: Towards a Theory of Identity in Performance." In *Tracing the Autobiographical,* edited by Marlene Kadar, Linda Warley, Jeanne Perreault, and Susanna Egan, 65–79. Waterloo, Ontario: Wilfrid Laurier University Press.

Gramsci, Antonio. 1985. *Selections from Cultural Writings.* Cambridge, Mass.: Harvard University Press.

———. 1995. *The Southern Question.* Translated by Pasquale Verdicchio. West Lafayette, Ind.: Bordighera.

Gribaudi, Gabriella. 1997. "Images of the South: The Mezzogiorno as Seen by Insiders and Outsiders." In *The New History of the Italian South: The Mezzogiorno Revisited,* edited by Robert Lumley and Jonathan Morris, 83–113. Devon: University of Exeter Press.

Gurzau, Elba Farabegoli. 1964. *Folk Dances, Costumes, and Customs of Italy.* Newark, N.J.: Folkraft Press.

Guss, David M. 2000. *The Festive State: Race, Ethnicity, and Nationalism as Cultural Performance.* Berkeley: University of California Press.

Hall, Stuart. 1981. "Notes on Deconstructing the Popular." In *People's History and Socialist Theory*, edited by Raphael Samuel, 227–40. London: Routledge and Kegan Paul.

———. 1991. "The Local and the Global: Globalization and Ethnicity." In *Culture, Globalization and the World-System: Contemporary Conditions for the Representation of Identity*, edited by Anthony D. King, 19–40. Binghamton: State University of New York Press; London: Macmillan.

Hanegraaf, Wouter J. 1996. *New Age Religion and Western Culture*. Albany: State University of New York Press.

Hardt, Michael, and Paolo Virno. 2006. *Radical Thought in Italy: A Potential Politics*. Minneapolis: University of Minnesota Press.

Hobsbawm, Eric J. 1959. *Primitive Rebels*. Manchester: University Press of Manchester.

Hobsbawm, Eric, and Terence Ranger, eds. 1992. *The Invention of Tradition*. New York: Cambridge University Press.

Istituto Ernesto De Martino. 1978. *Il Nuovo Canzoniere Italiano dal 1962 al 1968*. Milan: Mazzotta.

Ivanova-Nyberg, Daniela. 2014. "Bulgarian Recreational Folk Dance Repertoire Today: Field Studies in Bulgaria and North America." Paper presented at the annual meeting of the American Folklore Society, Santa Fe, N.M., October.

J. Paul Getty Trust. 2011. "Enzo Avitabile & the Sacro Sud Project." *Getty Center* (April 25).

Kapchan, Deborah A. 1996. "Performance." *Journal of American Folklore* 108, no. 430: 479–508.

———. 2007. *Traveling Spirit Masters: Moroccan Gnawa Trance and Music in the Global Marketplace*. Middletown, Conn.: Wesleyan University Press.

Kirshenblatt-Gimblett, Barbara. 1998. *Destination Culture: Tourism, Museums, and Heritage*. Berkeley: University of California Press.

La Barbera, John T. 2009. "'That's Not Italian Music!': My Musical Journey from New York to Italy and Back Again." In *Oral History, Oral Culture, and Italian Americans*, edited by Luisa Del Giudice, 101–18. New York: Palgrave Macmillan.

Lamanna, Antonello. 2004. Introduction to *Tammurriate: Canti, musiche e devozioni in Campania*, edited by Antonello Lamanna, 10–19. Rome: Adnkronos.

Lapassade, George. 2001. "Gnawa, tarantismo e neotarantismo." In *Tarantismo e neotarantismo: Musica, dance, transe; Bisogni di oggi, bisogni di sempre*, edited by Anna Nacci, 25–36. Nardò, Italy: Besa.

Laviosa, Flavia. 2010. "The Frontier Apulia and Its Filmmakers after 1989." *California Italian Studies Journal* 1, no. 1.

———. 2011. "Tarantula Myths and Music: Popular Culture and Ancient Rituals in Italian Cinema." In *Popular Italian Cinema: Culture and Politics in a Postwar Society*, edited by Flavia Brizio-Skov. London: I. B. Tauris.

Leydi, Roberto. 1972. *Il folk revival italiano*. Palermo: Flaccovio.

Lomax, Alan, and Luigi Chiriatti. 2006. *Alan Lomax in Salento: Le fotografie del 1954*. Lecce, Italy: Karamuny.

Lombardi-Diop, Cristina, and Caterina Romeo. 2012. *Postcolonial Italy: Challenging National Homogeneity.* New York: Palgrave.

Lombardi-Satriani, Luigi. 1974. "Folklore as Culture of Contestation." *Journal of the Folklore Institute* 11: 99–121.

Lüdtke, Karen. 2009. *Dances with Spiders: Crisis, Celebrity and Celebration in Southern Italy.* New York: Berghahn Books.

Lumley, Robert, and Jonathan Morris. 1997. "Chronology of Events in Southern Italy, 1799–1915." In *The New History of the Italian South: The Mezzogiorno Revisited.* Devon: University of Exeter Press.

Lundgren, Jodi. 2008. "Dancing the Spider: Tarantism and Transnationalism." *Canadian Dance Studies Conference Proceedings.*

MacCannell, Dean. 1999. *The Tourist: A New Theory of the Leisure Class.* Berkeley: University of California Press.

MacLeod, Nicola E. 2006. "The Placeless Festival: Identity and Place in the Postmodern Festival." In *Festivals, Tourism and Social Change: Remaking Worlds,* edited by David Picard and Mike Robinson, 222–37. Bristol, UK: Channel View.

Magliocco, Sabina. 2004. *Witching Culture: Folklore and Neo-Paganism in America.* Philadelphia: University of Pennsylvania Press.

———. 2006. *The Two Madonnas: The Politics of Festival in a Sardinian Community.* 2nd ed. Long Grove, Ill.: Waveland Press.

———. 2011. "Imagining the Strega: Folklore Reclamation and the Construction of Italian-American Witchcraft." In *Italian Folk: Vernacular Culture in Italian-American Lives,* edited by Joseph Sciorra, 197–214. New York: Fordham University Press.

Magrini, Tullia. 1988. "Women's 'Work of Pain' in Christian Mediterranean Europe." *Music & Anthropology* 3.

———. 1994. "The Contribution of Ernesto De Martino to the Anthropology of Italian Music." *Yearbook of the International Council for Traditional Music* 26: 66–80.

———. 2003. *Music and Gender: Perspectives from the Mediterranean.* Chicago: University of Chicago Press.

Mandese, Francesca. 2015. "Sergio Blasi: 'Io mi fermo qui'; Si dimette il 'padre' della Taranta." *Corriere del Mezzogiorno,* September 15. http://corrieredelmezzogiorno.corriere.it/.

Manzotti, Michele. 2005. "La nuova compagnia di canto popolare da Napoli all'Europa." *Drammatugia.it,* January 3. http://drammaturgia.fupress.net/.

Marchesano, Nino. 2000. "Zezi, l'altra musica di Napoli." *Repubblica,* February 5. http://ricerca.repubblica.it/repubblica/archivio/repubblica/2000/02/05/zezi-altra-musica-di-napoli.html.

Mauro, Giuseppe. 2004. "La tammurriata: Intervista con Vicidomini, 'O Lione e Colasurdo." In *Tammurriate: Canti, musiche e devozioni in Campania,* edited by Antonello Lamanna, 212–25. Rome: Adnkronos.

Melchionda, Marina. 2009. "Puglia Film Festival, 2009: Italy's Heel on the Big Screen." *i-italy: Italian/American Digital Project,* July 14.

Melton, J. Gordon, ed. 1998. *The Encyclopedia of American Religions and Religious Creeds.* Detroit: Gale Research.

Merkling, Frank. 1993. "Black Madonna Sets Sail for Danbury." *News-Times,* January 24, 3–4.

Mignone, Mario B. 1998. "The Two Italies and the Southern Question." In *Italy Today: At the Crossroads of the New Millennium,* 173–99. New York: Peter Lang.

———. 2008. *Italy Today: Facing the Challenges of the New Millennium.* New York: Peter Lang.

Moe, Nelson. 2002. *View from Vesuvius: Representations of the South in Nineteenth-Century Italy.* Berkeley: University of California Press.

Morris, Jonathan. 1997. "Challenging *Meridionalismo:* Constructing a New History for Southern Italy." In *The New History of the Italian South: The Mezzogiorno Revisited,* edited by Robert Lumley and Jonathan Morris, 1–19. Devon: University of Exeter Press.

Motherway, Susan. 2013. *Globalization of Irish Traditional Song Performance.* Abingdon, UK: Ashgate.

Murizzi, Faustiko. 2014. "Canto Antico: South Beat." *Rockit.it,* November 12.

"Musica Popolare." 1985. *Tradizioni: Newsletter of the Italian Folk Art Federation of America* 6, no. 1: 1–2.

Nacci, Anna, ed. 2001. *Tarantismo e neotarantismo: Musica, dance, transe; Bisogni di oggi, bisogni di sempre.* Nardò, Italy: Besa.

———. 2004. *Neotarantismo, pizzica, transe e riti dalle campagne alle metropoli.* Rome: Nuovi Equilibri.

Nava, Sergio. 2015. "Lavorare all'estero: Nel 2014 oltre 100mila in fuga dall'Italia." *IlSole24Ore,* March 23.

Noyes, Dorothy. 1995. "Group." *Journal of American Folklore* 108, no. 430: 449–78.

———. 2009. "Tradition: Three Traditions." *Journal of Folklore Research* 46, no. 3: 233–68.

Orizzonti Meridiani, ed. 2014. *Briganti o emigranti: Sud e movimenti tra conricerca e studi subalterni.* Florence: Ombre Corte.

Pacoda, Piefrancesco. 2012. *Tarantapatia: Le lunghe notti della taranta.* Calimera, Italy: Edizioni Kurumuny.

Paliotti, Vittorio. 1992. *Storia della canzone napoletana.* Rome: Newton Compton.

Pestelli, Carlo. 2013. "An Escape from Escapism: The Short History of Cantacronache." In *Made in Italy: Studies in Popular Culture,* edited by Goffredo Platino and Franco Fabbri, 153–61. New York: Routledge.

Picard, David, and Mike Robinson. 2006. *Festivals, Tourism and Social Change: Remaking Worlds.* Bristol, UK: Channel View.

Pizza, Giovanni. 2002. "Lettera a Sergio Torsello e Vincenzo Santoro sopra il tarantismo, l'antropologia e le politiche della cultura." In *Il ritmo meridiano: La pizzica e le identità danzanti del Salento,* edited by Vincenzo Santoro and Sergio Torsello, 43–63. Lecce, Italy: Edizioni Aramirè.

———. 2004. "Tarantism and the Politics of Tradition in Contemporary Salento." In *Memory, Politics and Religion: The Past Meets the Present in Europe,* edited by Frances Pine, Deema Kaneff, and Haldis Haukanes, 199–223. Münster: LIT.

——. 2015. *Il tarantismo oggi: Antropologia, politica, cultura.* Rome: Carocci Editore.

Plastino, Goffredo. 1996. *Mappa delle voci: Rap, raggamuffin e tradizione in Italia.* Rome: Meltemi.

——. 2002. *Mediterranean Mosaic: Popular Music and Global Sounds.* London: Routledge.

——. 2008. "Un sentimento antico." In *Alan Lomax: L'anno più felice della mia vita—un viaggio in Italia, 1954–1955,* edited by Goffredo Plastino, 16–86. Milan: Il Saggiatore.

——. 2013. "Naples Power: Neapolitan Sounds of the 1970s." In *Made in Italy: Studies in Popular Culture,* edited by Goffredo Platino and Franco Fabbri, 56–71. New York: Routledge.

Portelli, Alessandro. 2001. "The Center Cannot Hold: Music as Political Communication in Post-war Italy." In *The Art of Persuasion: Political Communication in Italy from 1945 to the 1990s,* edited by Luciano Cheles and Lucio Spolza, 258–77. Manchester: Manchester University Press.

Programma Integra. 2015. "Dossier IDOS—UNAR: Dopo 20 anni gli italiani all'estero crescono più degli immigrati." July 7. https://www.programmaintegra.it/wp/2015/07/dossier-idos-unar-dopo-20-anni-gli-italiani-allestero-crescono-piu-degli-immigrati/.

Rauche, Anthony. 1990. "The Tarantella: Musical and Ethnic Identity for Italian-Americans, in Italian Americans." In *Italian Americans in Transition: Proceedings of the XXI Annual Conference of the American Italian Historical Association, Held at the John D. Calandra Italian American Institute, the City University of New York, the Graduate School and University Center, New York, October 13–15, 1988,* edited by Joseph Vincent Scelsa, Salvatore John LaGumina, and Lydio F. Tomasi, 189–97. Staten Island, N.Y.: John D. Calandra Italian American Institute.

Rettura, Antonio. 2003. Review of *Che Il Mediterraneo Sia. Rockit.it,* September 6.

Romanazzi, Andrea. 2006. *Il ritorno del dio che balla: Culti e riti del tarantolismo in Italia.* Rome: Venexia.

Rossi, Annabella. 1994. *Lettere da una tarantata.* Lecce, Italy: Argo.

Rouget, Gilbert. 1985. *Music and Trance: A Theory of the Relations between Music and Possession.* Chicago: University of Chicago Press.

Saffioti, Francesca. 2010. "Il 'Sud' come frontiera geosimbolica." *California Italian Studies* 1, no. 1: 1–13.

Santoro, Vincenzo, ed. 2009. *Il ritorno della taranta: Storia della rinascita della musica popolare salentina.* Rome: Edizioni Squilibri.

——. 2015. "Vincenzo Santoro: Musiche e culture popolari dal Salento al Mediterraneo; Appuntamenti, pubblicazioni e iniziative." http://www.vincenzosantoro.it/.

Santoro, Vincenzo, and Sergio Torsello. 2002. Introduction to *Il ritmo meridiano: La pizzica e le identità danzanti del Salento,* edited by Vincenzo Santoro and Sergio Torsello, 5–10. Lecce, Italy: Edizioni Aramirè.

Saunders, George R. 1993. "'Critical Ethnocentrism' and the Ethnology of Ernesto De Martino." *American Anthropologist* 95, no. 4: 875–93.

Savigliano, Marta. 1995. *Tango and the Political Economy of Passion.* Boulder, Colo.: West-view Press.

Schneider, Jane, ed. 1998. *Italy's "Southern Question": Orientalism in One Country.* Oxford: Berg.

Sciorra, Joseph. 2004. "The Black Madonna of East Thirteenth Street." *Voices: The Journal of New York Folklore* 30.

———. 2008a. "La Madonna Nera of New York City." *i-Italy,* September 2.

———. 2008b. "What's So Funny about the Virgin Mary?" *i-Italy,* September 20.

———, ed. 2011. *Italian Folk: Vernacular Culture in Italian-American Lives.* New York: Fordham University Press.

Shay, Anthony. 2006. *Choreographing Identities: Folk Dance, Ethnicity and Festival in the United States and Canada.* Jefferson, N.C.: McFarland.

Shay, Anthony, and Barbara Sellers-Young, eds. 2005. *Belly Dance: Orientalism, Transnationalism, and Harem Fantasy.* Costa Mesa, Calif.: Mazda.

Sherreitt, Kumari. 2007. "Pagan-Catholic Dance Takes a Spin." *Ka Leo,* May 14.

Sigerist, Henry E. 2003. *Breve storia del tarantismo.* Nardò, Italy: Besa.

Siikala, Anna-Leena. 2000. "From Sacrificial Rituals into National Festivals: Post-Soviet Transformations of Udmurt Tradition." In *Folklore, Heritage Politics and Ethnic Diversity: A Festschrift for Barbro Klein,* edited by Pertti J. Anttonen et al., 57–85. Botkyrka, Sweden: Multicultural Centre.

Silverman, Carol. 2012. *Romani Routes: Cultural Politics and Balkan Music in Diaspora.* Oxford: Oxford University Press.

Stokes, Martin, ed. 1994. *Ethnicity, Identity, and Music: The Musical Construction of Place.* Oxford: Berg.

———. 2003. "Globalization and the Politics of World Music." In *The Cultural Study of Music,* edited by Martin Clayton, Trevor Herbert, and Richard Middleton, 297–308. New York: Routledge.

Taylor, Timothy D. 1997. *Global Pop: World Music, World Markets.* New York: Routledge.

———. 2007. *Beyond Exoticism: Western Music and the World.* Durham, N.C.: Duke University Press.

Torsello, Sergio. 2006a. "Lomax l'irregolare." In *Alan Lomax in Salento: Le fotografie del 1954,* 7–8. Calimera, Italy: Kurumuny Edizioni.

———. 2006b. "Panorami e percorsi: La letteratura sul tarantismo dopo *La Terra Del Rimorso.*" In *La tela infinita: Bibliografia degli studi sul tarantismo mediterraneo, 1945–2006,* edited by Gabriele Mina and Sergio Torsello, 25–48. Nardò, Italy: Besa.

UNESCO. 1995–2010. *UNESCO Atlas of the World's Languages in Danger.* http://www.unesco.org/languages-atlas/.

Urry, John. 1990. *The Tourist Gaze: Leisure and Travel in Contemporary Societies.* London: Sage.

Vacca, Giovanni. 1999. *Il Vesuvio nel motore: L'avventura del gruppo musicale operaio "E Zézi" di Pomigliano d'Arco.* Rome: Manifestolibri.

Valentino, Gianni. 2004. "Il canzoniere di Pomigliano: La musica dei Zezi ha trent'anni." *Repubblica,* December 1, 11.

Verdicchio, Pasquale. 1997. *Bound by Distance: Rethinking Nationalism through the Italian Diaspora.* Madison, N.J.: Fairleigh Dickinson University Press.

Vicinanza, Pia. 2005. *Tammurriata anima e corpo: Il ballo sul tamburo; Espressione e comunicazione sociale.* Sorrento, Italy: Franco Di Mauro.

Whiteley, Sheila, Andy Bennett, and Stan Hawkins. 2005. Introduction to *Music, Space and Place: Popular Music and Cultural Identity,* edited by Sheila Whiteley, Andy Bennett, and Stan Hawkins, 1–24. Surrey, UK: Ashgate.

Wood, Anna L. 2011. "Giuseppe De Franco (1933–2010): A Remembrance of an Immigrant Folk Musician." *Italian American Review* 1, no. 2: 177–84.

Discography

Avitabile, Enzo. 2006. *Sacro Sud.* Folk Club Etnosuoni.

Belloni, Alessandra. 2000. *Tarantata: Dance of the Ancient Spider.* Sounds True.

———. 2003. *Tarantelle & Canti D'amore.* Naxos of America.

Bennato, Eugenio. 1980. *Brigante Se More.* Lucky Planets.

———. 1999. *Taranta Power Collection.* Rai Trade—Taranta Power.

———. 2002. *Che il Mediterraneo Sia.* Taranta Power—Rai Trade, 2002.

———. 2009. *Sponda Sud.* Taranta Power, Radio Fandango, Lucky Planets.

Bennato, Eugenio, and Carlo D'Angiò. 1978. *Musicanova.* Lucky Planets.

Bordello, Gogol. 2007. *Super Taranta.* INGrooves.

Chairetakis, Anna L. 1979a. *Calabria bella dove t'hai lasciate: Italian Folk Music Collected in New York, New Jersey, and Rhode Island.* Folkways Records.

———. 1979b. *In mezz' una strada trovai una pianta di rosa.* New York: Folkways.

D'Addario, Marty. 1980. *Oh Mother It Hurts Me So: Traditional Music from Central Pennsylvania.* Lewisburg, Pa.: Union County Historical Society, Oral Traditions Project.

The Godfather. 1972. Geffe.

Gruppo Operaio E Zézi di Pomigliano D'Arco. 1976. *Tammurriata dell'Alfasud.* I dischi del sole.

———. 1994. *Auciello ro mio: Posa e sorde.* Tide Records.

———. 1995. *Pummarola Black.* Lyrichord.

Lomax, Alan, and Carla Bianco, eds. 1965. *Italian Folk Songs: Collected in Italian-Speaking Communities in New York City and Chicago.* Folkway Records.

Lomax, Alan, Carla Bianco, and Diego Carpitella. 1972. *Italian Folk Music.* Vols. 1–5. Folkways.

Lomax, Alan, and Diego Carpitella. 1957. *The Folk Music of Southern Italy.* Columbia.

———. 1958. *Music and Song of Italy.* Tradition Records.

———. 1999. *Italian Treasury: Folk Music and Song of Italy.* Edited by A. Chairetakis and G. Plastino. Rounder Records.

Musolino, Michela, and Wilson Montuori. 2003. *Songs of Trinacria.* ALFAMUSIC.

NCCP. 1972. *Cicerenella.* Ricordi.

———. 1974. *Li Sarracini Adorano lu Sole.* EMI.

———. 1992. *Medina.* CGD.

Petrosino, Joe. 2009. *Rockammorra.* Club Inferno.

Pizzica la taranta (Il folklore del salento). 2012, 2013, 2014. Swithmuse.

Spaccanapoli. 2000. *Aneme perze—Lost Souls.* Real World Records.

Traditional Music from across Italy. 1958. Recorded by Alan Lomax and Diego Carpitella in 1954 and 1955. Tradition.

Filmography

Avitabile, Enzo. 2013. *Music Life.* CNI Music.

L'eredità della priora. 1980. Directed by Anton Giulio Majano. RAI Radio Televisione Italiana.

Li chiamarono . . . briganti! 1999. Directed by Pasquale Squitieri. *V.I.D.I.* and Ministero per i Beni e le Attività Culturali (MiBAC).

Mangiacake. 2015. Directed by Nathan Estabrooks. Wet Umbrella.

Nuovomondo. 2008. Directed by Emanuele Crialese.

Passione. 2010. Directed by Joe Turturro.

Pizzicata. 1996. Directed by Edoardo Winspeare.

Sangue vivo. 2000. Directed by Edoardo Winspeare.

The Tammorra Displaced. 2005. Directed by Paolo Favero and Augusto Ferraiuolo.

Tam-Tam Tammorra. 1999. Directed by Salvatore Raiola.

Tarantella. 1995. Directed by Helen de Michiel.

Terraferma. 2011. Directed by Emanuele Crialese.

Voci del popolo contadino. 2007. Directed by Salvatore Raiola. SalvatoreRaiola Communication.

Index

INCORONATA INSERRA is a lecturer at the University of Hawaiʻi at Mānoa.

FOLKLORE STUDIES
IN A MULTICULTURAL
WORLD

Storytelling in Siberia: The Olonkho Epic in a Changing World
    Robin P. Harris
    (University of Illinois Press)
Ukrainian Otherlands: Diaspora, Homeland, and Folk Imagination in the Twentieth Century
    Natalia Khanenko-Friesen
    (University Press of Mississippi)
A Vulgar Art: A New Approach to Stand-Up Comedy
    Ian Brodie
    (University Press of Mississippi)

The University of Illinois Press
is a founding member of the
Association of American University Presses.

University of Illinois Press
1325 South Oak Street
Champaign, IL 61820-6903
www.press.uillinois.edu